Edward IV and the Wars of the Roses

Edward IV and the Wars of the Roses

David Santiuste

Pen & Sword
MILITARY

First published in Great Britain in 2010 by
Pen & Sword Military
an imprint of
Pen & Sword Books Ltd
47 Church Street
Barnsley
South Yorkshire
S70 2AS

Copyright © David Santiuste 2010

ISBN 978-1-84415-930-7

The right of David Santiuste to be identified as Author
of this Work has been asserted by him in accordance
with the Copyright, Designs and Patents Act 1988.

A CIP catalogue record for this book is
available from the British Library.

Typeset in 11/13 Ehrhardt by Concept, Huddersfield, West Yorkshire
Printed and bound in England by CPI UK

Pen & Sword Books Ltd incorporates the imprints of Pen & Sword
Aviation, Pen & Sword Maritime, Pen & Sword Military, Wharncliffe
Local History, Pen & Sword Select, Pen & Sword Military Classics,
Leo Cooper, Remember When, Seaforth Publishing and Frontline
Publishing.

For a complete list of Pen & Sword titles please contact
PEN & SWORD BOOKS LIMITED
47 Church Street, Barnsley, South Yorkshire, S70 2AS, England
E-mail: enquiries@pen-and-sword.co.uk
Website: www.pen-and-sword.co.uk

Contents

List of Illustrations

Acknowledgements

First I would like to thank Rupert Harding of Pen and Sword Books, for his suggestion that I should write this book and for considerate guidance thereafter. Christopher Summerville edited the manuscript with skill and care.

I owe much, of course, to the scholarship of others. The biographies of Edward IV by Cora Scofield and Charles Ross have been particularly helpful. (Unfortunately the most recent biography, by Hannes Kleineke, was published after I had carried out most of my research.) I must also acknowledge the influence of John Gillingham, Anthony Goodman, A.J. Pollard and Livia Visser-Fuchs. In addition *The Great Warbow*, by Robert Hardy and Matthew Strickland, has justly been described as a 'soldiers' bible' for the late medieval period. My debts to the work of three other scholars – Chris Given-Wilson, Michael Hicks and Michael K. Jones – will be obvious throughout the text, but I would also like to thank them here for their help and encouragement over a number of years. Professor Given-Wilson deserves particular thanks for acting as a patient and tolerant supervisor of my postgraduate studies, during which time I had the opportunity to explore many of the sources on which this work is based. Any errors are my own.

The patrons of the Richard III Foundation have taken a keen interest in my work since I was a student, but they have also provided support in other ways. Among many others I must single out John Davey (now sadly departed), Judi Dickson, and, above all, Joe Ann Ricca. Mark Taylor of the Towton Battlefield Society helped me on several occasions, and I have greatly enjoyed my conversations with other members of the 'TBS' (especially Scowen Sykes). Steve Goodchild of the Tewkesbury Battle-field Society provided photographs and was kind enough to share some useful local knowledge. The artistic talents of Christopher Summerville (again), Rae Tan and Geoffrey Wheeler have immeasurably enriched the book. [A generous grant from the Authors' Foundation allowed me to visit some of the sites of Edward IV's battles. Gary Sawyer allowed me to consult books from his personal library.]

But the last word must be reserved for family. I would therefore like to thank my parents, Harry and Marion Santiuste, and my partner, Caroline Proctor, whose support and understanding means more than I can say. This book is for them, with much love.

York & Lancaster: The English Royal Family in the Later Middle Ages

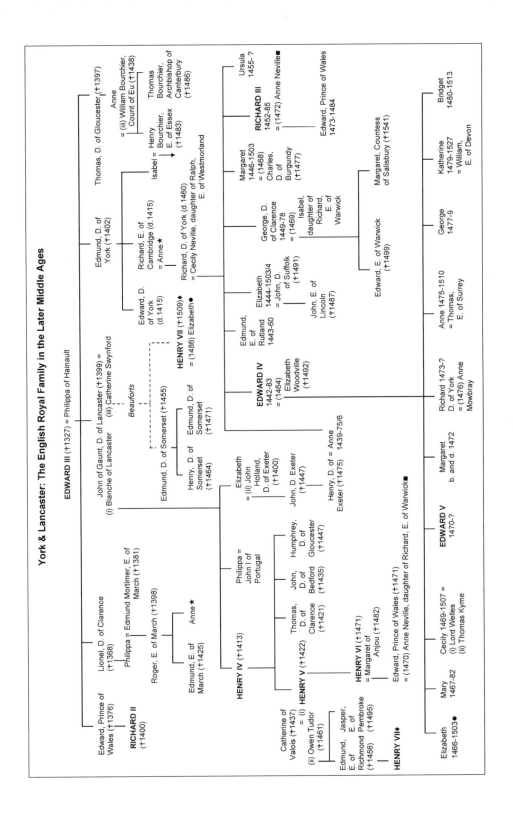

Maps

**England in the Wars of the Roses:
Major Towns, Castles and Battlefields**

0   150
Kilometres

N

R. Tweed

Berwick
Norham
Bamburgh
Dunstanburgh
Hedgeley
Moor (1464)
Alnwick
Warkworth
Hexham
(1464)
Newcastle
Carlisle
Durham

Middleham

Towton
(1461)
York
Hull
Wakefield
(1460)
Doncaster

R. Trent

Blore Heath
(1459)
Nottingham
Cromer
Harlech
Empingham
(1470)
Shrewsbury
Lynn
Norwich
Ludlow
(1459)
R. Severn
Mortimer's
Cross (1461)
Coventry
Fotheringhay
Kenilworth
Northampton
(1460)
Warwick
Edgecote
(1469)
Olney
Tewkesbury
(1471)
St Albans
(1455 & 1461)
Pembroke
Barnet
(1471)
Windsor
Bristol
LONDON
Canterbury
Sandwich
Dover
Southampton
Calais
Guines
Exeter
St Omer
Dartmouth

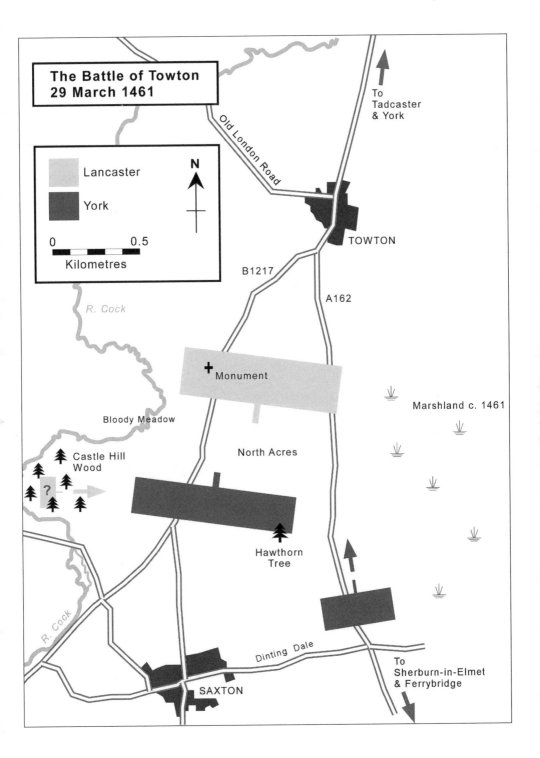

**The Battle of Towton
29 March 1461**

Lancaster

York

N

0   0.5
Kilometres

R. Cock

Old London Road

To
Tadcaster
& York

TOWTON

B1217

A162

+ Monument

Marshland c. 1461

Bloody Meadow

North Acres

Castle Hill
Wood

?

Hawthorn
Tree

R. Cock

Dinting Dale

SAXTON

To
Sherburn-in-Elmet
& Ferrybridge

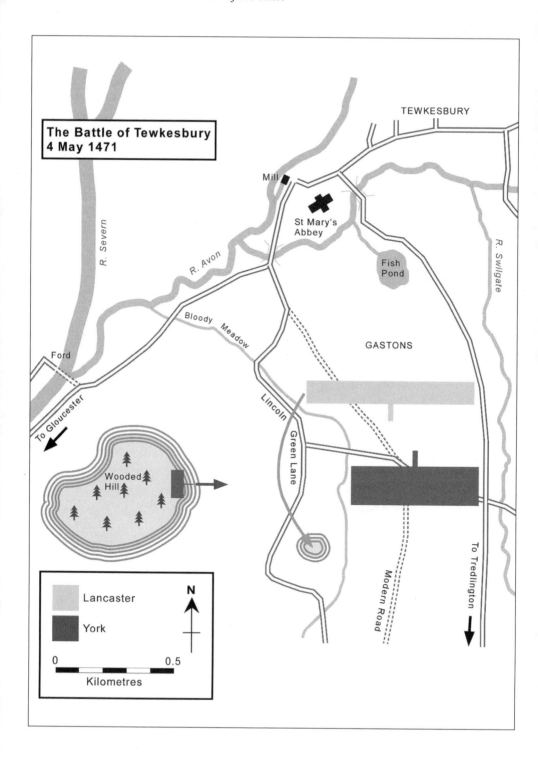

The Battle of Tewkesbury
4 May 1471

TEWKESBURY

Mill

St Mary's
Abbey

R. Severn

R. Avon

R. Swilgate

Fish
Pond

Bloody Meadow

GASTONS

Ford

To Gloucester

Lincoln Green Lane

Wooded
Hill

Lancaster

York

N

To Tredlington

Modern Road

0   0.5
Kilometres

Introduction

On 22 May 1455 a thirteen-year-old boy stood on a battlefield. This, we must assume, was his first exposure to warfare, although the sights he witnessed on that day would become sadly familiar. The boy was Edward, Earl of March, later to be known as King Edward IV. He was to play a vital role in the conflicts we know today as the Wars of the Roses. Traditionally the Wars of the Roses have been seen as a time of bloody battles and larger-than-life characters: England, traumatised by its defeat in the Hundred Years' War, is ripped apart by the treacherous machinations of 'overmighty' magnates. But this view owes much to the work of Shakespeare. In his *Henry VI* the King wanders in a daze as chaos erupts around him. The culmination of Shakespeare's history cycle, *Richard III*, is an orgy of mayhem and murder before peace is restored by Henry Tudor. Modern historians have attempted to provide a more nuanced interpretation. John Gillingham, for example, has argued that wider society was largely unaffected by the wars.[1] John Watts, in the most original recent interpretation of the Wars of the Roses, has characterised the English nobility not as bloodthirsty schemers but as 'victims, driven by the hideous logic of a dysfunctional system to the fruitless creation and defence of an authority which could not be exercised'.[2] Nevertheless, the battles of the Wars of the Roses were bloody indeed, and there *were* large characters – although contemporaries might not have recognised their depictions in Shakespeare! These were extraordinary times, when anything must have seemed possible: it is no surprise that 'Fortune's Wheel' was a popular device in contemporary literature. There were few larger characters, I would suggest, than King Edward IV.

This is not a conventional biography, although my intention is to illuminate Edward's personal role during the Wars of the Roses. The focus will be on Edward's military career, but in order to understand Edward as a commander I believe we must also try to understand Edward as a man. Context will be provided via a thorough discussion of political and diplomatic events.

The origins of the Wars of the Roses will be discussed in some detail below. However, before we progress any further, it may be helpful to explain some of the more important aspects of military organisation during this period. The following section provides an introduction to matters such as the conventions of military recruitment, motivation, and the equipment used by warriors, before moving on to a discussion of the sources.

First, how were armies raised?[3] It used to be thought that 'overmighty magnates' consistently maintained hordes of armed men – essentially private armies – although this view is now largely discredited. Most noble households did contain carefully selected 'tall men', who acted as bodyguards and fought close to their lord on the field, but their numbers were never great. But in times of crisis a great nobleman could call on his *affinity*, a broad network of tenants, servants and 'well willers', who would in turn call for support from within their own smaller networks. Existing administrative structures (maintained, for example, by estate officials) would help to ensure that men could be recruited quickly. Common soldiers would usually expect to be paid; sometimes gentlemen were *retained*, under the terms of an *indenture*, in return for cash payments. Often, however, these formal arrangements merely acknowledged existing relationships.[4] Noblemen augmented their forces from various sources – foreign mercenaries fought at many battles, and several towns sent well-equipped detachments to support armies on both sides – but this fluid system, traditionally known as *bastard feudalism*, was the primary means of recruitment for nobles' armies. The greatest noblemen, such as the Duke of York, or the Earl of Warwick, could raise hundreds, and even thousands of men in this way.

Perhaps surprisingly, royal armies would have been raised in a broadly similar manner. There was no standing army at this time, although the King did maintain a permanent garrison at Calais. Many members of the garrison were veterans of the Hundred Years' War. Yet even during foreign wars the crown largely relied on the nobility, exploiting the 'bastard feudal' networks that have already been described.[5] In times of dire necessity, however, the King could also call on the service of all able-bodied men for the defence of the realm. Assuming the system functioned well, each village and *hundred* would be expected to send a specified number of men. Traditionally the county sheriff was expected to raise these troops, but often the responsibility was delegated to local nobles and gentry, whose authority was based on a *commission of array*. Arrayed men would usually be paid, although there were occasions when they appear to have been pressed into service. Sometimes arrayed men are dismissed by historians as little more than a rabble, although there were many occasions, even in the absence of established noble leaders, when they displayed a high degree of organisation.[6] There was also considerable overlap with the 'bastard feudal' networks already described.

The King could appeal to an instinctive loyalty from all sections of society, although it must be stressed that even kings could not take support for granted. There were a lot of men during the Wars of the Roses who preferred, whenever possible, to avoid making commitments to either side.[7] Even so, it would be simplistic to suggest that when men *did* fight they were motivated only by material ambition, or, in the case of the commons, by legal obligations or fear. It is also clear that the nobles and gentry could be driven to act by family ties or more abstract principles.[8] Honour mattered, not least because the ideals of 'chivalry' continued to shape expectations of aristocratic behaviour.[9] But the motives of common men were just as complex. The dissemination of propaganda, within an increasingly literate society, helped ensure that common people would answer a call to arms of their own free will. Some rebel noblemen sought to convince a wide public that their actions were motivated in defence of the 'common weal'.[10] Motivations were complex, as ever, but we can assume that often men of all social classes joined armies because they felt morally obliged to do so.

Next, we turn to equipment and weapons.[11] The aristocracy usually fought on foot, in full armour. Plate armour was now at the height of its development, and it did not physically restrict the wearer as much as might be supposed. Knights at tournaments would often leap before they entered the lists, to show how little they were affected by wearing armour.[12] That said, armour was uncomfortable to wear for long periods due to the heat and fatigue generated; and breathing could be difficult – men often risked death by removing their visor or *bevor* (throat protection) at critical moments. Nevertheless, the best plate armour, produced by German or Italian specialists, provided effective protection from missiles and close-quarter weapons. Developments in armour meant that noble warriors increasingly favoured 'crushing' weapons, such as maces, which would be more likely to incapacitate an enemy than a blade, even if they did not kill him outright. Then smaller weapons such as a dagger could be brought into play, focusing on weak points such as the visor or the armpit – if the assailant had time. Swords were used extensively, but another popular weapon was the poleaxe. This was a truly formidable staff weapon, which usually incorporated a blade, a point and a 'beak'. The latter was designed to punch through plate armour – and bone.

As we move down the social scale there was, unsurprisingly, more variety in the type of equipment used, but 'ordinary' soldiers should not be underrated. The Italian Domenic Mancini witnessed the arrival at London in 1483 of Duke Richard of Gloucester's northern archers – presumably chosen men. Mancini was deeply impressed:

> There is hardly any without a helmet, and none without bows and arrows: their bows and arrows are thicker than those used by other nations, just as their bodies are stronger than other peoples', for they seem to have hands and arms of iron [...] there hangs by the side of each one a sword no less long than ours, but heavy and thick as well. The sword is always accompanied by an iron shield. They do not wear any armour on their breast [...] the common soldiers have more comfortable tunics that reach down below the loins and are stuffed with tow or some other soft material. They say that the softer the tunics the better do they withstand the blows of arrows and swords, and besides that in summer they are lighter and in winter more serviceable than iron.[13]

The 'comfortable tunic' referred to was known as a *jack*, although some common soldiers may have worn more (or less) armour than this. It is intriguing that Mancini tells us that *almost* every man has a helmet, even in this relatively well equipped group. The longbow was, of course, the weapon most associated with the English common soldier during this period. Ideally made from a yew bowstave imported from the Continent,[14] 6 feet long, and just as heavy as Mancini implies, the longbow was a powerful weapon. It required constant practice for an archer to draw a bow effectively. It is generally accepted that a reasonably skilled archer could shoot at least ten arrows a minute during combat, although some men may have shot more. English archers were feared throughout Europe because their 'arrow storms' had been a feature of the greatest English victories against the French during the Hundred Years' War.[15] Not all the common soldiers would have been archers, however. Some would have wielded staff weapons such as the *glaive* or the *langdebeve*.[16] Archers would also have been expected to fight in the *mêlée* with hand weapons, including the sword and buckler noted by Mancini or the *maul* (lead hammer).

Such then (briefly), were armies during the Wars of the Roses, although it is important to realise that arms and armour were constantly evolving. For example, there were regional variations in armour, though even knights of modest means would buy imported suits of armour from foreign specialists. In England, for instance, men came to prefer a version of the *sallet* (helmet) that was taller than the original German versions. But the most rapid changes appeared in the field of gunpowder weapons.[17] England did not take the lead in these developments and chroniclers' references to 'gonnes' – such as the *culverin*, a light artillery piece that could be used in the field – are often obtuse. Nevertheless, as we shall see, gunpowder weapons did play a role in the Wars of the Roses. English commanders, especially Edward IV, were evidently keen to learn about gunpowder technologies and to employ the new weapons on campaign.

The historian of the Wars of the Roses has recourse to a wide range of sources.[18] Record sources often provide us with our chronology, especially with regard to political events, and some historians are able to weave extraordinary stories from the most unpromising materials. This book is not based on extensive archival research, although I am building on solid foundations provided by others. The smooth narratives produced by modern historians often gloss over the long years of painstaking work in the archives, undertaken by generations of scholars. Yet records often lack the human element that appears in letters or chronicles, although these sources present their own problems. For example, the diplomatic correspondence preserved in the *Calendar of State Papers* related to Milan can be remarkably vivid, but it quickly becomes clear that much of it is based on gossip and rumour. The wonderful *Paston Letters* provide an incredible insight into the world of the English gentry, although the letters are a chance survival and are not fully representative. It is rare for personal letters to survive even from the greatest of noblemen and kings.

When historians use chronicles as sources they face a number of challenges.[19] Few chronicles provide eyewitness accounts, for example, and it is very difficult to determine how chroniclers obtained their information. Even when two (or more) chronicles say the same thing, this does not mean we are necessarily dealing with a 'fact'; it is just as likely that one chronicler was copying the other or that both had access to the same source. Many chroniclers derived their information about military affairs from newsletters, which circulated widely, although some writers were better than others at weaving such pieces into their own work. Livia Visser-Fuchs has studied the way in which the Burgundian nobleman Jean de Wavrin incorporated a wide range of material into his work, much of which originated in England.[20] Some of Wavrin's *Receuil* is independent – he was present on the field at Agincourt – yet, paradoxically, the great value of his work is in his willingness to use (and therefore preserve) the work of others. Wavrin did not lack discernment, however. Indeed many chronicles were carefully constructed by their authors: they are not merely repositories of information. One of the most intelligent writers of the period is the author of 'Gregory's Chronicle' (*c.* 1470), possibly a cleric with a background in writing sermons. This chronicler carefully *selected* his material and his approach is anecdotal. Warriors, including 'ordinary' people, are judged according to a sliding scale of honour and shame.[21] Such accounts provide a fascinating insight into contemporary *mores*, although they do not always make it easy for the modern historian to determine causal relationships. It can also be difficult to determine the exact sequence of events. But this is not to say, though, that 'Gregory' (and others) entirely ignored the more practical aspects of warfare. His account of the second Battle of St Albans (although it may be derived from another source) provides some interesting comments about the equipment used and also displays an awareness of tactical issues.

The best military source for the period is almost certainly the *Arrivall*, written by one of Edward's clerks shortly after the 1471 campaign. Unusually, for a medieval source, it provides valuable accounts of military councils and strategic decisions. Such details usually have to be inferred from events. We must not forget that the *Arrivall* was an 'official' production, designed to commemorate and propagandise Edward's recovery of his throne, but the author was an acute observer of military affairs. Moreover, few other sources were written so close to the centres of power, although a notable exception is the second continuation of the *Crowland Chronicle*. The writer was certainly well informed, and it is usually assumed he was a Yorkist 'civil servant'. Other important English sources include the *Chronicle of the Rebellion in Lincolnshire* (another official tract), *Annales Rerum Anglicarum* (which provides a valuable, albeit unfinished, account focusing on the activities of the Nevilles), the *English Chronicle*, the first continuation of the *Crowland Chronicle* (written by the abbey's prior), and *Warkworth's Chronicle* (the latter was possibly written *c.* 1480 by the master of Peterhouse College, Cambridge). From the Continent, the works of Georges Chastelain and Philippe de Commynes are important for the light they shed on European views of the English. Commynes, indeed, was personally involved in diplomacy, although he is scarcely objective. The Italian Domenic Mancini visited England close to the end of Edward's reign and, as we have seen, took advantage of the opportunity to observe the English at close hand. A number of later English sources also provide interesting details, although it becomes ever more difficult to determine where they obtained their sources and why they were writing. The influential work of Edward Hall will be discussed in some detail below. Another intriguing later source is *Hearne's Fragment*, written *c.* 1520 by a (presumably) elderly man who claims to have been a servant of the dukes of Norfolk. It is likely, unfortunately, that the most valuable section of this work no longer survives.

How may historians fill in the gaps in the written evidence, or determine between conflicting accounts? One solution, in a military context, has been provided by Lieutenant-Colonel Alfred Burne, writing in the mid twentieth century. Burne's approach was to employ a method he called *Inherent Military Probability*.[22] Burne determined what he considered to be indisputable 'facts'; he would then put himself 'in the shoes' of each commander in turn, considering what he would have done in their situation. If the 'I.M.P.' could be reconciled with the sources he would then move on to 'the next debatable or obscure point in the battle and repeat the operation'. To some extent, therefore, Burne's approach was simply to employ logic and 'common sense', in the light of his military training. On occasion, however, Burne is given to surprising flights of fancy.[23] His reconstructions are essentially intellectual exercises which prioritise one factor, the tactical, over others that are equally important. Battles were often decided, at least partly, by factors over which the commander had no control, most notably the weather. The best military minds could not be prepared for unexpected acts of treachery. Most importantly, Burne's accounts also give little sense of the chaos of battle, which could sometimes be overcome only by willpower and courage, not by tactics.[24]

Nevertheless, Burne's work remains valuable and thought-provoking. For example, a survey of the terrain was an important aspect of Burne's approach, and naturally this remains important today. Most battlefields have changed, of course, although modern scientific methods, allied to painstaking research in the archives, have made it possible to understand the medieval landscape as never before. At Towton, moreover, the battle-field continues to give up its secrets to archaeologists. Most notably in 1996 there was a chance discovery, during building work, of a mass grave, which held the skeletons of sixty-one men who died in the battle. The skeletons have been subjected to modern forensic techniques, in the light of research into medieval arms and armour, and the results have been startling.[25] Yet as Robert Hardy has eloquently reminded us, even when no bodies have been discovered, *every* battlefield is 'a tomb [...] a perpetual shrine and memorial which should engage our thought and our reverence'.[26] Walking in the gentle countryside between Kingsland and Mortimer's Cross, bathed in sunshine, I found it difficult to imagine that men once struggled there for their lives. But when I visited the plain at Towton for the first time, battered by the cold wind on a winter's day, it was not so difficult to envisage that this was once the site of a great and terrible battle. Ultimately we should not be surprised that historians have reached different conclusions about the Wars of the Roses. Much as we may wish the writing of history to entail only an 'objective' examination of the 'facts', it also requires imagination and many silent choices. The sources of history are open to many interpretations.

Modern historians have offered many different interpretations of Edward IV himself. Was Edward 'playboy or politician?' asks Keith Dockray, in a lucid survey of the historiography.[27] Dockray appears to conclude that Edward was a bit of both, although others have offered more robust views – as we shall see. Contemporary writers were also divided in their assessment of Edward's character, although few doubted his courage or his great skill in war. Thomas More, writing some years after Edward's death, was fulsome in his praise. More was by no means an impartial observer – he was a writer with a complex agenda – but his description of Edward provides an apt introduction:

> He was [...] of heart courageous, politic in counsel, in adversity nothing abashed, in prosperity rather joyful than proud, in peace just and merciful, in war sharp and fierce, in the field bold and hardy.[28]

Was Thomas More right? It is for the reader to decide.

Chapter 1

Rouen, April 1442

Edward Plantagenet was born at Rouen, in Normandy, on 28 April 1442. His father was Richard Duke of York, the greatest English nobleman after the King. York was a 'prince of the blood', descended from King Edward III on both sides of his family. Edward's mother, Duchess Cecily, was a member of the powerful Neville family, who had steadily increased their influence throughout the century. Cecily herself, traditionally known as 'Proud Cis' and 'The Rose of Raby', gained a reputation as a beautiful and formidable woman. The duke and duchess were rarely parted, and yet, as we shall see, rumours were later to emerge that Edward was not York's son.[1] Of course, it is now impossible to resolve the question of York's paternity either way, although there is little evidence to suggest that Duke Richard treated Edward any differently from the rest of his children. An elder boy, Henry, died as an infant, so Edward became York's heir. Over the next few years, more children would join Edward and his older sister, Anne, and the duke and duchess produced a large family; Edward had three brothers and four sisters. Edward's three younger brothers – Edmund, George and Richard – will all feature prominently in our story.

At this time, the Duke of York was King Henry VI's lieutenant-general, responsible for the direction of England's war with France. By 1442 the English and French had been at war, intermittently, for more than a hundred years.[2] The war was reopened in earnest in 1413, by Henry V, who had recently attained the throne. Henry V, the victor of Agincourt, was a great military commander but he was aided by internal divisions within France. The ageing French King, Charles VI, suffered from mental illness (he sometimes believed himself to be made of glass). The French political community struggled to cope with the effects of their King's incapacity; eventually this led to feuding between the highest nobility. The culmination, in 1419, was the murder of Duke John of

Burgundy in the presence of the *Dauphin*, Prince Charles. This pushed Duke John's young son, Duke Philip, into an alliance with the English. By 1420 Henry had conquered much of Northern France. He must have appeared invincible, and so the French came to terms. Henry married Charles VI's daughter, Katherine. The Treaty of Troyes disinherited the Dauphin, making Henry heir to the French throne in his stead. But in 1422 Henry contracted dysentery. The King died on 31 August, only thirty-five years old, at the height of his powers. Henry's son, Henry VI, succeeded to the English throne unchallenged but he was still an infant. All Henry V's achievements were therefore placed in jeopardy, although the English cause in France continued to prosper. Effective leadership was provided by Henry V's brother, John Duke of Bedford. But then, in 1429, everything changed. A small French force, ostensibly under the command of the remarkable Joan of Arc, broke the English siege of Orléans. Later that year, the Dauphin was crowned King Charles VII at Rheims, while Joan looked on in rapture.[3] Joan's 'ministry' was short-lived though: she was captured by the Burgundians the following year, and the English burned her alive as a witch. In 1431, Henry VI, although still a small child, was in turn crowned King of France at Paris. Yet Joan's intervention had turned the tide of the war. In 1435 the English received a crushing blow when Duke Philip formally repudiated the Anglo-Burgundian alliance.[4]

By the early 1440s, therefore, the English were very much on the defensive. Charles VII surprised his subjects (and perhaps himself) by proving to be an effective king,[5] and France's superior resources now began to tell. But the English resisted bitterly, and there were some victories in these years. The Duke of York himself led a particularly successful expedition in 1441, the year before Edward's birth. York's main purpose was to relieve the town of Pontoise, which had been besieged by Charles VII's army.[6] During this campaign York exhibited dynamic leadership, and his audacious conduct – including night marches and surprise river crossings – so discomfited the French that every time the English appeared 'they ran hard in the other direction'. On one occasion York almost captured Charles, finding the King's bed still warm. Such successes were rare though, and much of York's time in France was spent in a grim struggle to hold the line. Moreover, it was also clear by now that Henry VI was unlikely to follow in his father's illustrious footsteps. Henry had achieved his majority in 1437, but he left most affairs in the hands of his chief minister, the Duke of Suffolk. Henry showed no inclination to lead an army in person. Insofar as he was interested in the war at all, he was inclined towards peace.

Suffolk also wanted peace, although perhaps on more pragmatic grounds. In 1445 Henry married Margaret, the daughter of Count René of Anjou, and this was the price of a truce. Henry's government also ceded the territory of Maine. This was done in the teeth of 'hawks' such as the Duke of Gloucester, who was now Henry V's only surviving brother. In the years after Henry V's death Gloucester had played a prominent role, although by this time he was effectively marginalised. Gloucester's downfall was completed in February 1447, when he was arrested and charged with treason. He was never tried, but died shortly afterwards in mysterious circumstances. Suffolk's major rival had been removed, although his dominance would soon come to an end. A series of diplomatic blunders, which culminated in the English sack of Fougères, gave Charles a pretext to reopen the war.[7] York had been succeeded as lieutenant by another kinsman of King Henry, Edmund Beaufort Duke of Somerset. Somerset had a distinguished war record but proved a disaster as lieutenant. In October 1449 Somerset was compelled to surrender Rouen; English Normandy was overrun. The loss of Normandy was a national disgrace, for which Suffolk paid the price. He was impeached by Parliament, although the death sentence that was sought was commuted to banishment. But Suffolk's ship was intercepted – it remains unclear on whose orders – and Suffolk was brutally put to death. Worse was to follow for King Henry when the commons of the south-east rose in rebellion under an Irish soldier, Jack Cade. The revolt was eventually suppressed with great cruelty, although not until some of Henry's ministers had been captured and murdered.

Thus it was a troubled kingdom to which Richard Duke of York returned in September 1450. Following the end of his tenure in France he had been appointed Lieutenant of Ireland, where he had enjoyed some success. But he now considered his presence in England to be essential. First, because he was enraged by the conduct of Somerset. York was vexed by a matter of honour: he believed that Somerset's actions in France had breached the chivalric code.[8] Nevertheless, Somerset remained in favour at court. He had replaced Suffolk as Henry's principal counsellor, notwithstanding his miserable failure in France. Second, York wished to disassociate himself from Cade's revolt, because the rebels had called for him to be given a greater place in government. Suspicions of York were particularly aroused at court because Cade, posing as a kinsman of the Duke, referred to himself as 'John Mortimer'. In order to understand the significance of Cade's claims we need to go back to 1399, when Richard II was deposed by his cousin Henry Bolingbroke. Bolingbroke, who was Henry VI's grandfather, took the throne as King Henry IV. But a claim to the throne on behalf of Edmund Mortimer, the young Earl of March, which was arguably stronger than Henry's, had been passed over.[9] The House of Mortimer and their descendants therefore acted as a magnet for anyone with a grievance against the Lancastrian kings. York was now the Mortimers' heir.[10] York's father had been executed for his part in a rebellion against Henry V, but Duke Richard himself had been conspicuously loyal. Gloucester's death had brought the Duke of York a step closer to the throne, although it is unlikely that he could have contemplated the removal of Henry at this stage.[11] York's motives remain opaque, although he was now to devote the rest of his life to high politics in England.

But there were no simple remedies. Late medieval England was a mature political society.[12] Its institutions, including Parliament, were of long standing. It was, moreover, a complex society, which combined political, cultural, religious and economic factors within a continued state of flux. However, the position of the monarchy was unchallenged: even the most radical political thinkers of the time could not conceive of a state which had no king. The King's role was complex and multi-faceted. He was administrator, war leader and judge – the 'chief executive' of the realm – although this does no justice to the awesome majesty of king-ship as it was perceived by medieval people. A medieval ruler was *rex et sacerdus*, king and priest. He ruled through hereditary right, but also because he was thought to be ordained by God. The King's link with the divine did not mean, though, that his powers were completely unchecked. In his coronation oath the King swore to rule for the benefit of his subjects. It was also crucial that a king maintained good relations with his magnates, who expected the right to offer counsel and that their advice would be duly considered. Indeed, much of the political power in the country rested with the aristocracy – the peers, lords and gentry – the few hundred families, whose authority was derived from ownership of land and hereditary right.[13] Yet if the King was considered to be divinely ordained, then how could he be *compelled* to act in the best interests of his realm?

It is clear that the political system depended heavily on the personal attributes of the King. One of the most difficult dilemmas that faced the political community during the later Middle Ages, therefore, was how to proceed when the King was unable, or unwilling, to provide effective leadership. Deposition, the ultimate solution, was never taken lightly, although it was now accepted that a king who ruled as a tyrant could be justifiably removed. Two medieval English kings had been deposed: Edward II, in 1327, and Richard II, in 1399, as we have seen. Henry VI's minority – another hazard of medieval politics – had been navigated without the system breaking down, but as an adult king, at least until 1453, Henry posed a different set of problems. Henry was not actively malign, but he largely abdicated responsibility, first to Suffolk, and then to Somerset. Why he did so remains a matter of debate.[14] Many contemporary writers believed Henry to be a good, simple and pious man: according to his chaplain, John Blacman, he was 'like a second Job'. These are not necessarily negative qualities, of course, but the implication was that Henry was better suited to life in a monastery than to kingship. More seriously, however, Henry was also thought to be naïve and lacking in judgement. Abbot Whethamstede of St Albans, for example (albeit writing with hindsight), described him as 'a mild-spoken, pious king, but half-witted in affairs of state'.

The Duke of York launched an energetic campaign aimed at removing the Duke of Somerset from power. But he made little progress – and obviously the King would not act against Somerset in person – so he retired to his castle of Ludlow, in the Welsh Marches. York held lands throughout England, Ireland and, until 1449 of course, in France, but his greatest power lay in the Marches, the Mortimers' patrimony. The duke's marcher lordships brought him great wealth and here, like other marcher lords, he enjoyed quasi-regal powers. Ludlow, then a large and impressive castle, was the Duke of York's principal seat. We may assume that York was reunited with his young son, Edward, because it was here, rather than in the household of another great noble, that Edward was destined to grow up. Edward would never forget his youth at Ludlow, nor the town's long-standing loyalty to the House of York.[15] The Duke of York's power in the Marches brought him little comfort though. His sense of frustration grew, and York's self-imposed exile from court gave his enemies the chance to brief against him. In February 1452 York, supported by the Earl of Devon and Lord Cobham, resorted to arms for the first time. By the end of the month York, denied entry to London, had taken up a strongly fortified position at Dartford, in north-west Kent. Here, he awaited the arrival of the King's forces. This was not a course to be taken lightly. Theoretically, only the sovereign had the right to levy war, and to defy the King openly was treason. Nevertheless, on this occasion both sides were reluctant to engage in bloodshed. A series of noble emissaries, including York's kinsmen, the Nevilles, were sent to persuade York to disarm. Eventually, York agreed to disband his army on the understanding that the King would hear his petition against Somerset; this was agreed. However, after presenting his case to the King, York was taken into custody. He was compelled to renew his oath of allegiance publicly, and also to swear that he would eschew 'the way of feat' [arms] thereafter.[16] Further reprisals against York may have been planned, although it was now that Edward made his debut on the public stage, and thereby saved his father from further humiliation. It was said that Edward, now Earl of March, had raised an army, although he was still only ten years old, and was coming to York's aid.[17]

During the next year it must be said that Henry's government was energetic, particularly in the field of law and order, although the King's own role is unclear. Henry's councillors also turned their attention to the war in France. An expeditionary force was despatched to Aquitaine, under the redoubtable John Talbot, Earl of Shrewsbury. The English enjoyed initial success but Charles VII reacted swiftly and despatched a powerful force. On 17 July 1453, Talbot, aggressive as usual, attacked the French at Castillon, near Bordeaux, where they had fortified their encampment. The French were well supplied with artillery, which was expertly deployed, and the English attackers were blown to pieces; Talbot himself was slain. The Battle of Castillon has traditionally been regarded as the end of the Hundred Years' War, and the English 'Empire' in France would henceforth be limited to the Calais Pale. The disaster at Castillon had further repercussions. Up to this point, Henry had given no indication that he wanted to follow his father's martial example, but he had shown no clear signs of mental illness. But the news of Shrewsbury's death had a catastrophic effect. When word of the English defeat was brought to Henry at Clarendon he suffered a breakdown.[18] Henry was completely incapacitated. Even when Queen Margaret bore Henry a son, Edward, their first and only child, he remained oblivious.

At Dartford York had been left isolated by a lack of support from the nobility, but now he forged a valuable alliance with the Nevilles. The family included Richard Earl of Salisbury, his brother – the veteran William Lord Fauconberg – and Salisbury's brood of able sons. The eldest of Salisbury's sons, also named Richard, held the title Earl of Warwick through his marriage to Anne Beauchamp. Warwick's brothers included John, who was destined to become a great warrior, and George, who was destined for a career in the Church. The Nevilles were motivated purely by self-interest: they needed support to help them in their feud with the Percys, who held much influence at court. Acrimony between the two great northern families was long-standing, dating back to the late fourteenth century, but their quarrel had become increasingly bitter as Henry VI's reign progressed. Matters came to a head in August 1453. The wedding party of Salisbury's other son, Thomas, traversing Heworth Moor, was attacked by a Percy force under Lord Egremont.[19] In these testing times York also won the support of other lords. An attempt by Queen Margaret to claim the regency was rebuffed, and on 27 March 1454 York was accepted as Lord Protector by his peers. Unsurprisingly, York's supporters were rewarded and his enemies were excluded from government. Salisbury, for instance, became Chancellor, an office that was usually held by a churchman; Somerset was imprisoned in the Tower, although he was never brought to trial. However, having opposed government by a court clique for so long, York did not wish to appear to be the prisoner of a faction. Intriguingly, York displayed his impartiality through a rebuke to his own son, Edward.[20] In a letter of May 1454 York upbraids Edward, 'lamenting your misgovernance to my great sorrow'. York expresses concern that Edward was raising an army, 'to what intent it is not known, but marvelled [. . .] whereof'. It is difficult to know what to make of this document: Edward was still only twelve years old. Even though the lines between childhood and adulthood were not as distinct as they are today, it seems unlikely that Edward would have taken the initiative to raise troops at this time. However, Edward had already accompanied his father to London in 1454, riding at the head of 'cleanly beseen [equipped] and likely men',[21] which suggests he could easily have acted as a figurehead for a recruiting drive in the Marches; this would also explain the reports of Edward's earlier activities in 1452. Perhaps York had feared that he might need to call on troops, but now that his position was secure there was no need for a show of armed force. It is therefore likely that York's letter was really a propagandist text, designed to reassure those who were concerned about his motives.[22]

York's authority appeared to be well established, but at Christmas of 1454 King Henry suddenly recovered his reason. The results were predictable. By February 1455 Somerset was released from prison and restored to his offices; in March, Salisbury was compelled to resign as Chancellor. Understandably, now that Somerset was restored to favour, York and his supporters considered their position to be precarious. York and the Nevilles retired from London to the north. But shortly afterwards they were summoned to a Great Council, at Leicester, where they feared there would be further reprisals. Notwithstanding York's oath to forgo 'the way of feat', to which he considered he had been unduly constrained, he and the Nevilles quickly raised an army. This time Edward did come to join his father, riding at the head of a force from the Marches. Edward had now just reached his teens, but it was common for youths to join a military campaign in order to gain experience, even if they were not actually expected to fight.[23] An embassy despatched by Somerset was ignored and York's army moved rapidly south. On 22 May 1455 York encountered Henry and his entourage at St Albans. Once again there would be negotiations, but this time they were destined to fail. The Wars of the Roses were about to begin.

Henry, *en route* to the Midlands as planned, arrived at St Albans in the morning.[24] The Yorkist army was already nearby, encamped in Key Field to the south-east of the town. The Yorkist forces were markedly superior to Henry's own. Somerset had envisaged a political solution to his struggle with York, so there had been no time to raise a significant force on Henry's behalf. Few of the lords who had responded to Henry's summons would have been truly prepared for war, and others, such as the Earl of Oxford, did not arrive in time. Presumably many of the lords still hoped to avoid bloodshed: could York be persuaded to disarm? Henry took up a position in the town centre, by the Market Cross, and the Duke of Buckingham was sent to negotiate on the King's behalf. No compromise could be reached, however, because York insisted that Somerset should be given up for judgement. The royal banner was raised, which signified a state of war, and the Yorkists moved to the attack.[25] Despite their inferior numbers, the royalists' position was relatively strong. St Albans had no walls, but the houses grouped around the market square provided fortifications of a kind; the roads into the town were barred. The Earl of Northumberland and his ally, Lord Clifford, were in command at the barricades. For an hour, the royal army put up a stout defence, but then Warwick finally discovered a way into the town. Accompanied by Sir Robert Ogle, with 600 men from the Scottish Marches, Warwick bypassed the barricades, making his way into the gardens behind Holywell Hill. From here, Warwick's men burst into the market square:

> They ferociously broke in by the garden sides between the sign
> of The Key and the sign of The Chequer in Holywell Street,
> and immediately they were within the town, suddenly they
> blew up trumpets, and set a cry with a shout and a great voice
> 'A Warwick! A Warwick!'[26]

Northumberland and Clifford despatched many of their troops to defend King Henry, so eventually their forces were overwhelmed. Both lords were killed, to the Nevilles' great satisfaction. The Yorkists rained arrows into the market square and the royalists were routed. Henry took shelter in a tanner's cottage, while Somerset sought refuge in the Castle Inn. Once he was aware the battle was won, York gave orders that King Henry – who had been wounded by an arrow – should be conveyed to the safety of the Abbey. Now York's thoughts turned to his great rival, Somerset. Yorkist soldiers surrounded the inn and battered down the doors. With no hope of escape or mercy, Somerset resolved to die fighting. According to one report he killed four men before he was cut down. Somerset's body was left lying in the street, until York was prompted by Abbot Whethamstede to allow an honourable burial. Did Edward witness Somerset's death? Edward must have seen something of war at St Albans, although whether he was traumatised or exhilarated is impossible to say.

On 23 May Richard Duke of York entered London in triumph, riding at the right hand of Henry VI. Henry had pardoned York: what else could he have done? Shortly afterwards York would once again receive the protectorate – possibly the shock of St Albans had caused Henry to suffer another mental collapse. But Edward returned to Ludlow, to complete his education. By the age of fourteen this would have certainly included training in arms. Edward would have become accustomed to wearing 'harness' – armour – and would have learned to handle weapons. Edward would have learned to use the sword, which remained the weapon most associated with nobility, although we have seen that the nobility also favoured the poleaxe. Fighting with an axe did not only require brute strength: a surviving fifteenth-century French treatise is solely devoted to using an axe in combat.[27] It encourages warriors to consider, for example, the problems associated with fighting a left-handed opponent, and to master feints. It also teaches more underhand methods, such as jamming the haft of the axe between an opponent's thighs. But of course physical attributes were also important. The biography of the French nobleman Jean le Meingre (1366–1415), better known as 'Boucicaut', provides an idealised account of the training regime of a youth.[28] Boucicaut, it is said, ran for miles in full armour. He put in hours of practice with his axe, to strengthen his arms. Boucicaut also took pains to improve his agility: he did gymnastics, including somersaults, again fully armed, and could jump onto his horse without touching the stirrups. Yet few youths could ever have lived up to Boucicaut's discipline, and his biographer is obliged to end his account with the phrase 'and these things are true'. Indeed, William Worcester, who presented his *Boke of Noblesse* to Edward in 1475, was rather scathing of the English aristocracy's readiness for war:

> Of late days, the greater pity is, many one that is descended of noble blood and born to arms, as knights' sons, esquires, and of other gentle blood, set himself to singular practice, strange from that feat, as to learn the practice of law or custom of land, or of civil matters, and so wasting greatly their time on such needless business . . .[29]

But Worcester was writing a polemic. It was designed to exalt the experience of veterans of the Hundred Years' War, and *pour encourager les autres*.[30] We may assume the reality lay somewhere between these two extremes. Noble education was designed to be holistic, in that it would incorporate physical training *and* book learning.

The education of a noble youth was overseen by a 'master'. In Edward's case this was almost certainly a man of knightly rank, although he could also have been a cleric. Edward shared his education with his younger brother Edmund, to whom he was closest in age. A great noble's son would usually be joined by a number of aristocratic youths, forming a household in miniature. Edward was no exception, although not all of his companions were to his liking. Edward was particularly vexed by the behaviour of two local boys, the Crofts.[31] The group of boys would have spent the morning learning grammar and languages. Some relief might have come in the form of romance literature. It was hoped that tales of 'knights and chivalry' would inspire youths to carry out deeds of arms. Edward's youngest brother, Richard, was the scholar of the family, but Edward appears to have learnt his lessons well enough. In 1454 Edward and Edmund assured their father in a letter that 'we have attended our learning sith [until] we come hither, and shall hereafter'.[32] Edward was evidently literate and, according to Commynes, he spoke 'quite good French'.[33] As a youth, he also owned a well-known Latin text, the *Secreta Secretorum*.[34] It is possible that the lessons contained within this work – a classic of the pervasive 'Mirrors for Princes' genre – were to inform his conduct as king. Scholastic learning was therefore encouraged and valued, although the boys would have been released from their books relatively early each day. It would then fall on the master to supervise knightly training. According to the *Liber Niger*, which stipulated the routine of Edward IV's household as King, the master of the 'henchmen' – noble pages – was expected to 'learn them to wear their harness' and to teach them 'to ride cleanly and surely, to draw them also to jousts'.[35] Mock tournaments could be dangerous, and were evidently not taken lightly. In 1389 John Hastings, Earl of Pembroke, then in his late teens, was accidentally killed by his jousting partner.

In many respects Edward's education would have resembled that of his son, also named Edward, who was sent to be educated at Ludlow in his turn. Prince Edward, it is often suggested, was a frail, scholarly youth, with a 'special knowledge of literature' but it is frequently overlooked that he also 'devoted himself to horses and dogs and other youthful exercises to invigorate his body'.[36] His father, as a boy, would have done the same. The active pursuits of the aristocracy, just as much as swordplay, could also be regarded as military training. Archery, for example, was a popular pastime among noblemen of all ages, even though they did not use bows in battle.[37] But the most significant activity was hunting. In the woods of the Marches there was much good hunting to be found. Deer and fox, and perhaps also boar, would have been plentiful. The Mortimer stronghold of Wigmore, a castle Edward would have known well, derives its name from the Welsh *Guig Mawr* – Great Forest. Edward enjoyed hunting throughout his life, and his delight in the chase was surely fostered as a youth. The aristocracy hunted on horseback, with hounds. It was regarded as a noble pursuit in itself, and to know the technical terms associated with hunting was seen as a mark of good breeding.[38] However, medieval writers also described hunting specifically as training for war. The poet and historian John Hardyng, writing in the 1450s, advocated that youths should learn to hunt as the stage of their education prior to training in arms. They were:

> For deer to hunt and slay and see them bleed,
> And hardiment giveth to his courage,
> And also in his wit he taketh heed,
> Imagining to take them at advantage.[39]

Above all, therefore, Hardyng saw the hunt as mental training. The hunt encouraged strategic and tactical thinking, as well as spatial awareness, and also exposed the youth to the psychological trauma of shedding blood. It would also have given him experience of the emotional 'rush' experienced in combat, or at least something close to it.

It is easy to imagine that Edward enjoyed an idyllic time at Ludlow. Yet as Edward studied, hunted, and learned the martial arts, England once again followed the path towards civil war. Duke Richard's victory proved short-lived: in February 1456 he was once again compelled to resign the protectorate. York had a new rival. The removal of Somerset had led to the emergence of Margaret of Anjou as a real political force. After her marriage to Henry, Margaret had quickly mastered English, but her political role remained limited. As we have seen, her first significant attempt to assert herself politically, in 1453, was a failure. Now, though, Margaret revealed herself clearly to be a 'great and strong-laboured woman'.[40] For the rest of the 1450s Margaret largely withdrew from London to the Midlands, at Coventry, where she was frequently joined by her husband. As Margaret's influence grew, the great offices of state were given to her allies. But Margaret also made an original claim to political authority, which was based on her position as mother to the Prince of Wales.[41] The result, unsurprisingly, was a clear polarisation in English politics, even though few of the lords were firmly committed to York's or Margaret's cause.[42] This was not the only cause of division. The young heirs of the dead at St Albans, namely Somerset, Clifford and Northumberland, had their own agenda – vengeance – which Queen Margaret did nothing to discourage. Somerset had been seriously wounded at St Albans and had watched his father die. The volatile Duke of Exeter also became associated with the young lords, and they appeared at court accompanied by unruly retinues. On one occasion Somerset and Sir John Neville, Warwick's younger brother, had 'great visaging [*sic*] together and mustered for to bicker in Chepe'.[43] The Duke of York was threatened several times; in October 1456, for instance, Somerset had to be restrained from attacking York at Coventry.

In some respects the late 1450s may be seen as a 'phoney war'. It is striking, for example, that in 1456 the Lancastrian government began to assemble artillery at Kenilworth Castle, under the supervision of a London merchant, John Judde.[44] An opportunity was also taken to diminish York's influence in the Marches, when several of his adherents were punished for their role in disturbances in South Wales. These included Sir William Herbert, of whom more shall be heard. However, although York's power had been curtailed once again, his young ally, Richard Earl of Warwick, was growing in strength. Warwick has acquired a mythic reputation, and it was at this time that his legend was born. One of the few acts of York's second protectorate that was allowed to stand was the appointment of Warwick as Captain of Calais. Warwick's lands and affinity brought him great power, but it was the Captaincy of Calais that would allow him to become such a force during the coming years. Unusually, Warwick resided in person, which allowed him fully to exploit the advantages of this office. Most notably, Warwick came to understand the value of seapower: if Warwick was 'overmighty' anywhere, it was on the sea.[45] Henry VI's government had neglected naval defence. This meant that, as the war turned against the English, French squadrons began to menace English ships and even the south coast of England itself. And then, on 28 August 1457, the celebrated French warrior Pierre de Brézé raided Sandwich, a key English port at this time. Warwick's response was to assemble an impressive fleet, but this was done at his own cost, and its loyalty was to him alone. Furthermore, Warwick's subsequent success at sea – including blatant acts of piracy – won him popular renown, especially in the south-east of England. According to *Bale's Chronicle*, 'he was named and taken in all places for the most courageous and manliest knight living'.[46] To some extent, though, Warwick's reputation was his own creation. His most recent biographer has noted that a 'chivalric' reputation entailed a certain amount of 'self-fashioning', and Warwick sponsored the dissemination of propagandist texts.[47] Warwick also won support through his liberality: according to the *Great Chronicle* Warwick 'was ever had in great favour of the commons of this land, by reason of the exceeding household which he daily kept in all countries'.[48]

With political tensions rising, King Henry intervened in person, in one of his few kingly acts. In March 1458 Henry brokered an agreement designed to bring peace.[49] Talks – which we must assume were difficult and fractious – took place in London. All of the nobles present were accompanied by substantial retinues, and serious precautions were necessary to keep peace in the streets.[50] Yet, eventually, all parties were compelled to accept Henry's arbitration. York and the Nevilles were to pay compensation to the heirs of the dead Somerset and Clifford, and a *chantry* was to be endowed at St Albans.[51] A further series of agreements bound the Percys and Nevilles to keep the peace, and all parties were liable to pay large fines if the terms of the agreement were breached. On 25 March, the feast of the Annunciation, a solemn ritual took place to consecrate the settlement. Henry led a procession to St Paul's, where a Mass was celebrated. York walked hand in hand with Queen Margaret, Salisbury walked beside Somerset, and Warwick walked with Exeter.

Many historians have been contemptuous of Henry's achievement, and some contemporaries, too, were scathing: one preacher at Coventry, William Ive, claimed Henry had 'made lovedays as Judas made with a kiss with Christ'. But the 'Love Day' should not be so easily dismissed; both sides made real concessions. Leaving aside the material reparations, the Yorkists were forced to accept a share of responsibility for the events at St Albans, and the young Lancastrian lords were expected to forgo vengeance. Moreover, public expressions of intimacy were a crucial part of any political reconciliation.[52] For medieval people, such rituals did not merely reflect or even reinforce political realities, they were supposed to *create* them too. Yet, ultimately, it does seem clear that reconciliation on Henry's authority could not hold. Sadly, Henry's intervention had come too late, for both himself and his realm. In autumn 1458, Warwick was summoned to London, presumably to account for his piratical activities. Warwick obeyed the summons, although somewhat tardily, and arrived in November. But there was a brawl at Westminster Palace – said to have begun when one of Warwick's men trod on the foot of a royal servant – and Warwick was lucky to escape alive. Warwick was convinced that a plan had been made in advance to murder him, and he withdrew in fury to Calais. By the spring of 1459 Queen Margaret and her allies, notably the Earl of Wiltshire and Viscount Beaumont, were ready to strike against their enemies. A great council was convened to meet at Coventry, but the Yorkist lords were pointedly excluded. According to *Benet's Chronicle*, they were indicted there for treason.[53] York and the Nevilles once again resorted to arms.

At Middleham, the Earl of Salisbury mustered his tough northern affinity; Warwick sailed from Calais with a veteran force from the garrison.[54] At Ludlow, however, the Duke of York raised fewer men than he had hoped. Some of his adherents had been cowed by their punishment in 1456; of the powerful Devereux family only the young Walter joined the duke. Others, including Sir William Herbert, had received royal pardons and were not willing to risk all in rebellion. Nevertheless, York's morale would have been improved by the presence of his two eldest sons, Edward and Edmund, who were now both old enough to fight. Edward, in particular, must have looked every inch the young warrior, like a hero of romance. Many contemporary writers commented on Edward's good looks.[55] After the German visitor Gabriel Tetzel met Edward in 1466, for example, he described him as a 'handsome upstanding man'. Philippe de Commynes was often critical of Edward, and considered him to be unduly obsessed with women, but he was nevertheless impressed by Edward's appearance. Commynes met Edward in Burgundy in 1470, and he could 'not recall ever having seen such a fine looking man'. Perhaps surviving portraits do not do Edward justice, although observers were often impressed by his physique as much as his face. When Edward's coffin was opened in the eighteenth century his skeleton was measured at 6 feet 3½ inches and it was broadly proportioned. Edward had a tremendous presence, of which he was keenly aware. Even later in life, when his looks had faded and he had put on weight, the Italian observer Mancini records that Edward 'was wont to show himself to those who wished to watch him, and seized any opportunity occasion offered of revealing his fine stature more protractedly and more evidently to onlookers'. In 1459 Edward was still untested, but his potential was clear: Yorkist verses from the following year were to describe him as 'Edward, Earl of March, whose fame the earth shall spread'.[56]

The Yorkists hoped to surprise the King at Kenilworth, but the royal forces were well prepared. Warwick made for Warwick Castle, via London, where the Yorkists had intended to gather their forces. But Warwick found the King already on the move, to the north. At Coleshill, near Birmingham, Warwick narrowly escaped an ambush laid by the Duke of Somerset. Warwick moved west, to join with the Duke of York, although the Lancastrians' strategy was initially focused on the Earl of Salisbury; it was the Yorkists' northern troops, of course, who had performed so effectively at St Albans. On 23 September Salisbury was intercepted by a strong force under Lord Audley, at Blore Heath in Shropshire, which had been raised in the name of the Prince of Wales. Although Salisbury was heavily outnumbered, Audley was killed and his men put to flight. Salisbury was able to join the other Yorkists at Ludlow. Blore Heath was a blow to Henry's supporters, although the force defeated by Salisbury was nothing compared to the main royal army. Henry's army was vast, one of the largest forces ever raised during the Wars of the Roses. Henry was accompanied by at least eighteen peers, together with their 'fellowships', although there may have been more, together with arrayed 'naked [unarmed] men' who may have numbered thousands. Furthermore, notwithstanding his characteristic offers of pardon, Henry VI was in an unusually determined mood, and this would have given heart to his men.[57] The Yorkists advanced to Worcester, but in the face of the royal host the Yorkists retreated first to Tewkesbury, and then to Ludlow. This was presumably a position of last resort, although fortifications, by Ludford Bridge, may have been prepared in advance. The royal army arrived here on the evening of 12 October.

The Yorkists had taken up a strong position and they were well supplied with artillery, but morale within their camp was low. Throughout the night York defiantly fired his guns, to bolster his army's flagging spirits. But according to Wavrin, it was at this point that a contingent of the Calais garrison, under the veteran Andrew Trollope, defected to the royal army. They were induced by 'an extremely well written' letter from the young Duke of Somerset.[58] Apparently the Calais men were shocked to learn they were expected to face the King in battle, although it is difficult to believe they could have been so naïve – even if the sight of the royal banner caused them to experience genuine doubts. Whatever their motives, this was a crushing blow, which rendered the Yorkist position untenable. The Duke of York, together with the other leaders, took flight. York would surely have sought counsel from the other lords, including his sons; no accounts survive to suggest the decision caused any debate. However, the debacle at Ludford Bridge was a cruel blow to York's reputation. His exploits at Pontoise were now almost twenty years in the past and must have seemed a distant memory indeed. Still, the duke remained the head of the House of York, and the Yorkist party's acknowledged leader. Yet in the following weeks and months Edward was to step out of his father's shadow, and he would emerge as a powerful and important figure in his own right. Edward Earl of March, at the age of eighteen, was about to prove himself a man.

Chapter 2

Calais, November 1459

The Yorkist lords disappeared into the night, leaving their men and their banners at the mercy of their enemies. Whether by accident or design, they broke into two groups. York was accompanied by his second son Edmund – they immediately fled by sea to Ireland – but Edward joined the Nevilles. Edward's party acquired a ship with the help of Lady Dinham, and it appears they may also have tried to reach Ireland. However:

> when they had gone to sea, my Lord of Warwick asked the captain and the others whether they knew the way westward, and they answered they did not, they did not know these waters for they had never been there. The whole noble company then became fearful, but the Earl of Warwick, seeing his father and all the others were afraid, said to comfort them that if it pleased God and St George, he would lead them to a safe haven. And indeed, he took off his pourpoint [tunic], went over to the rudder and had the sails hoisted. The wind took them to Guernsey, where they waited for the wind, until by the grace of God they reached Calais.[1]

The exiles were greeted by Lord Fauconberg: Warwick had left Calais in his care. Yorkist control of Calais, where Edward and the Nevilles arrived on 2 November, would prove crucial. Warwick's prowess at sea would ensure the Yorkists possessed a secure base from which they could plot their return.

Back in England, a Parliament was held at Coventry: the so-called 'Parliament of Devils'. The Yorkist leaders, including Edward, were declared traitors. Execution was not possible but the Yorkists were *attainted*, meaning their blood was deemed corrupt. Consequently, their descendants would not be permitted to inherit their lands and titles. The Yorkist lords were now legally 'dead', although the Lancastrian government continued to pursue them. Steps were also taken to deny the Yorkists a refuge: the young Duke of Somerset, supported by Andrew Trollope, was charged with the task of bringing Calais to heel. As we have seen, Somerset was a determined and aggressive man who passionately desired to avenge his father. He also possessed great charisma, and knew how to win and keep men's loyalty.[2] Somerset would prove a formidable adversary. Fortunately for the Yorkist lords, however, by the time Somerset was able to put to sea they were already safely ensconced at Calais. When Somerset approached Calais he was greeted by artillery fire from the Rysbank tower. Yet, refusing to admit defeat, Somerset moved down the coast and put ashore at Guines. He promised to pay the garrison their long overdue wages and was admitted to the fortress.

From his new base at Guines, Somerset did his best to harass the Yorkist garrison at Calais – 'full manly he made sorties', according to 'Gregory' – but without further support his mission could not succeed. Some of his supplies and men had already fallen into the Yorkists' hands, weakening his position considerably. In December a fleet was assembled at Sandwich to go to Somerset's aid.[3] Lord Rivers and Sir Gervase Clifton were in command. But there was much sympathy for Warwick within the coastal towns and he was kept well informed of the Lancastrian plans. On 15 January 1460, in the early hours of the morning, a Yorkist fleet descended on the port. Lord Rivers, his wife and son were all taken captive. More importantly, Warwick's men captured most of the Lancastrian fleet. Edward did not take any part in this daring exploit, but the surviving sources do suggest a growing prominence. William Paston recorded that Lord Rivers and his son Anthony were brought to Calais by the light of 'eight score torches'.[4] Then, according to Paston, Edward joined the other Yorkist lords in 'rating' [berating] the Woodvilles for their perceived pretensions. Perhaps this episode does not reflect especially well on Edward – and, as we shall see, there is a certain irony given the events that were to come! – but evidently 'my Lord of March' was now considered a person of substance whose activities were worth reporting.

By March 1460 the Yorkists were growing in confidence. It must have seemed clear that the Lancastrian government did not possess the necessary resources, or even the will, to displace them. Indeed, at this time Warwick felt secure enough to sail to Ireland, in order to consult the Duke of York, by now well established at Dublin. At Guines, however, the Duke of Somerset experienced immense frustration. A further Lancastrian expedition under the new Lord Audley was driven ashore by bad weather near Calais and Audley taken captive. Somerset's position was now precarious, but he remained a tenacious opponent. Although Somerset was almost crippled by lack of funds and supplies, Warwick's absence from Calais offered Somerset a glimmer of hope. On 23 April, St George's Day, Lancastrian forces attacked Newnham Bridge, the gateway to Calais itself.[5] The date is significant – doubtless Somerset wished to inspire his men by appealing to England's patron saint – and this was a determined assault. But the Lancastrians were repulsed with heavy loss. Unfortunately, the details of this engagement are obscure, but is it possible that Edward was involved in the fighting? Assuming that Somerset attacked in strength, the Yorkist lords still at Calais would surely have gone out to meet him.[6] Perhaps it was here that Edward first drew blood from an enemy. Shortly afterwards Warwick returned to Calais, despite the attentions of a fleet under the Duke of Exeter, who declined to engage. Warwick brought news of his talks with York, and the result had been profound. Edward was soon to be released from exile at Calais: the Yorkist lords would return to England.

In hard fighting, Lord Fauconberg and Sir John Wenlock won a bridgehead at Sandwich. On 26 June, Edward and Warwick took ship at Calais; with them were Salisbury, Lord Audley (who had defected to the Yorkists) and 1,500 soldiers. The Yorkists had also gained a useful ally in the person of Francesco Coppini, Bishop of Terni. Coppini had been sent by the Pope to preach a crusade in England, but he had now espoused the Yorkist cause. The weather was kind and the Yorkists 'arrived graciously at Sandwich'.[7] Propaganda had been disseminated in advance, which meant that a large number of Kentishmen rapidly answered their call to arms. At Canterbury, the three 'captains' who had been ordered to hold the city – John Fogge, John Scott and Robert Horne – decided instead to join the Yorkists.[8] The Yorkist army reached London on 2 July. After some debate they were greeted by the mayor and the Archbishop of Canterbury, although the City Fathers tactfully suggested to the Yorkist earls that their stay in London should be brief. Doubtless they were worried about the prospect of conflict in London itself, because there was still a Lancastrian garrison in the Tower, under the command of the veteran Lord Scales. However, it is also likely that the Yorkist leaders wished to confront King Henry as soon as possible, before he had time to gather substantial forces. They were themselves desperately short of money and supplies, but in two days of whirlwind activity the Yorkist earls raised loans from within the city and organised everything necessary for the campaign to come, including horses and baggage. By 4 July the

Yorkist army was ready to march and their vanguard led the way. A force under the Earl of Salisbury was detailed to keep watch on the activities of the Lancastrian garrison in the Tower, but the rest of the army followed the day after.

The Lancastrian court was at Coventry, as was common during this period, but on hearing of the Yorkist advance, King Henry and his supporters – who had already been raising troops – moved to Northampton.[9] Initially, Henry may have lodged at Delapré Abbey, south of the town, although his army would have camped in the open. Henry was accompanied by a number of peers – the Duke of Buckingham, the Earl of Shrewsbury, and Lords Beaumont, Egremont, and Grey of Ruthin – although there had been no time to raise a truly formidable force. But the Lancastrians were confident they were capable of making a stand. By 10 July, when the large Yorkist army arrived on the scene, the Lancastrians had taken up a fortified position with their rear protected by the River Nene. They 'ordained there a strong and mighty field [...] armed and arrayed with guns'. Banks and ditches would have been dug to the front and the Lancastrians would have been well supplied with artillery from their arsenal at Kenilworth. Although the Yorkists outnumbered the Lancastrians, the army must have looked on their enemy's strong position with trepidation.

The Yorkists' propaganda had always stressed that their argument was with Henry's courtiers, not with Henry himself. Therefore they needed to give the impression of wanting to present their case. Henry had now joined his army in the field. A delegation headed by Richard Beauchamp, Bishop of Salisbury, approached the Lancastrian camp, offering the Archbishop of Canterbury and Coppini as mediators. Perhaps Henry, even now, would have granted the Yorkist lords an audience but his noble supporters were in no mood to parley. The Duke of Buckingham was particularly belligerent. He has traditionally been regarded as a moderate influence, but by now he had lost all patience with the Yorkists. Buckingham angrily denounced the bishop's delegation as 'men of war' – because they came with an armed guard – and curtly cut off their protestations to the contrary. 'Forsooth,' said the duke, 'the Earl of Warwick shall not come to the King's presence; if he comes he shall die.' Yet remarkably, Warwick sent another herald, and it was not until this emissary was refused access to the King that the charade of negotiation finally came to an end. One last Yorkist messenger announced that 'at two hours after noon he [Warwick] would speak with him or else die in the field'.

Conflict was now certain. Realistically, had it ever been in doubt? As was customary, the Yorkists ordained three 'battles', although quite what this meant in practice is not always clear. It is often assumed that armies during the Wars of the Roses were crudely split into three large units, probably because the sources rarely tell us more. It has been plausibly suggested that further organisation may have been provided, albeit in a rather haphazard way, by grouping the men according to lordships or localities.[10] Yet evidence does exist to suggest that medieval battle plans – and dispositions – could be much more complex.[11] For example, the surviving battle plans drawn up by the Marshal Boucicaut and by Duke John 'the Fearless' of Burgundy clearly demonstrate that tactical considerations were taken very seriously. It was also considered how an army should be organised when not made up of seasoned warriors.[12] But on this occasion tactical factors were not crucial, although dispositions will be discussed more thoroughly below, when the sources allow this. The Battle of Northampton was partly to be decided by a factor sometimes neglected by historians, but which played a part in almost all of the battles and campaigns of the Wars of the Roses: namely, the weather. The Yorkists would also profit from an act of treachery. But what of Edward's own role in the battle? It is contested in the sources. Most chroniclers agree that 'little Fauconberg' was accorded the honour of leading the vanguard, consisting of the men of Kent. According to Wavrin, Warwick and Edward then jointly 'directed' the rest of the army, although Whethamstede tells us that Edward led one of the three 'battles'. At Northampton, the army probably looked to Warwick for overall direction, although it is clear that Edward held a position of responsibility. Perhaps Edward had already 'won his spurs' in the skirmish at Newnham Bridge, but now there was more at stake. What is certain is that here, for the first time, Edward would have stood under his own banner with a group of men looking to him for leadership.

According to Whethamstede, Warwick, Edward and Fauconberg made a simultaneous assault on the Lancastrian position, presumably hoping to win the day through sheer force of numbers. The assault took place in driving rain, which must have made the going difficult, and at around 400 yards the Yorkists would have come within range of the Lancastrians' artillery. This was a critical moment: the Yorkists might suffer heavy casualties and panic would surely ensue . . . Yet, inexplicably, the Lancastrian guns did not fire. According to the *English Chronicle*, 'the ordnance of the King's guns availed not', because they 'lay deep in the water, and so were quenched, and might not be shot'. The Yorkists' relief would have been countered by Lancastrian alarm. Worse was to come. There must have been archers in the Lancastrian camp but they made little impact and the Yorkists quickly arrived at the Lancastrians' fortifications. Lord Grey of Ruthin was in command of the Lancastrian 'vaward', which would have been expected to offer fierce resistance. But in a quite extraordinary move, Grey changed sides and went over to the Yorkists:

> the attacking squadrons came to the ditch before the royalist rampart and wanted to climb over it, which they could not do quickly because of the height [but] Lord Grey and his men met them and, seizing them by the hand, hauled them into the embattled field.[13]

The Yorkists now poured into the Lancastrian camp. According to Wavrin, Edward's own troops were the first inside. With their fortifications now useless, most Lancastrian soldiers seem to have thrown down their arms or taken flight. The Lancastrian nobles made a stand around King Henry's tent but, assailed from all sides, they stood little chance. Buckingham, Shrewsbury, Beaumont and Egremont were all killed. King Henry himself was captured by an archer, Henry Mountfort. The Yorkist victory was complete.

Clearly Grey's treachery was crucial: how can his actions be explained? The Yorkist *English Chronicle* argues that Grey was responsible for the 'saving of many a man's life', but later commentators have been less kind. In the words of H.T. Evans, 'in the sordid annals of even these sterile wars there is no deed of shame so foul'.[14] Yet Grey's motives remain shrouded in mystery. According to Wavrin, Grey's treachery had been arranged in advance, but if this is true it seems curious that Grey did not receive any immediate benefits from his 'foul' deed. Much later he became Earl of Kent, although for now survival was his only reward. Perhaps, as R.I. Jack has suggested, Grey's actions simply represent 'an inspired gamble' in the heat of the moment.[15] But it is also a puzzle why Lord Grey was entrusted with the 'vaward' in the first place. He was not an especially important magnate, and, unlike Fauconberg on the other side, he did not have a military reputation. This is particularly significant bearing in mind that the other nobles present do not seem to have been adequately prepared for battle; another leader, such as Buckingham, or the warlike Egremont, would surely have offered more defiance.

The battle lasted barely half an hour. Some royalist troops appear to have drowned in the river Nene while trying to escape, but losses on both sides were slight. As at St Albans the Yorkists' aim was to isolate and eliminate the Lancastrian leaders. Indeed, according to the *English Chronicle*, orders were given to spare the King and the commons, but to show no mercy to the lords and gentry. Probably neither Edward nor Warwick were heavily involved in the fighting; once it became clear the battle was won, and their chief rivals could not escape, doubtless their main concern was to ensure that the person of Henry VI was secured. This too was quickly achieved. Edward, as a soldier, was to face much greater challenges. Even so, his experience here may have strongly influenced his later conduct as both a strategist and a tactician. During the course of the French wars it had become received wisdom that defensive tactics would invariably prevail on the battlefield. Jean de Bueil, reflecting on his experience of fighting the English, counselled that 'a formation on foot should never march forward, but should always hold steady and await its enemies ...'[16] It is often suggested that the defensive approach adopted by York, at Ludford, and by Buckingham, at Northampton, was a legacy of their experience in France. For younger men such as Edward, however, the events at Northampton must have discredited the tactic of the entrenched encampment. If they did look to the Hundred Years' War for models, they would find them in the careers of men such as John Talbot, whose success depended on audacity and speed, not on dogged defence.

Following the battle the captive Henry was treated, ostensibly at least, with the deference due to a king; both Edward and Warwick kneeled before him, acknowledged him as their sovereign, and Henry was led with ceremony into Northampton. Although it was later alleged that Coppini had threatened to excommunicate the Lancastrians if they did not submit, the bodies of the dead Lancastrian lords were treated with respect. Buckingham, for instance, received honourable burial at the Grey Friars' Church; other victims were buried at St John's Hospital. On 14 July the Yorkists headed back to London, where the Earl of Salisbury, ably assisted by Sir John Wenlock, was now besieging the Tower. With the approach of the Yorkist army, Lancastrian resistance in the Tower quickly came to an end. Scales surrendered the Tower on 19 July. Some of the defenders would later be executed, but Lord Scales negotiated safe passage for himself and Lord Hungerford. But the Tower garrison had fired cannon into the city, which had enraged the citizens. Scales tried to reach sanctuary at Westminster but was recognised by a woman, taken captive by a party of Thames boatmen, and brutally put to death. Perhaps surprisingly, the Yorkist leaders are said to have much regretted these events, although of course there were many connections that could, under different circumstances, have brought together those who we today refer to as 'Yorkist' or 'Lancastrian'. Indeed, Lord Scales' death is said to have caused Edward particular grief; he was Edward's godfather.[17]

Edward and the Nevilles were now masters of the kingdom, but in the absence of the Duke of York it was not possible to pursue any of their long-term objectives. York landed at Chester on 8 September, however, and from here he made leisurely but regal progress, his sword borne upright before him like a king. For the last ten years, all of York's public statements had stressed that he was a loyal subject of Henry VI; his opposition was for the good of the 'common weal' and was not aimed at King Henry himself. But now York would propose a more radical solution to England's problems. He reached London on 15 October and upon arriving at Westminster Palace – where a Parliament had been hastily assembled – he immediately made his intentions clear. York placed his hand on the throne and looked for acclamation. But he was met with stunned silence. The Archbishop of Canterbury made a clumsy attempt at a greeting, asking York if he wished to see the King. York's reply was proud and haughty: 'I know of no one in the realm who would not more fitly come to me than I to him.'[18] Then he stormed out of the room, leaving consternation in his wake.

According to Wavrin, York's actions took Edward and the Nevilles by surprise, and they were appalled. Warwick went to remonstrate with the duke:

> and so [Warwick] entered the duke's chamber and found him leaning on a dresser. When the duke saw him he came forward and they greeted each other and there was some strong language between them, for the earl told the duke that the lords and the people disapproved of his intention to depose the King. While they were talking [Edmund] Earl of Rutland entered, the brother of the Earl of March, and he said to Warwick: 'Dear cousin, do not be angry, for you know that it belongs to my father, and he shall have it.' To this, the Earl of March, who was present, responded and said to the Earl of Rutland, 'Brother, offend nobody, for all shall be well.' After these words, when the Earl of Warwick had heard the duke's wishes, he left in anger without taking leave of anybody, except the Earl of March, whom he asked very kindly to come the next day to London, where a council meeting would be held. March said he would not fail to be there.[19]

This is a fascinating passage. It provides evidence of a rapport between Warwick and Edward, which had presumably developed in exile, but also evidence of Edward's growing influence, which was to a certain extent independent of York *or* Warwick. Wavrin's account has not been generally regarded as reliable, however.[20] Were Edward and Warwick really surprised or appalled by York's actions? It seems extremely unlikely.[21] Nevertheless, it may be that Warwick, ever the politician, quickly realised that the lords were still reluctant to depose Henry VI. Edward, a much more subtle and sensitive man than his father, would surely have reached the same conclusion. Perhaps, then, the cause of the arguments reported by Wavrin was not that Duke Richard had sought the throne, but that he had (literally) shown his hand too soon.

In truth there were flaws and inconsistencies in the claims of both York and Lancaster. The lords, who were mindful of the oaths they had sworn to Henry but also of the power that York now held, eventually offered a curious compromise. York reluctantly agreed to the terms of the 'Act of Accord', which was similar to the Treaty of Troyes, whereby Henry would remain king for the rest of his life, but thereafter the crown would pass to York and his descendants. Henry, of course, had little choice but to acquiesce, although his queen was still at large and would scarcely have been expected to honour such an agreement. Margaret and her adherents were scattered – the Queen had herself fled to Wales in precarious circumstances – but she quickly took steps to gather her supporters.[22] By early December York was preparing for war. The Yorkists split their existing forces, although of course they expected to raise fresh troops for the struggle to come. York went north, Warwick was to remain in London, and Edward was sent to the Marches; it was to be his first independent command.

Edward reached the Marches in time for the seasonal festivities, and spent Christmas at Shrewsbury.[23] Shrewsbury was the traditional mustering point for English armies that were about to campaign in Wales, and we may assume that Edward was expected to bring order to the principality. Edward's intended opponents – if they would stand against him – would have been retainers and allies of Jasper Tudor, Earl of Pembroke, King Henry's half-brother.[24] During the late 1450s Pembroke, helped by his personal connections to the Lancastrian court, had become immensely powerful throughout Wales. He had consolidated his position during the Yorkists' exile, and, although he now had fled to Brittany, his influence endured. One of Edward's main aims would have been to take the northern Welsh fortresses of Harlech and Denbigh.[25] These castles, along with the Tudor strongholds of Pembroke and Tenby in the south, were now crucial to Lancastrian communications and provided a possible gateway for invasion forces. Like Henry V before him, it appears to have been envisaged that Edward should gain his first experience of leading an army in Wales; it was now conceivable, of course, that Edward would shortly become Wales's prince.

Edward was accompanied from London by a number of lords and gentry, such as Lords Audley and FitzWalter and Humphrey Stafford. If they were not with him already, he was shortly to be joined by Lord Grey of Wilton and Sir Walter Devereux, among others. The 'odious' Croft brothers also joined Edward; presumably they now treated him with more respect! But the most significant of his supporters was surely Sir William Herbert of Raglan, who was accompanied by his younger brother Richard. As we have seen, Herbert had declined to support the Duke of York during the Ludford Bridge campaign, but he was now firmly committed to the Yorkist cause. Moreover, Herbert was a veteran – he had served in France with the formidable Matthew Gough – and evidently the support he offered Edward at this time was vital. Herbert was an able, ambitious, and thoroughly ruthless man, and he was to become a pillar of the Yorkist regime. Important military and administrative tasks would be delegated to his charge, and Edward's patronage would allow him to become the most powerful man in Wales.[26]

Edward was accompanied by the nucleus of an effective and cohesive force, but recruitment in the Marches allowed him quickly to increase his numbers. Most of the men who joined him came from Herefordshire. Edward might have known many of them from his time at Ludlow. Crucially, Edward was able to call on the services of seasoned warriors, many of whom had seen service in France. William Worcester recorded the presence of several veterans in Edward's army during this campaign.[27] They included, for example, Henry ap Griffith, John Mylewater and Philip Vaughan of Hay. Worcester also gives the names of sons who were following in their fathers' traditions, such as James Ash, whose father Hopkin, 'a handsome man', was 'of war'. At this early stage in the Wars of the Roses there must also have been many unnamed veterans of lower status who would have answered Edward's call; some of the unfortunate men from the mass grave at Towton appear to have been experienced soldiers. One of these, whose remains were recorded as 'Towton 16', has excited particular comment.[28] He was a tall and robust man, probably in his late forties. Abnormal developments in the elbow are consistent with sustained practice of archery. At some stage in his career he had sustained a horrific blade wound to his jaw that would have left him permanently disfigured. But the wound was well healed: testimony to the skills of a medieval surgeon. Based in the Welsh Marches, Edward would have been able to recruit skilled bowmen like Towton 16, and the experience of veteran archers would have been extremely valuable. Strength and a good eye could perhaps be taken for granted, but these men would also have understood how bowmen should be deployed on the battlefield. Command was invariably held by aristocrats, but experience was always highly valued.

Edward must have looked forward to the coming campaign with confidence, but early in the New Year a messenger brought him shattering news. Although Margaret of Anjou was currently in Scotland,[29] northern Lancastrian supporters – notably the Earl of Northumberland – had quickly raised an army. They were reinforced by the Duke of Somerset, who had now returned to England,[30] and the Duke of Exeter, who had led their retinues on a lightning march from the West Country. On 30 December, at Wakefield in Yorkshire, Edward's father had engaged the Lancastrian forces and been utterly defeated.[31] York himself had been killed on the field. Edward's brother, Edmund, with whom he had spent his boyhood and to whom he seems to have been close, had also been slain.[32] Warwick's brother, Thomas, was another fatality. Edward's uncle, the Earl of Salisbury, had been captured and executed after the battle. The heads of the fallen were displayed on the gates of York at Micklegate Bar; the head of the duke himself was mockingly adorned with a paper crown. The Wars of the Roses would now enter an especially vicious phase: prisoners could rarely expect mercy and the mutilation of the dead would become commonplace.

Edward made a rapid and instinctive response to the disaster at Wakefield. Edward was moving into England – although to what immediate purpose is unclear – but he then received news of a Lancastrian landing in Pembrokeshire, in West Wales. The Earl of Pembroke had returned, and he was joined by the Earl of Wiltshire. According to the *Short English Chronicle*, the two earls arrived by sea with 'Frenchmen and Bretons, and Irishmen'.[33] We may assume that Pembroke brought the Bretons and Frenchmen. Wiltshire, who had briefly fled to exile in Flanders, had returned via Ireland, where he held extensive estates as Earl of Ormond. Wiltshire's contingent would therefore have included Irish *galloglass* (from the Irish plural *galloglaigh* or 'foreign soldiers') – heavily armed professional soldiers – and less well equipped light infantry or *kerns*.[34] It is not clear when the Lancastrians landed or when Edward received warning, but we can assume that news of the Lancastrians' movements was brought to Edward by the Yorkist retainer, John Dwnn. Based at Kidwelly, the Dwnns were well placed to track and monitor Lancastrian movements, much to Pembroke's chagrin. If the news did come from the Dwnns, evidently the intelligence they brought to Edward was crucial: Pembroke was later to attribute his defeat to the actions of 'March, Herbert and the Dwnns'.[35]

Presumably the Dwnns encountered messengers from Pembroke who were seeking support. Pembroke and Wiltshire quickly began to raise troops from the surrounding area. Chief among the men who answered Pembroke's call were the Scudamore brothers, Sir John and Sir William, who, like many of those in Edward's army, had experience of war in France. Sir John, described by Worcester as 'the most valiant' of the family, is said to have brought thirty men, some of whom may also have been veterans. Why men chose one side over the other, was, as ever, often determined by local factors: Ralph Griffiths has suggested this campaign was greatly concerned with 'the waging of old feuds and the settling of old scores'.[36] The last decade had seen much conflict between Welshmen who could now be regarded as 'Yorkist' or 'Lancastrian', but some of these enmities had deeper roots. How significant was it, for example, that the Scudamores were grandsons of Owain Glyndwr, whereas the Herberts were grandsons of his enemy Dafydd ap Llewelyn?[37] Of course family honour mattered in England too – the significance of 'feudlike' behaviour may have been underestimated – but in Wales kinship links were always crucial. Family histories – and family hatreds – were kept alive by the bards, which meant that minor squabbles could receive an epic treatment that transcended their often petty origins.[38]

Edward and his advisors cannot have predicted Pembroke's movements with certainty. Ultimately, of course, Pembroke would have aimed to join the main Lancastrian force, but several options remained open to him. If Edward was aware the Lancastrians were making for Llandovery (which they did) – a move into mid Wales – this could have suggested a further destination in the English Midlands: perhaps Pembroke was intending to make for Coventry, which would undoubtedly have opened its gates to a Lancastrian army at this time. There, the Lancastrians would have been able to rest securely, before joining Margaret's army for a final push towards London. But there was another plausible route, with disturbing implications for the Yorkists near Shrewsbury. Although Pembroke's 'country' was in the south, he was also influential in the north, where his supporters still held the important castle of Denbigh, as we have seen.

Pembroke could have planned to join with Lancastrian sympathisers in north Wales and the north-west of England, before then joining Margaret (like everyone he must have been surprised by the speed of events in Yorkshire). With harsh winter conditions precluding a journey through the mountainous heart of Wales, the best way would have been to move east and then north, following the Severn valley. This would have meant that the Mortimers' heartland – Ludlow and the surrounding area – would lie in the Lancastrians' path.

Throughout the Wars of the Roses Lancastrian armies gained a reputation for cruelty and violence that was carried out away from the field of battle; this must have affected Edward's thinking. The previous year, following the Yorkist leaders' flight at the Rout of Ludford, the Lancastrian army had moved on to Ludlow and sacked the town:

> When they had drunken enough of wine that was in taverns and other places, they full ungodly smote out the heads of the pipes and hog's heads of wine, [so] that men went wet-shod in wine, and then they robbed the town, and bore away bedding, clothes and other stuff, and defouled many women.[39]

The presence of foreign troops in the Lancastrian army would have heightened fears of ill discipline. Indeed, the Kern had gained a reputation for terror throughout Europe. In the Hundred Years' War kerns are said to have returned from raids with heads, and even dead babies, as trophies.[40] The later invasion of England by the Earl of Lincoln, in 1487, shows the Irish were quite capable of discipline, but on this occasion enmities between local men could have ensured that the Lancastrian leaders would fail to keep the Irish troops in check. Potentially, therefore, Edward faced two serious problems, if he was to continue his advance into England. First, he risked being trapped between enemy armies. Second, he would be asking men to follow him in the knowledge that their homes and families could be at risk.

Pembroke's army had therefore to be confronted for reasons of both strategy and morale. It made sense to meet them in the area of Mortimer's Cross, a crossroads to the south of Ludlow, where he could intercept the Lancastrians wherever they were headed. Many of his men could be dispersed back to their homes, but they could easily be called upon when needed. Furthermore, Edward would be able to fight on ground he knew well, where he might even have hunted as a youth. Doubtless he retired to Ludlow, or perhaps to Wigmore, in order to wait in comfort for his prey.

On 2 February, the eve of battle, Edward would have risen in the knowledge that his enemies were close at hand. Probably Edward was now at Wigmore or Croft Castle. He would have expected to spend the day making preparations, waiting for the reports of scouts. But his plans were interrupted by an extraordinary event. Let the author of the *English Chronicle* take up the story:

> And the Monday before the day of battle, that is to say on the feast of the Purification of Our Blessed Lady, about ten o' clock before noon, were seen three suns in the firmament shining clear, whereof the people had great marvel, and thereof were aghast. The noble Earl Edward them comforted, and said 'Be of good comfort, and dreadeth not; this is a good sign, for these three suns betoken the Father, the Son, and the Holy Ghost, and therefore let us have a good heart, and in the name of Almighty God, go we against our enemies.'[41]

The phenomenon described by the chronicler has been explained by modern science. The additional two 'suns' are called *parhelia* or *sun dogs*: they come into being, on cold days, when the sun is low in the sky. Light is refracted through ice crystals, creating the illusion of three suns. Parhelia are beautiful and they may still provoke wonder, but in a modern person they would not cause the sense of terror recounted in the chronicle. The medieval understanding of such events therefore needs to be explained. It is easy to poke fun at medieval people's ignorance of the natural world, but educated people did provide rational explanations for the cause and effect of natural wonders. In short, they were seen as examples of divine providence, evidence of God's presence in the world. They were regarded as signs of God's favour and of impending change. The great Roger Bacon, for instance, considered parhelia to be signs of particular significance.[42]

The *Illustrated Life of Edward IV* presents Edward, at the moment the parhelia appear, appealing to God for guidance, just like Paul at Damascus: 'Lord, what will you have me do?'[43] Coppini had described Edward as 'prudent and magnanimous',[44] but we should remember that Edward was still only eighteen years old. The loss of his father and brother must have shaken him to the core. For Edward, then, this was a moment of great personal significance. He afterwards adopted the 'rose-en-soleil' as his badge, and he would use this as a personal emblem for the rest of his life.[45] However, the passage quoted above also provides evidence of Edward's precocious abilities as a leader. Medieval battles were chaotic and confusing. Tactics *were* important, as was military train-ing, but willpower and motivation became increasingly important as the battle progressed. Although he would be able to inspire those around him by 'feats of arms', if the commander was to be in the thick of the action it was therefore crucial for him to communicate a clear sense of motivation before battle was joined. This is not controversial, but how could this be achieved? Evidently it required a commander to convey a message that would appeal to contemporary *mores*.[46] On this occasion Edward convincingly presented the parhelia as a sign from God that his cause was good and just. On the day of the battle, he and his men would fight as one.

From Llandovery the Lancastrians moved on to Brecon, and from there they followed the north bank of the Wye, via Hay and Weobley (the alternative route, which would have brought them directly to Mortimer's Cross, via the 1,250-foot pass at Forest Inn, must have seemed forbidding in the depths of winter). This meant, assuming that Edward was based somewhere near Wigmore, that the road to Hereford, and thence to England, was still open. It might have been tempting to evade the Yorkists and to push on. But Pembroke must have been aware that the Yorkists were familiar with the local area and they were fresh. Pembroke would have been concerned that the Yorkists could fall on them at any time. He therefore decided to engage the Yorkists, even though he must have known his polyglot force did not hold any significant advantages. On the morning of 3 February the Lancastrians approached Mortimer's Cross from the south, in the certain knowledge that they would meet the Yorkists on the way.

Almost certainly the Yorkists had the choice of ground, and they would have wanted to find a position that would allow them to make use of their advantage in archers. Local historian Geoffrey Hodges has identified a plausible site that would have suited them well. This is just to the south of the crossroads itself, and Hodges' case is supported by place-name evidence.[47] Here, Edward's army would have been able to take up a position with well protected flanks. The River Lugg would have been to their left, and to the right there is a bank with steep wooded slopes. Yorkist archers would certainly have been deployed on the flanks, although perhaps also, initially, to the front.[48] In truth we know little for certain about either side's dispositions, although Edward himself would have taken position in the centre, under his personal standard. This was Edward's first experience of overall command, but he had now seen battle at first hand on more than one occasion; at Northampton he had taken a leading role. He knew what he was about to see, and what was expected of him. Edward also took the field in the knowledge that he was surrounded by men he had known since childhood, and this must have been a great comfort. There would have been comfort, too, in the fact that his men seemed in good heart. Even if he still nursed doubts and fears behind the mask of command, he had successfully used the omen of the parhelia to inspire his men and to stiffen their resolve. Perhaps the Croft brothers, watching this young giant leading his troops with confidence onto the field, thought wryly of the times they had bullied him at Ludlow.

If the Yorkists adopted 'traditional' English tactics, relying heavily on their archers, then the onus was on the Lancastrians to attack. According to the Elizabethan poet Michael Drayton, whose work may preserve earlier oral traditions, Wiltshire and his Irishmen formed the Lancastrians' van. Wiltshire and his personal retinue would have been 'harnessed' and armed in the same manner as their peers. The gallowglass, although they must have looked archaic to English eyes, with two-handed axes and conical helmets, would also have been heavily armoured. However, the Irish light infantry would have been less well equipped. Few, if any, would have worn armour. Although some would have been armed with broadswords, others might have carried only 'darts' (javelins) and *skeins*.[49] Of course, Drayton cannot be regarded as a reliable guide to events, but his poem, which suggests the Irish fought with great courage, does evoke their experience at Stoke which is better documented:

> The Earl of Ormond [. . .] came in the vanguard with his
>   Irishmen,
> With darts and skains [skeins]; those of the British blood,
> With shafts and gleaves [glaives], them seconding again,
> And as they fall still make their places good,
> That it amazed the Marchers to behold
> Men so ill-armed, upon their bows so bold.[50]

Yet if the Irish showed immense bravery under fire, their leader could not match their courage. His father had been a noted war captain in France, serving under both Bedford and Talbot, but the Earl of Wiltshire gained a reputation for cowardice. Discussing the first Battle of St Albans 'Gregory' disparagingly refers to him fighting 'manly with the heels, because he was afraid of losing [his] beauty',[51] Wiltshire did not redeem himself at Mortimer's Cross. He fled once again, leaving his men to their fate.[52]

An 'arrow storm' would have taken a terrible toll on the Lancastrians, but even on occasions when English archery was at its most deadly – for example at Agincourt or Halidon Hill – the two armies invariably came 'to hands'. We must assume that the Battle of Mortimer's Cross eventually ended in a *mêlée*, with the soldiers on both sides – including the archers – fighting with hand weapons. Edward himself, perhaps wielding the pole-axe that would have allowed him to make use of his great height and strength, would have been a conspicuous target. He would therefore have been in the thick of the action. He would have been surrounded by picked men, determined to protect their lord and his banner, but they could not have sheltered him from every danger. Did Edward know the relief – then exhilaration – that followed when he survived death by a hair's breadth?

It was, of course, during the chaos of the *mêlée* that morale, as well as skills and numbers, would be crucial. In this, as in every other aspect, the Yorkists held the advantage. Eventually, the Lancastrian line must have wavered; then it would have broken as men fled in all directions, discarding weapons and equipment as they ran.[53] Probably the Yorkist lords took to horse in order to pursue their fleeing enemies. Some did escape, most notably Pembroke, whose elusive qualities were more generously regarded than Wiltshire's. However, a number of the Lancastrian leaders seem to have made a desperate last stand, before they were forced to surrender. The prisoners included Henry Scudamore (Sir John's son) and Pembroke's famous father, Owen Tudor. According to the *English Chronicle*, 4,000 of the Lancastrians lay dead.[54] The field belonged to the Yorkists.

Edward's victory was almost complete, but not quite. Surely Edward had Wakefield in mind when he now resolved how to deal with his prisoners. Perhaps the Lancastrian prisoners still expected to be treated according to the laws of chivalric combat, but Edward would show no mercy. After the Yorkist army had rested – possibly Edward retired to Wigmore for the evening – the most notable of the prisoners, including Owen Tudor, were taken to Hereford, where they were to be beheaded. The old Welshman was evidently shocked at his treatment, but eventually resolved to meet his death with stoicism. This was a quality the chronicler 'Gregory' particularly admired. Tudor was

> trusting always that he should not be headed [*sic*] till he saw the axe and the block; and [even] when he was in his doublet, he trusted on pardon and grace till the collar of his red doublet was ripped off. [But] then he said 'That head shall lie on the stock that was wont to lie on Queen Katherine's lap,' and put his heart and mind wholly unto God and full meekly took his death.[55]

For Owen Tudor, who had married a queen while still a mere squire, fortune's wheel had turned full circle. The Yorkists' left Tudor's head in Hereford, 'on the highest grice [step] of the market cross', as a grim symbol of their victory.

Edward remained in the area for over two weeks, and his actions at this time have led to some debate. The main Lancastrian army was now moving south at a furious pace. Why did Edward not hurry to support Warwick? Evans has argued that Edward was expecting, and perhaps even *hoping*, that Warwick would be defeated.[56] However, this is implausible. Evans's argument is based on the assumption that Warwick had been opposed in principle to Henry VI's deposition, but, as we have seen, this is doubtful. It is more likely that Edward decided to wait on events and was expecting to receive news, and instructions, from Warwick. On 12 February Warwick despatched a commission of array to Edward, which empowered him to raise more troops, but there is no indication that Warwick exhorted Edward to come to his aid at once.[57]

Possibly Warwick had underestimated the speed of the Lancastrian advance. The Lancastrian army, now joined by Queen Margaret herself, had swept south, leaving a trail of plundered towns in its wake. Warwick, perhaps responding to the fears of terrified Londoners, moved northwards to St Albans in order to bar the Lancastrians' way. Here, on 17 February, Warwick's army met the Lancastrians, but was heavily defeated.[58] The Lancastrians regained custody of King Henry. Warwick's younger brother, John, recently created Lord Montagu, was captured.[59] The earl himself was forced to flee. In Wavrin's account and the *English Chronicle*, which may preserve Warwick's own justifications, the Yorkist defeat is attributed to the treachery of an obscure Kentish esquire called Lovelace. However, the author of 'Gregory's Chronicle', who appears to have been present at the battle in some capacity, implies Warwick's own preparations were to blame, and that he was comprehensively out-manoeuvred by the Lancastrians. Warwick may have been let down by his scouts, but it can also be argued that his cautious, defensive tactics played into the hands of the Lancastrian commanders, whose own tactics relied, as they did at Wakefield, on speed, aggression and surprise. It is strange, however, that the Lancastrians did not take immediate advantage of their victory and failed to march on London. Instead, Margaret sought to negotiate entry with the City Fathers, who stalled by sending a delegation of noble ladies. This delay would have far-reaching consequences, as the historian Charles Ross makes clear: 'control of the capital, with its departments of state, its financial power, and its symbolic prestige, was again denied to the Queen's party'.[60] Margaret's loss was to be Edward's gain.

Edward could have known of Warwick's defeat by 19 February. Now, at last, he moved with decision. Warwick would have taken pains to reassure Edward that all was not lost but Edward's new sense of purpose was surely self-inspired. Edward no longer bowed to Warwick's authority. The defeats suffered by his father and Warwick must have made Edward realise that his destiny lay in his own hands. His victory at Mortimer's Cross – which appeared divinely ordained – would have given him new belief in his own powers. It is also striking that Edward retained the confidence of his men, even after Warwick's defeat had made their prospects uncertain. Edward met Warwick, who had managed to extricate at least some of his army from the disaster at St Albans, in the Cotswolds. From here, the Yorkists now moved at speed: not to engage Margaret, but to get to London. Edward and Warwick were approaching London by 26 February. By now the Lancastrians had grown impatient and there had been minor skirmishes in the outskirts of the city. Nevertheless, because there was still no indication that the Lancastrians were preparing a serious assault, this only served to harden opinion against Margaret's forces. London opened its gates to the Yorkist army. On hearing this news, the Lancastrians withdrew north.

In London, the Yorkist lords quickly came to a momentous decision. If there had been any genuine doubts whether Henry could legitimately be deposed, these were now set aside.[61] It was argued that Henry, by choosing to rejoin his wife, had broken his oath. As Margaret's army was responsible for York's death it therefore followed that Henry had breached the Act of Accord. Edward, now heir under the terms of the agreement, was, of course, next in line to the throne. Edward's own claim to the throne was explained during his first Parliament, in November 1461, and presumably the same arguments were put forward at this time. Edward's legitimate descent from Lionel of Clarence was stressed, and it was argued that Henry – deemed a usurper, like all the Lancastrian kings – had presided over chaos. Henry's deposition would be to the 'universal comfort and consolation' of all Englishmen, because it would allow Edward, their 'rightwise and natural liege and sovereign lord', to take the throne in his stead.

But it was important, of course, to ensure that protocol was seen to be observed, and to convey that Edward's accession had popular support. To this end, there were a number of carefully orchestrated ceremonies, starting on 1 March. First, George Neville (now Bishop of Exeter) addressed a crowd – allegedly 3,000–4,000 strong – at St George's Fields. When the crowd (perhaps with some prompting) called for Edward to be king, their 'captains' took this news to Edward at Baynard's Castle, the York family's London residence. On the next day Edward's title was formally proclaimed throughout the city. The following day (3 March) a 'great council', including the Nevilles, John Duke of Norfolk, the Archbishop of Canterbury, Herbert, Devereux, and 'many others' un-named, was hastily convened to 'agree and conclude' that Edward should take the throne. On 4 March Edward heard Mass at St Paul's, before proceeding to the Great Hall at Westminster Palace. Here, Edward took the oath, and wore the robes of state for the first time. Taking his seat on the marble chair called the 'King's Bench', he was acclaimed once again by those present and formally 'took possession of the realm of England'.

Doubtless the Nevilles took a hand in the stage-management of these ceremonies, and Warwick has traditionally received the credit for Edward's accession to the throne. Certainly, contemporary foreign observers did believe Warwick was fully in control of events, and they would continue to do so for many years to come.[62] However, modern historians have been more sceptical of Warwick's influence: did Edward really need a 'kingmaker'?[63] Of course, Edward's Mortimer claim was not enough – his title ultimately depended on military power – but much of the army at his back was his own. These soldiers had followed him from the Marches, many of them at their own cost,[64] and now they trusted to a bond forged in battle. Edward, not Warwick, had won the hard-fought victory that saved the Yorkist cause. People cannot have failed to compare Edward's victory at Mortimer's Cross to Warwick's miserable failure at St Albans, even though the latter's popularity with the commons appears to have remained intact.

However, the choice people had to make was not between Edward and Warwick, but between Edward and Henry VI. Edward's good looks, noble bearing, and affable manner – and also his newly-proven military prowess – provided a sharp contrast to the monkish King Henry. Evidently the verses recorded for posterity in 'Gregory's Chronicle' are propagandist, but they may genuinely reflect the dominant feeling of optimism in London at this time:

> Let us walk in a new vineyard, and let us make a gay garden
> in the month of March with this fair white rose and herb, the
> Earl of March.[65]

Yet Henry, for all his faults, had been the anointed king, and how could Edward's throne be secure when the main Lancastrian army – including much of the English aristocracy – remained undefeated? At his inauguration Edward held the sceptre of state but he did not wear the crown. This conveyed a clear message: Edward would seek divine sanction for his claim in a colossal trial by combat. It was to be the bloodiest battle ever fought on British soil.

Chapter 3

London, March 1461

There was no time to waste; the Yorkists set to work almost immediately. Edward was already in command of an army, but a much greater force would be required if the Yorkists were to confront and defeat the vast Lancastrian host to the north. On 6 March, two days after Edward became King, proclamations were issued explaining Edward's claim to the throne and calling for support.[1] The Earl of Warwick and the Duke of Norfolk set out to raise forces in their own 'countries'. Presumably lesser captains such as John Fogge were also sent into the regions to raise troops. Meanwhile, Edward remained in London, the hub of Yorkist activity. One of Edward's most important tasks was to raise funds. The mayor and aldermen of London had already advanced £4,666 to the Yorkists since July, but in the first three days of Edward's reign they were prevailed on to loan a further £4,048.[2] Individuals also contributed further sums.[3] The merchant Hugh Wyche, for example, who was soon to become Mayor of London, loaned Edward £100. Bishop George Neville contributed to the war effort by pawning some of his jewels to a grocer. Sadly for Bishop Neville, he was never to see the jewels again: the grocer intended the jewels to be delivered to Calais, but the ship in which they were stowed, as it lay in the harbour at Sandwich, was captured and plundered by pirates.

The money raised by the Yorkists was required to pay soldiers, but also to buy equipment and supplies. The town records of Lydd, for example, note payments received 'for victuals sent to London, to the journey of York'.[4] It was, of course, a major undertaking to feed an army on the march. As John Gillingham suggests, in the fifteenth century an army consisting of 10,000 soldiers would have been the equivalent of one of the country's major cities on the move.[5] Presumably armies would also have been followed by a multitude of non-combatants, including priests, merchants, even prostitutes. On this occasion Edward's administrators appear to have done their work thoroughly – Wavrin writes of the large number of wagons stuffed with supplies and ordnance gathered in the fields outside the city – but it was simply not practical for an army to carry all the supplies it required.[6] Otherwise we must assume part of the wagon train would have lagged several days behind the vanguard. Commanders therefore expected to replenish their supplies *en route*. During the campaigns of 1460–1, however, the commanders of both sides struggled to find adequate provisions for their armies. It was rare for medieval campaigns to take place during the colder months. Seasonal shortages, in a particularly hard winter, made life hard for both men and animals. Prior to the second Battle of St Albans, for example, the large army raised by the Earl of Warwick is said to have suffered from hunger, which led to desertions. The sarcastic comments made by 'Gregory' about the Yorkist 'spears' suggest the army was forced to rely on daily foraging: 'spearmen they be good to ride before the footmen and eat and drink up their victuals'.[7]

The Lancastrian army must also have suffered during the winter campaigns. They would have been well supplied in the north from their bases at York and Hull, but as they moved south they may have found provisions harder to come by.[8] If they resorted to increasingly brutal expedients in order to acquire food and other supplies then this may, at least in part, explain the stories that appear in several chronicles of Lancastrian atrocities. Whethamstede, for example, compared the northerners in the Lancastrian army to Attila's Huns; the first Crowland Continuator described the Lancastrians as a 'whirlwind from the north [...] a plague of locusts covering the whole surface of the earth'.[9] But the chroniclers' accounts are generally rather vague, and it has been suggested that behind the high-flown rhetoric we may glimpse nothing more than the usual activities of an army on the march.[10] Even so, perhaps we should not belittle the experiences of local communities that found themselves in the Lancastrians' path. Moreover, although it is clear that reports of Lancastrian activities may be exaggerated, some evidence does exist which implies the Lancastrian commanders struggled to maintain discipline. After the Battle of Wakefield it is said that the Duke of Somerset agreed to ransom the Earl of Salisbury, 'but the common people of the country, which loved him not, took him out of the castle by violence and smote off his head'.[11] Lancastrian successes in the field may be attributed to a disciplined core made up of the aristocratic retinues and the soldiers of the Calais garrison. As 'Gregory' noted of the second Battle of St Albans, 'the substance that got that field were household men and feed men.

I wene [*sic*] there were not 5,000 men who fought in the Queen's party, for the most part of [the] northern men fled away'.[12]

Edward's clerks, in the proclamations noted above, made an appeal for popular support, exploiting the fears caused by the Lancastrian advance. The civil war was characterised as a battle between north and south, with the dividing line at the Trent. The first of Edward's proclamations was sent out to the sheriffs of thirty-three counties: with the curious exception of Northumberland, all were in the south. It was said that the Lancastrian leaders, 'moved and stirred by the spirit of the Devil', had permitted acts 'in such detestable wise and cruelness as hath not been heard done among the Saracens or Turks to any Christian men'. It was alleged that churches had been plundered and desecrated; women, including nuns, raped; men murdered or maimed. Edward commanded that no man in his own army should act thus, on pain of death, and he called on every man between the ages of sixteen and sixty to help him resist the depredations of the Lancastrians. Incentives were also offered. A second proclamation stated that any supporter of Henry VI who submitted within ten days would be given a full pardon. Significantly, however, this offer was not extended to anyone with an income of over 100 marks a year, which meant that Henry's aristocratic supporters were excluded. Presumably the intention was to disturb the relationship between the Lancastrian lords and their more humble supporters – an extension of the Yorkist policy at Northampton.[13] Rewards of £100 were placed on the heads of a number of notable Lancastrian leaders. These included Andrew Trollope, who had been knighted as a reward for his services to the Lancastrian cause.

On 11 March Lord Fauconberg marched out of London, in command of the Welsh and Kentish foot. Edward followed two days later. From London Edward's progress north was slow, presumably in order to allow recruits to join the army *en route*. Edward received reports that the Lancastrians were based at Nottingham, although he soon discovered they had withdrawn across the Trent to York. This gave Edward a chance to join forces with Warwick, somewhere in Yorkshire, although the Duke of Norfolk appears to have remained at least a day's march behind. By now Edward must have been in command of a truly substantial army, although both sides' forces must have been huge by the standards of the time. Everyone understood how much was at stake; most people must have assumed the coming battle would settle the quarrel once and for all. The Lancastrian army included at least nineteen peers.[14] Men had joined the Lancastrian army from all over England, not just from the north as Yorkist propaganda would suggest.[15] The burghers of York, who usually sent contingents of 400 men to join campaigns, are said to have sent 1,000 men to join the Lancastrian army at Towton.[16] Bishop Richard Beauchamp of Salisbury and the author of *Benet's Chronicle* both believed that Edward's army consisted of 200,000 men, although this figure is surely exaggerated.[17] Most modern historians have accepted a more plausible estimate of 50,000 men to account for the numbers on both sides,[18] but it is impossible to give an exact figure.

It is usually assumed the Yorkists were outnumbered during the Towton campaign, although if Norfolk's forces are taken into account this is uncertain. Only eight peers are thought to have joined the Yorkist army,[19] although the personal resources of Edward and Warwick equated to those of several earls. Large numbers of gentry joined the Yorkists, including Edward's supporters from the Marches such as Sir William Herbert. Others included Walter Blount, William Hastings, John Howard and Humphrey Stafford, all of whom were knighted after Towton and were to become important members of the Yorkist regime. A contemporary poem, *The Rose of Rouen*, which pays tribute to Edward's prowess during this campaign, suggests that Edward also succeeded in attracting substantial urban support.[20] Contingents are said to have been sent from London, Bristol, Canterbury, Coventry, Gloucester, Leicester, Nottingham and Salisbury.

On Friday 27 March Edward was based just south of the River Aire, probably at Pontefract. From here the Yorkists planned to advance north, crossing the Aire at Ferrybridge, although the Lancastrians were now moving south to meet them. Over the next two days there were to be two substantial engagements, at Ferrybridge and Towton, although there may also have been a number of other smaller skirmishes. Perhaps surprisingly, however, the written sources are limited. Historians will always be indebted to the experts who worked on the Towton Project, although naturally it is not possible to provide an account based on archaeological evidence alone. Of the most contemporary written sources, the most detailed account is provided by Jean de Wavrin.[21] Wavrin's narrative may be supplemented by two letters sent to Coppini after the battle (both dated 7 April), written respectively by Bishop George Neville and Bishop Richard Beauchamp.[22] Several contemporary English chroniclers, including 'Gregory', Whethamstede and the author of the 'Brief Latin Chronicle' provide short accounts of the two battles.[23] With the exception of Wavrin, however, none of the contemporary sources offer many useful details about the fighting itself. Most previous historians have therefore been influenced by the substantial narrative provided by Edward Hall, who was writing in the 1530s.[24] But since Hall was writing many years after the events he describes, his account must be used with care. Yet just as we cannot take his word as a sure guide to events, it is too simplistic to dismiss his account as 'unreliable'. Rather, we should regard Hall as an early interpreter of the Wars of the Roses. He evidently took a keen interest in the mentality of fighting men, as well as the course of events. Moreover, Hall was a thoughtful and industrious scholar; it is clear that Hall had immersed himself in the sources, some of which may now be lost. Hall also appears to have drawn on local oral traditions, although how he acquired all of this knowledge is unclear.

Hall provides the most vivid account of the events at Ferrybridge. Lord FitzWalter is sent to guard the crossing at Ferrybridge, in order to secure the passage for the Yorkist army. This presumably takes place towards the end of the day on Friday 27 March. Secure in the knowledge that the great Lancastrian army is still some way off to the north, making its ponderous way south from York, FitzWalter and his men settle down for the night. However:

> after many comparisons were made between the Earl of Northumberland and the Lord Clifford, both being lusty in youth, and of frank courage, the Lord Clifford determined with his light horsemen to make an assault [on] such as kept the passage of Ferrybridge, and so departed from the great army on the Saturday before Palm Sunday, and early before his enemies were awake, got the bridge, and slew the keepers of the same, and all such as would withstand him.

Lord FitzWalter is hastily aroused from sleep:

> The Lord FitzWalter hearing the noise, suddenly rose out of his bed, and unarmed [i.e. without armour], with a poleaxe in his hand, thinking that it had been an affray amongst his own men, came down to appease the same, but before he could say a word, or knew what the matter was, he was slain.

The news quickly reaches the Earl of Warwick:

> When the Earl of Warwick was informed of this feat [Clifford's assault] he, like a man desperate, mounted on his hackney, and came blowing [in tears] to King Edward, saying 'Sir, I pray God have mercy on their souls, which in the beginning of your

enterprise have lost their lives, and because I see no success of the world, I remit the vengeance and punishment to God our creator and redeemer,' and with that he alighted down and slew his horse with his sword, saying 'let him fly that will. For surely I will tarry with him that will tarry with me,' and he kissed the cross hilt of his sword.

Warwick's bravado has the desired effect, and the Yorkists are moved to avenge their fallen comrades. However, Clifford and his men are equally determined to defend the bridge and the Yorkists sustain heavy casualties. Edward, despairing of the possibility of success through a frontal assault, sends a substantial body of men to cross the river further downstream at Castleford. This force, under Fauconberg, Robert Horne and Walter Blount, is therefore able to attack Clifford's flank, and the Lancastrians are forced to retreat. Clifford and his men withdraw several miles to the north, but are pursued by the Yorkists. A further skirmish takes place at Dinting Dale, to the north-east of the village of Saxton. Clifford removes his 'gorget' (throat protection),[25] either through 'heat or pain' and he is shot and killed by an enterprising Yorkist archer. The Earl of Westmorland's brother, Lord John Neville (from a different branch of the Neville family), is also killed.

Hall's account of the action at Ferrybridge is packed with colourful, plausible details. Warwick's stirring speech has become famous, but it is not so well known that Hall almost certainly derived this anecdote from Continental sources: the same story appears in the work of both Jacques Duclercq and the Monstrelet-Continuator.[26] Not all of Hall's sources can be traced, although some of his stories might have been inspired by other accounts of battles. For example, Clifford's boldness calls to mind Thomas of Clarence at Baugé, who met his death because he was desperate to prove himself in battle.[27] Other sources do confirm that a serious engagement took place at Ferrybridge, although they invariably offer fewer details than Hall's account. 'Gregory', for example, tells us that the Battle of Ferrybridge was fought on 'Palm Sunday Eve', that Lord FitzWalter was killed, as in Hall's narrative, and that Warwick was wounded by an arrow in his leg. According to Bishop Neville:

> Our adversaries had broken the bridge, which was our way across, and were strongly posted on the other side, so that our men could only cross by a narrow way, which they had made themselves after the bridge was broken. But our men forced a

way by the sword, and many were slain on both sides. Finally
the enemy took to flight, and very many of them were slain as
they fled.

Wavrin tells us that a skirmish involving the Duke of Suffolk's scouts
escalated into a more substantial encounter in which 3,000 men were
killed. In this account the fighting lasts several hours before the Yorkists
eventually gain control of the crossing. But it remains unclear what exactly
the Lancastrians were trying to achieve, and what proportion of their army
was committed. Was the Lancastrians' intention merely to hinder the
Yorkist advance, or was control of the bridge originally conceived as part
of a larger plan?

Bishop Neville's account implies that the battles of Ferrybridge and
Towton took place on the same day, although this is difficult to understand. If the bridge was indeed broken it would have taken considerable
time for the whole Yorkist army to cross the river, even though Edward
had now secured the passage. Although the 'narrow way' made by
the Yorkists would have allowed men to cross it would not have been
sufficient for horses, nor for the carts that carried the crucial supplies
and ordnance. Perhaps the Yorkists made hasty repairs to the bridge, or
constructed a pontoon,[28] although it is possible that some of the army was
forced to take a detour via Castleford. This would have taken up much
of the day, whichever solution to the problem was chosen. Wavrin tells
us that, having crossed the river, Edward and his army made camp for
the night. Edward might have secured lodgings at Sherburn-in-Elmet,
although it is doubtful that the small town could have provided shelter
for the whole army. Many of his soldiers must have camped in the open,
spending a miserable night. The weather was unseasonably cold – there
was snow and hail – and provisions were now running short. According
to Wavrin, both men and horses suffered terribly. Moreover, although
the Yorkist soldiers would have been exhausted, their minds must have
remained active, thinking of the fight to come. Somewhere to the north,
their Lancastrian enemies endured a similar experience.[29] On the next
day Edward received reports from his scouts that the main Lancastrian
army was taking position nearby, and that the fields were filling with
armed men. At this news Edward was 'overjoyed, because he wished for
nothing more than to fight them', even though the Duke of Norfolk's
forces had still not joined him. The Yorkist army prepared for battle.

Contemporaries referred to the Battle of Towton by a number of
names. It was also known, for example, as Palm Sunday Field or the Battle

of Sherburn. However, the location of the battlefield is unusually well defined. In the Act of Attainder passed by Parliament later in the year the battle is said to have taken place 'in a field between the towns of Sherburn-in-Elmet and Tadcaster [...] called Saxtonfield and Towton-field, in the Shire of York'.[30] Wavrin's account suggests the Lancastrians chose the ground. We may therefore presume the Lancastrians took a position somewhere between the villages of Saxton and Towton, which are roughly 1½ miles apart.[31] To the south of Towton there is a plateau that rises to an average height of 150 feet; a wide, windswept plain. To the west is a steep-sided valley, through which flows the Cock Beck; to the east the plateau descends more gently towards what, in 1461, would have been heavy, sodden ground. In the fifteenth century there would have been substantial woods on both sides.[32] The plateau is bisected by a shallow depression at North Acres; this becomes progressively deeper to the west, as Towton Dale intersects with the Cock Valley. At the time of the battle the plateau is likely to have been unenclosed agricultural land, crossed by roads and tracks – much, indeed, as the landscape is today. It is generally accepted that the Lancastrians 'took their field' overlooking North Acres, on the line marked by the present-day monument: a relatively strong position with well protected flanks. The Yorkists took position on a ridge to the south. The extent of their line is probably marked by a hawthorn tree, which serves today as a trigonometric point.

Wavrin depicts Edward acting as an inspirational leader prior to the battle, attempting to give heart to his cold and hungry men:

> When the said earl [Edward] was informed by his men of the disposition of his enemies he went along the length of his battles until he reached his horsemen, which he had placed on his wing, and he said to them with a smile, 'My children, I pray you that today you will be good and true to each other, because we are fighting in a good and just cause!' And then each of them replied in a loud voice that they wished to do this.

This emphasis on Edward's leadership is suggestive, not least because his opponent, Henry VI, was not at the battle in person. It is doubtful that anybody ever expected him to fight, but Henry had been present on the field, as a figurehead, at the first Battle of St Albans, Ludford Bridge and Northampton. Henry's presence, as rightful king, was intended not only to inspire his own men but also to deter his opponents. In the early battles of the Wars of the Roses, rebels may have experienced a genuine feeling of anxiety when opposing the royal banner. But now that Edward had claimed the throne, this latter advantage was lost to the Lancastrians, and Henry would have become a primary target for elimination. It therefore made sense, in purely pragmatic terms, for Henry to remain behind at York, where he was accompanied by his wife and son. Henry's royal banner would still have flown on the field at Towton, but one of the most important uses of a banner in battle was to signify the position of its owner. There were, though, a number of brave and experienced noblemen on the Lancastrian side, whose banners would have provided rallying points for their own troops. It is usually assumed the Lancastrian commander was Henry Duke of Somerset, on account of his rank and because he appears relatively prominently in the sources.[33] However, it is uncertain which of the Lancastrian leaders, if any, was acknowledged as overall commander in Henry's absence.[34] At Towton, men on both sides would have been acutely aware that Henry VI was *not* present, and this surely means that his banner would have lost some of its power. Conversely, when *Edward's* banner advanced, this would be a sign to the Yorkist army that their leader had thrown himself into the thick of the fray.

None of the sources refer to gunpowder weapons at Towton, although the bad weather may again have rendered them useless.[35] We may assume the battle would have begun with an archery duel. In Hall's account Lord Fauconberg once again commands the vanguard, including the Yorkist archers, as he had done at Northampton. Fauconberg draws upon his intelligence and vast experience to turn the bad weather to the Yorkists' advantage:

> The Lord Fauconberg, which [*sic*] led the forward [foreward] of King Edward's battle, being a man of great policy and of much experience in martial feats, caused every archer under his standard to shoot one flight and then made them stand still. The northern men, feeling the shot, but by reason of the snow not perfectly viewing the distance between them and their enemies, like hardy men shot their sheaf arrows as fast as they might, but all their shot was lost, and their labour in vain, for they came not near the southern men by forty tailor's yards. When their shot was almost spent the Lord Fauconberg marched forward with his archers, who not only shot their own sheaves, but also gathered the arrows of their enemies and let a great part of them fly against their own masters, and another part they let stand on the ground, which sore annoyed the legs of the owners when battle was joined.

This has become one of the best-known elements of the Towton story. Hall's account has been followed by many previous writers without question, even though Fauconberg's quick-witted actions are not recorded in any contemporary sources. However, the importance of the weather *was* noted in a more strictly contemporary account, the *Registrum* of Abbot Whethamstede. Whethamstede tells us that at a crucial moment the wind changed – he ascribes this to divine grace – by which means the Lancastrian archers were 'nullified and frustrated'. Although it cannot be proved that Hall read Whethamstede's narrative, it is possible, as on other occasions, that Hall amplified his original sources in order to create a more dramatic and convincing account.

Most sources suggest that the Lancastrians abandoned their defensive position and attacked. According to Wavrin, the Duke of Somerset, accompanied by Trollope, Lord Rivers and Rivers' son, Lord Scales, led a furious charge and routed part of the Yorkist army. A tradition has arisen that some of the Lancastrian forces had been concealed in Castle Hill Wood, to the west of the battlefield, although there is no direct evidence for this.[36] As Edward's 'horsemen' are said to have been put to flight – and pursued for 11 miles – this suggests that at least some of the Lancastrians must also have been mounted. It is generally accepted that light cavalry had a valuable role during the Wars of the Roses as scouts; we may also safely assume that men mounted to pursue their enemies, as, indeed, we have already seen.[37] Later there will be some discussion of how, at the Battle of Tewkesbury, a small group of mounted 'spears' could wreak havoc against demoralised men on foot. Nevertheless, few historians have been willing to consider the possibility that cavalry frequently played an important role during the battles of the Wars of the Roses.[38] Perhaps this is strange, because cavalry, presumably employed in flanking attacks, would have provided a useful option to a commander facing large numbers of archers. Yet in the absence of more substantial evidence it is difficult to pursue this argument any further.

We cannot be certain of the Lancastrians' tactics, therefore, although a number of sources do support Wavrin's view that the Yorkists came under serious pressure. The 'Brief Latin Chronicle' tells us that many of Edward's soldiers 'turned their backs'. According to Bishop Beauchamp there was 'a moment when [. . .] almost all our followers despaired [. . .] so great was the power and impetus of the enemy'. The Yorkists would surely have been defeated had not Edward, 'with the utmost of human courage', thrown himself into the fray. Wavrin also stresses the importance of Edward's personal role. In his account Edward rallies the troops, riding up and down his lines, reminding them of his right to the crown. This done, Edward 'dismounted his horse, saying to them, sword in hand, that this day he wished to live or die with them, and so he gave them greater courage, and then he placed himself in front of his standard'. It is quite possible, of course, that Edward's personal role has been exaggerated. But other sources suggest that leaders could inspire their men by ostentatiously choosing to fight on foot. Commynes, writing of the Battle of Montlhéry in 1465, at which he was present, describes the behaviour of Sir Philip de Lalaing:

> Sir Philip de Lalaing dismounted because it was then the most honourable practice amongst the Burgundians that they should dismount with the archers, and always a great number of gentlemen did so in order that the common soldiers might be reassured and fight better. They had learnt this method from the English, with whom Duke Philip had fought in his youth for thirty-two years [*sic*] in his youth.[39]

Most English noblemen fought on foot, of course, but we may assume it remained a symbolic moment when a commander dismounted from his horse. It is not difficult to imagine how a charismatic leader such as Edward could have exploited this to his advantage.

From this point the *mêlée* was long and bitterly contested. Wavrin tells us the fighting at Towton was fiercest in the quarter of the Earl of Warwick, notwithstanding his wound.[40] Medieval sources often claim that battles lasted for hours, and Towton was no exception. But of course, the warriors at Towton could not have fought continuously for such a length of time. Fatigue and dehydration would have made this impossible. As Anne Curry points out, chroniclers' accounts of battles do not often record repetitive actions; they are usually episodic, focused on the most crucial details.[41] They rarely provide details of the waves of attacks, withdrawals, regroupings, and lulls in the fighting, although these must have taken place. Strange as it may seem, there may even have been periods of respite agreed by both sides. At the Battle of Neville's Cross, for example, fought in 1346 between the English and the Scots, it was said of the two sides that 'three times they drew apart from one another for rest so as to fight again more strongly'.[42] Yet it is difficult to understand how such agreements were made, because the fighting in a *mêlée* was chaotic. A major problem was the extremely close nature of the fighting, because men were invariably tightly pressed together; warriors in the front line would often be put under pressure by the forward momentum of the men following.

Weapons and fighting techniques needed to be adaptable, in order for men to cope adequately with a range of combat situations.[43] The poleaxe was a particularly versatile weapon. It was at its most deadly when used with two hands, like a woodsman's axe, although this required a warrior to have space of at least 3 feet behind him and to either side. In a tight press, therefore, the top spike would become most useful. It would be used like a bayonet and thrust into an opponent's face or perhaps into the armpit, where armoured protection would be limited. A sword could also be adapted if space was limited. When warriors were fighting shoulder to shoulder one hand would be placed on the blade, which would be used to thrust at opponents, whereas the crossguard and pommel could be used like a club. We have seen that common soldiers might use staff weapons such as the glaive, which could be used to hook an opponent to the ground. English archers became renowned in the French wars for their quick and nimble fighting,[44] and we may presume they also displayed these skills in the Wars of the Roses. During the *mêlée* they used a variety of arms including hatchets, the *maul* and a range of bladed weapons. The narrative accounts of the Battle of Agincourt suggest most wounds in the *mêlée* were suffered to the head, and this is borne out by the archaeological evidence from Towton[45] (most of the men from the mass grave appear to have been killed during close quarter fighting; evidence of wounds caused by projectiles is limited). The majority of wounds were inflicted by bladed weapons, although the use of other weapons has also been identified. Towton 41 received three wounds to the back of the head that are consistent with the top spike of a poleaxe, presumably delivered after the victim was lying face down and immobilised. Towton 16, an experienced soldier who may have been singled out for special attention, received no fewer than eight wounds to the head. One blow from a blunt object, perhaps a mace or a maul, had crushed his skull. The skeletons from Towton Hall provide graphic testimony to the bloody reality of medieval combat.

For a long time the battle was evenly poised, but then, suddenly, the Yorkists gained the advantage. According to *Hearne's Fragment*, the arrival of John Duke of Norfolk, 'with a fresh band of good men of war', was crucial. Edward must have been hoping and praying that Norfolk would arrive in time; the duke and his men gave renewed drive to the Yorkist assaults. The exhausted Lancastrians began to give ground and finally their lines were broken. Now the battle became a rout, although according to the *Crowland Chronicle* Edward did not share in the pursuit. Now secure in his victory, Edward remained on the field, surrounded by the heaps of dead. This is an arresting image, although there were sound practical reasons for Edward to stay on the battlefield. Although the Lancastrians had been defeated, Edward could not have been sure their army had been destroyed. Henry VI had stayed away from danger, at York, and could continue to act as a focus for resistance. Somerset, for instance, who survived the battle, might have rallied some of his men in order to continue the fight, as Warwick had done after St Albans. Edward needed to maintain a base to which his men could bring news. Edward may also have presided over the execution of Lancastrian prisoners. According to 'Gregory', forty-two Lancastrian knights were despatched on the field. Thus the brutal work continued, even after the battle was won.

The Yorkists offered no quarter to their enemies at Towton, regardless of rank. Some writers, notably Andrew Boardman, have argued for a sharp distinction between the conduct of warfare during the Wars of the Roses and that of the Hundred Years' War.[46] For the aristocracy, so the argument runs, the Wars of the Roses were brutal, merciless conflicts, whereas, in the French wars, defeated noblemen could expect to be treated with respect. There was, of course, a crucial difference between the two conflicts: it could be argued the suppression of rebellion was not war at all, strictly speaking, but justice. Now that Edward claimed to be the rightful king, anyone who resisted him could be deemed a traitor. But some qualifications are required because the picture is complex. Noble prisoners were not always slaughtered without mercy during the Wars of the Roses. For example, Warwick's brother, John Neville, was captured twice and still survived.[47] It must also be stressed that the 'chivalric code' did not always save as many noblemen in France as is sometimes assumed – and not only because French noblemen were mown down by arrows. Many captured nobles in France *were* spared, of course, and they were often forced to pay large ransoms to their captors, although it was unusual for there to be a large numbers of prisoners after a pitched battle. The Battle of Poitiers, fought in 1356, was a notable exception. Françoise Bériac and Chris Given-Wilson have surveyed the experiences of defeated armies at a number of other fourteenth-century battles, and their conclusions are stark:

> The predictable fate of a soldier, noble or otherwise, who, finding himself on the losing side of a fourteenth-century battle, failed to make good his escape, was not to be taken prisoner. It was to die.[48]

Fifteenth-century battles were usually no different. At Towton, a high proportion of the defeated army failed to make good their escape. On this occasion it appears no orders were given to 'spare the commons', and they died alongside the aristocratic leaders. Some of the men from the mass grave had suffered blows to the head from bladed weapons that were delivered from above or behind. This may suggest they were killed in flight – probably by mounted opponents.[49] If we may assume Norfolk smashed into the Lancastrian left flank then this would have turned the battle lines, pushing the Lancastrians back towards the steep slopes of the Cock Valley. In the snow, the slopes must have been slippery and treacherous. Some of the Lancastrians may have fallen to their deaths; others would have suffered terrible injuries that were to leave them at the mercy of their pursuers. Towton Dale offered a safer entrance to the valley. Presumably some of the Lancastrians sought to put the river between themselves and the Yorkists, and then to take shelter in the woods to the west. But it appears the river was not easy to cross, and there were few safe places to ford. Today the Cock Beck does not appear the most formidable of obstacles, although there has been considerable silting and it remains deep in parts. On the day of the battle, moreover, it is possible that the river was in spate. Towton Dale would have provided easy access to the Cock Valley for Yorkist horsemen, who relished the opportunity to ride down the desperate Lancastrians. The meadows beside the river became a killing ground. One of the fields has become known to this day as 'Bloody Meadow'. Deep into the sixteenth century local people remembered the slaughter that took place. Hall wrote of the carnage at the Cock Beck, where 'the common people there affirm that men alive passed the river upon dead carcasses, and that the great river of Wharfe, which is the great sewer of the brook, and all the water coming from Towton, was coloured with blood'. This, presumably, is the source of the infamous legend of the 'bridge of bodies'. Writing slightly later than Hall, John Leland claims to have seen the five large pits in which a great number of Lancastrian casualties were originally buried.[50]

Many died on the battlefield. Others were trapped and butchered in the Bloody Meadow. Yet we must assume that many of the Lancastrians escaped successfully from the battlefield, taking the road north towards Tadcaster, although the Yorkists continued to pursue them.[51] Bishop Neville claimed that 'so many dead bodies were seen as to cover an area six miles long by three broad and about four furlongs'. For those that fled towards Tadcaster, the River Wharfe – much deeper and wider than the Cock – now provided a barrier to safety. Here, as at Ferrybridge, Bishop

Neville tells us that the Lancastrians had deliberately broken the bridge before the battle, although it is difficult to understand what advantage they would have gained from this. Another possibility is that the bridge may have been damaged by the pressure caused by unusual levels of traffic. Gravett suggests the bridge might have been sabotaged by Lancastrian fugitives seeking to hinder the Yorkist pursuit.[52] But, if so, they condemned many of their comrades to death, either in the icy waters of the Wharfe or at the hands of their enemies. The pursuit was relentless.

On the Yorkist side, the only casualties of note were Lord FitzWalter and the Kentish captain, Robert Horne. Naturally the Lancastrian casualties were much higher. A number of the Lancastrian leaders were killed, including the Earl of Northumberland, and Lords Clifford, Dacre, Welles and Neville. Sir Andrew Trollope, who may still have been suffering from the wounds he received at St Albans, was also slain. We cannot know for certain how many others died. Several chroniclers assert that over 30,000 men were killed, although it is well known that medieval writers often exaggerated the numbers of dead at a battle.[53] A figure of 28,000 reached the Pastons.[54] Apparently this estimate was based on the reports of heralds who were present on the field, and this figure was widely circulated. Nevertheless, most modern historians remain sceptical. The figure quoted in *Annales* – 9,000 – is regarded as being much more credible, although there is no particular reason to assume the author was better informed than other writers. Perhaps it is enough to say that thousands died at Ferrybridge and Towton, when the casualties on both sides are taken into account. It is also necessary to consider those who died afterwards of their wounds, or possibly due to exposure in the bitter cold. We should also not forget those whose lives were ruined by the injuries they received. Indeed, some wounded men may have been killed by their own comrades, as 'mercy killings' were a feature of medieval battles.[55] The famous Amboise Paré, writing in the sixteenth century, was at first appalled by this practice when he was a young surgeon. As the French army approached Turin, in 1536, Paré encountered three men who had been badly burned:

> Beholding them with pity there came an old soldier who asked me if there was any means of curing them. I told him no. At once he approached them and cut their throats gently and, seeing this great cruelty, I shouted at him that he was a villain. He answered me that he prayed to God that should he be in such

a state he might find someone who would do the same for him, to the end that he might not languish miserably.[56]

If such actions did take place at Towton, then perhaps we may glimpse a rare moment of charity on this most brutal and bloody of fields.

The Battle of Towton will continue to provoke vigorous debate. But all those who have written about Towton throughout the ages have agreed that something terrible happened on 29 March 1461. Contemporaries were appalled. Wavrin wrote that 'the battle was furious and the slaughter great and piteous, because the father did not spare the son, nor the son the father'. Bishop Neville similarly lamented the tragedy of civil war:

> O miserable and luckless race and powerful people, would you have no spark of pity for our own blood, of which we have lost so much of fine quality by the civil war, even if you have no pity for the French!
>
> If it [Towton] had been fought under some capable and experienced captain against the Turks, the enemies of the Christian name, it would have been a great stroke and blow. But to tell the truth, owing to these civil discords, our riches are beginning to give out, and we are shedding our own blood copiously among ourselves [...] But the limitations of writing do not permit me to state my mind on all these things.

The last sentence speaks volumes. It is difficult for a writer to convey, in any real sense, the horrors of Towton. One of this period's most skilful writers, who was deeply interested in warfare, barely even tried. Yet 'Gregory' was clearly moved, observing that few men understand the realities of war 'until the thought be tried out'. His terse account of the battle concludes with a simple prayer for the dead: 'Jesu be thou merciful unto their souls. Amen.'

Chapter 4

York, March 1461

God had spoken; Edward had been anointed in the blood of Towton. Now – though Henry VI still lived – Edward was truly King. The day after Towton Edward entered York. Henry, Margaret and their son had taken to flight, but Edward captured the Earl of Devon and several others. They had taken refuge in the castle but were not able to offer any meaningful resistance. Devon was executed forthwith and the heads of dead Lancastrians replaced those of Edward's kinsmen on Micklegate Bar. Edward remained at York for three weeks and celebrated Easter (5 April) with great pomp. Doubtless Edward's army was exhausted, but many of his lieutenants remained active throughout Yorkshire at this time. They extracted submissions from a number of northern towns. Royal agents were also charged to find men to replace those who had died at Towton.[1] Evidently Edward planned to continue the pursuit of the Lancastrians. In the last week of April Edward marched north, to Durham. On 1 May Edward was at Newcastle, where he presided over the execution of the Earl of Wiltshire, whose luck had finally run out.[2] By now, however, Edward must have been aware that the Lancastrian royal family was out of his reach. They had sought exile in Scotland, where they were welcomed by Bishop James Kennedy of St Andrews. Henry and Margaret were quickly joined by many of their partisans, including Somerset, Exeter and Sir John Fortescue. Much of Northumberland remained under Lancastrian control, including the great castles of Bamburgh, Dunstanburgh and Alnwick, but Edward decided that the subjugation of the far north could wait. In time, this would be a task for the Nevilles. Warwick was to be assisted by his able younger brother, Lord Montagu, who had been released from captivity after Towton. Newcastle was left in the capable hands of Lord Fauconberg, soon to become Earl of Kent, with a garrison of 120 men. Edward himself turned south, towards his coronation.

Edward's experience as a leader was still limited, notwithstanding two important victories in the field, but he appears to have understood instinctively that the time had come to delegate. Or was he influenced by others? Surely Edward sought counsel, and it is tempting to conclude that Warwick was guiding the young King. Certainly, Warwick was never slow to offer advice. During the preparations for one campaign, probably in 1463, Warwick lectured Edward about the importance of logistics; he stressed that adequate victuals for the army would need to be purveyed in advance.[3] Edward's response is not recorded. However, Warwick was not the only person in a position to advise Edward. One man who won Edward's confidence early in the reign was Sir William Hastings, who would become Edward's intimate companion and one of his most effective servants. He was ennobled shortly after Edward's coronation, and Hastings' power would become immense. This was mainly because, as king's chamberlain, he controlled access to Edward.[4] Sir William Herbert was another whose power grew quickly. As early as 8 May 1461 Herbert received important offices in South Wales to reward him for his service.[5] Herbert was also ennobled after Edward's coronation, along with his associate Sir Walter Devereux; the latter became Lord Ferrers of Chartley. Other influential figures included Sir Humphrey Stafford, later Earl of Devon, John Tiptoft, Earl of Worcester, and Edward's kinsmen the Bourchiers. The Bourchiers included Henry, Earl of Essex, and Thomas, Archbishop of Canterbury.

Edward's coronation, which took place on 28 June 1461, was a spectacular occasion. In his early years as King, Edward was presented as a saviour who would heal the land. Iconography associated with Edward drew on biblical texts, prophecies and other esoteric material, including sources connected with alchemy.[6] Edward was compared, for example, to Moses, who led his people out of bondage, and to Joshua, another decisive general whose success was heralded by divine portents. The Italian diplomat Count Dallugo was dazzled by the young King, and came to believe that Edward's subjects worshipped him like a god.[7] Some former Lancastrians, such as the Woodville family, were now glad to take advantage of Edward's mercy and entered the Yorkist fold. There were still plenty of others, though, who refused to give up the Lancastrian cause, even though their position was now precarious. Many of the Lancastrians' most able military leaders, such as Clifford and Trollope, had perished in the carnage at Towton. Several of those who had survived, such as Somerset, found themselves in areas where they were strangers, cut off from their spheres of influence. Nevertheless, frequent commissions of array in the spring and summer of 1461 show that Towton had not ended the matter for good. One troublesome area was the March of Calais. Hammes Castle resisted the Yorkists until October. Both sides made use of artillery.[8] The garrison finally surrendered to Sir Walter Blount, now Treasurer of Calais, although not until he had given them £250, which he had to borrow from a Florentine merchant.[9]

In July 1461, even though most of the Lancastrian leaders were in exile in Scotland, both sides turned their attention to Wales. The irrepressible Jasper Tudor was still at large. He had been joined by the Duke of Exeter, and the Lancastrians still held a number of strong castles in the principality. Edward planned to lead an expedition in person to crush the resistance. On 8 July Herbert and Ferrers were commissioned to array the men of the marches, and on 12 July Edward instructed Philip Harveys, his newly appointed Master of the King's Ordnance, to make ready for the coming campaign.[10] The Lancastrians attempted to use diplomacy to counter Edward's preparations. An embassy was despatched to France from Scotland. Lord Hungerford was officially the leader of the delegation, although Somerset was also in the party.[11] The Lancastrians hoped to persuade King Charles to grant them a substantial loan and to send a force of 2,000 men to serve in Wales. Indeed, Charles had already adopted an aggressive policy towards the new Yorkist regime: a French force under Pierre de Brézé had landed on Jersey in May. But Charles died suddenly on 22 July, due to complications following dental surgery, before the Lancastrian embassy arrived. Charles's son and successor, Louis XI, had been on bad terms with his father and had therefore favoured the Yorkists. The Lancastrian diplomats found themselves in a difficult position. Lord Hungerford's safe conduct was no longer considered valid because it was in the name of Charles VII, not Louis, and he was arrested at Dieppe. The Duke of Somerset did not carry an official safe conduct; he was taken into custody at the castle of Arques. Moreover, Brézé's expedition was cancelled and he was out of favour at court. These were serious reverses for the Lancastrians, which improved the mood at the Yorkist court considerably. At the end of August Richard Woodville (Lord Rivers) who had only recently been a Lancastrian himself, told Count Dallugo that Henry VI's cause was now 'lost irretrievably'.[12]

With the risk of foreign intervention receding, this explains why Edward now pursued the planned expedition to Wales with less urgency. By the middle of August Harveys was on his way directly to Hereford; he was accompanied by Richard Garnet, the Sergeant of the King's Tents. But Edward took a more leisurely route, travelling circuitously via

Canterbury, Sandwich, Salisbury and Bristol. Edward reached Bristol on 4 September and here he was 'full honourably received in as worshipful wise as ever he was in any town or city'.[13] Edward spent a week at Bristol, where he enjoyed the hospitality of Mayor William Canynges, in the mayor's luxurious home. It must be said that not all of Edward's stay was given up to pleasure: he also presided over the execution of the Lancastrian Sir Baldwin Fulford, and his presence ensured that three of the city's ships were put at his disposal. Nevertheless, Edward did not arrive at Hereford until 17 September, nine days after his army had been instructed to meet him there. The next day he moved on to Ludlow, where he remained until the 26th. Edward's priority was the planned Parliament, which began at Westminster in early November, where he would reward his supporters and punish his enemies. Edward was content to delegate the war in Wales to Lord Herbert, assisted by Lord Ferrers, in whom he had the utmost trust. Herbert's first target was Pembroke Castle. He was supported by a fleet, including the ships from Bristol, to ensure that no assistance could reach the Lancastrians by sea. Pembroke was commanded by the veteran Sir John Scudamore, but Scudamore quickly concluded that his position was hopeless. On 30 September he surrendered the castle 'without any war or resistance'.[14] By 4 October the Paston correspondent Henry Windsor heard that the Yorkists had taken all the castles that had been held against them.[15] This was not quite true. Carreg Cennen continued to resist the Yorkists until May 1462, when it was captured by Herbert's younger brother Richard. Harlech, which could be provisioned by sea, would hold out until 1468. Yet by the middle of October 1461 the Earl of Pembroke and the Duke of Exeter were forced to retreat into the mountains of Snowdonia, like so many insurgents in Wales before them. Perhaps they were planning a guerrilla campaign, but on 16 October they were brought to bay at Twthill near Caernarfon. Although Pembroke and Exeter both escaped, their army was scattered. The Lancastrians in Wales ceased to be a major threat.

But it was in the north where the Lancastrian challenge was strongest. In the summer of 1461 the Lancastrians still controlled much of Northumberland, through their possession of northern castles, although the attitude of the Scots was also crucial. In the late 1450s the Scots, under the warlike James II, had sought to take advantage of English weakness. James raided northern England several times. In July 1460, following the Battle of Northampton, James led a large Scottish army over the border and besieged Roxburgh Castle. The Scots took Roxburgh but at the cost of their king's life: James was killed when a cannon exploded.

For Edward, James's death was extremely fortunate. If James II had lived it is possible that large swathes of northern England would have fallen under Scottish control, at least temporarily, as had occurred when previous Scottish kings had profited from English civil strife. But James II's heir, James III, was only eight years old at the time of his father's death. James II's widow, Queen Mary, became regent, although her authority was constantly undermined by the powerful Bishop Kennedy. Their respective supporters were referred to (with a degree of simplification) as the 'young' and 'old' lords. Mary was influenced by her uncle, Duke Philip of Burgundy, who Edward quickly came to regard as a staunch friend.[16] She was therefore inclined towards an accommodation with the Yorkists. Kennedy, on the other hand, in the bellicose tradition of Scottish medieval bishops, favoured an aggressive policy towards England. He therefore strongly supported the Lancastrians.

The impasse was broken when Margaret of Anjou offered Berwick to the Scots: the prospect of such a rich prize turned Mary's reluctant hospitality into active support. The Scots took possession of Berwick on 25 April. Margaret also agreed to cede Carlisle, the gateway to the Western March, although the city was now under Yorkist control. In June the Lancastrians besieged Carlisle with Scottish support. The Duke of Exeter was presumably in command, although Margaret is also said to have been present. Edward was concerned enough to bring forward the date of his coronation, so that he could return to the north, but Carlisle was quickly relieved by Lord Montagu. The besieging forces withdrew. Some of the Lancastrians made their way to the other side of the Pennines, where they joined a small force accompanied by Henry VI. Henry's standard was raised at Brancepeth, near Durham, but the Lancastrians were put to flight by levies raised by Bishop Laurence Booth.

Although the Lancastrians had failed to make any real progress, even with Scottish support, Yorkist authority in the far north remained limited. However, at the end of July Warwick was appointed Warden of both the East and West Marches, which suggests the subjugation of Northumberland was now considered a priority. In the autumn there were a number of Yorkist successes. The Percy stronghold of Alnwick surrendered, and a Yorkist garrison was put in place. Sir Ralph Percy (the younger brother of the Earl of Northumberland killed at Towton) submitted by the end of September and was received into Edward's grace. According to John Hardyng's chronicle, the Percys had 'the hearts of the people by north' during the Middle Ages and evidently Edward agreed.[17] Percy was entrusted with the keeping of the coastal castle of Dunstanburgh. Yet in the winter of 1461–2 it became clear that Yorkist control of Northumberland remained tenuous, notwithstanding Edward's willingness to come to terms with local men who had fought against him. Sir William Tailboys recaptured Alnwick, and the Lancastrian Lord Dacre took back his ancestral seat of Naworth, near Carlisle.

The ongoing state of affairs in the north did not seriously threaten Edward's position, but the Lancastrians would continue to drain his resources if they were allowed to maintain a secure base in Scotland. War was expensive and Edward had already accrued considerable debts. Edward therefore began to put more pressure on the Scots. For this he had a useful tool in the person of James Earl of Douglas, who had been an exile in England for over five years. Douglas was encouraged to regain what he saw as his rightful place, and to seek vengeance for his dead brother.[18] He sought the support of John MacDonald, Lord of the Isles, who ruled much of north-west Scotland in a state of near autonomy. In March 1462 a triple alliance was sealed between Douglas, MacDonald and MacDonald's kinsman Donald 'Balloch'. The Stewarts were to be expelled or destroyed, and Scotland divided between the three lords. Edward was to be acknowledged as overlord in return for his support.

This grand scheme was not as far-fetched as it might appear, although the rebels' chances were slim without active English help. However, like most other rulers of the period, in diplomacy Edward preferred to keep his options open. The situation at the Scottish court had now started to change in Edward's favour. Margaret of Anjou, despairing of further support from Mary, sailed to France in April. Mary had paid for Margaret's passage, although it is possible she was not too disappointed to see Margaret leave. Perhaps other personal relationships had broken down? While he was in France, the Duke of Somerset is said to have revealed that he and Mary had been lovers.[19] Shortly after Margaret's departure Mary agreed to meet Warwick at Dumfries, and Warwick was encouraged by her attitude. He even suggested that Mary could be a suitable bride for Edward, but, unsurprisingly, this proposal was obstructed by Bishop Kennedy. No agreement was reached, so Warwick launched a raid into southern Scotland, where Douglas was also active. At the same time the MacDonalds were wreaking havoc in Atholl. With the Scots under pressure from the north and south, Kennedy and his faction could not object to Mary's decision to meet Warwick again. This time a short truce was agreed, from June until the end of August, and this gave the Yorkist commanders opportunity to move against the Lancastrian rebels. By the end of the summer Alnwick, Bamburgh and Naworth were once again in Yorkist hands.

Meanwhile, Margaret of Anjou had arrived safely in France, and was attempting to convert her cousin Louis XI to her cause. By now, Edward had realised that Louis XI was not really a 'Yorkist': the French King had already begun to weave the political webs for which he became notorious, baffling and infuriating his contemporaries. He earned the soubriquet 'the universal spider'. His main objective, with regard to England, was to keep her weak and divided. It was therefore little surprise when, on 24 June 1462, Louis and Margaret came to terms at Chinon. At the Truce of Tours (28 June) Louis agreed to release Brézé to lead an expedition, and also to provide funds, in return for the cession of Calais. But Calais was under Yorkist control: a serious French assault on the port was impossible unless the Duke of Burgundy gave Louis' troops permission to pass through his lands. This, understandably, Duke Philip would *not* do. Margaret's concessions, therefore, brought Louis little in practical terms and he consequently reneged on most of his own promises. Brézé's support was still worth having – he was described by Warkworth as 'the best warrior of all that time' – but Margaret's French army was limited to 800 men.[20] Ultimately, much of the cost of the expedition was borne by Brézé, not Louis. Margaret sailed first for Scotland, where she was joined by Henry VI and others. Then the fleet made for Northumberland, landing near Bamburgh. At first, the Lancastrians enjoyed some success. Bamburgh opened its gates and Somerset was placed in command.[21] Sir Ralph Percy, at Dunstanburgh, quickly reverted to his former allegiance. The Yorkist garrison at Alnwick surrendered after a short siege. Yet when Henry VI's standard was raised few of the local gentry rallied to his cause.

Edward's reaction was swift. Perhaps, lacking accurate intelligence, he overestimated the extent of the Lancastrian threat. By 30 October, only five days after the Lancastrian landing at Bamburgh, Warwick was hurrying north. Warwick was commissioned to raise the northern levies; supplies and artillery were despatched by sea to Newcastle. The Earl of Douglas was once again unleashed to raid southern Scotland. By 4 November, Edward himself was moving north, giving every indication that he intended to campaign in person. Edward had formed a great army, possibly one of the largest ever raised by a medieval king. According to one contemporary source he was joined by two dukes, seven earls, thirty-one barons and fifty-nine knights, together with numerous levies.[22] Alarmed by Edward's movements, and also by the lukewarm response to their appeals for support, Margaret and her commanders decided she and Henry should return to Scotland. Presumably they intended to regroup, and to solicit Scottish reinforcements. Garrisons were left in the northern castles, including most of the Lancastrian nobles. The castles were 'victualled and stuffed both [*sic*] with Englishmen, Frenchmen and Scotsmen'.[23] But winter storms scattered Margaret's fleet. Four ships were wrecked, including Margaret's own. Margaret, Henry and Brézé reached Berwick in an open boat but many of the French troops were stranded on Lindisfarne. The French were thoroughly demoralised by their experience. They quickly surrendered to a force under two local gentlemen loyal to Edward. Edward himself reached Durham on 16 November but was struck down by illness.[24] Evidently Edward's condition was serious. Although he continued to issue orders from his sickbed he did not take the field. Active command was therefore delegated to Warwick, who supervised simultaneous operations against all three Northumbrian castles from a base at Warkworth Castle.

Edward's forces quickly achieved an effective blockade of the northern castles but his great guns were silent. It has often been argued that Edward wanted to obtain the northern castles unscathed. This was an issue raised two years later, when these fortresses were once again in Lancastrian hands.[25] Nevertheless, during the later Middle Ages, the firing of cannon at a siege was also a symbolic act. Thereafter, if the castle fell, it would be deemed to have succumbed to assault. This meant, according to the laws of war, that once the besieging commander had fired his guns only he had the right to accept or even propose terms. In theory (if not always in practice), if a castle or town was taken by assault, a defeated garrison could then be slaughtered without mercy.[26] But until the guns had fired it was possible for the defenders to surrender the castle by an *appointement* or treaty. The lack of bombardment therefore conveyed a clear message to the garrisons that Edward was willing to come to terms. This may appear a radical departure from the conduct of war during the Towton campaign, but Edward was always keen to pursue a conciliatory policy during the early years of his reign. Moreover, it should be remembered that many of Edward's enemies during this campaign were foreigners: French and Scots. As we have seen, the distinctions between 'foreign' and 'civil' war were not as great as sometimes assumed, but it is significant that these men were not Edward's subjects. Even if they fought under the Lancastrian banner it would be difficult to argue they were traitors, and to justify their treatment accordingly. The French and Scots therefore had less to lose than their English comrades, so we might assume they would be less willing to fight to the death.

John Paston III was present with the Yorkist forces, in the retinue of
the Duke of Norfolk. His letters vividly portray the work of the army
under Warwick's command, and also Warwick's skills as an administrator:

> My Lord of Warwick rides daily to all these castles to oversee
> the sieges. If they need victuals or anything else, he is ready
> to supply them. The king commanded my Lord of Norfolk to
> send victuals and the ordnance from Newcastle to Warkworth
> Castle to my Lord of Warwick; and so my Lord of Norfolk
> commanded Sir John Howard, Sir William Perche, Sir Robert
> Chamberlain, Ralph Asheton and me, Calthorpe and Gorge
> and others to escort the victuals and ordnance; and so yesterday
> [10 December 1462] we were with my Lord of Norfolk at
> Newcastle. We have people enough here. In case we stay longer
> I pray you see that more money is sent here to me by Christmas
> Eve at the latest, for I cannot obtain leave to send any of my
> waged men home. No one can depart – unless, of course, they
> steal away without permission, but if this were to be detected
> they would be sharply punished.[27]

Warwick was in his element, although Paston hints at tensions within the
Yorkist camp, and also the prospect of desertions. Ironically, it appears
likely, in one crucial sense, that Edward's army was *too* large, because
supplies quickly began to run short. This might explain Warwick's later
concerns about Edward's logistical preparations, as noted above, although
it is unlikely that Edward would have been blind to the problem. Lack of
supplies would provide another explanation of why Edward wished to
bring matters to a speedy conclusion.

The Yorkist commanders were also aware that a Scottish army, under
the Earl of Angus, was gathering across the border. The army included
Brézé, who would have been particularly keen to relieve Alnwick because
his son was a member of the garrison. But the news of the impending
Scottish invasion was concealed from the Lancastrian garrisons at Bamburgh
and Dunstanburgh, who were now reduced to eating their horses. On
Christmas Eve the commanders of Bamburgh and Dunstanburgh offered
their surrender. Their conditions were accepted and the Yorkists took
possession of both castles by 27 December. Somerset, Percy and a number
of others submitted to Edward. They were taken to the King at Durham,
where they swore oaths of allegiance. Somerset was required immediately
to prove his loyalty. He therefore joined Edward's army at Alnwick,
where he served with some distinction. Percy was given custody of the

two other northern castles, according to the terms that had been agreed. There were others, though, who still refused to accept Edward's kingship, including Jasper Tudor and Somerset's kinsman, Lord Roos.[28] They were permitted to retire to Scotland under safe conduct.

Now the Yorkists were free to concentrate all their forces against Alnwick, but then, on 5 January, the Scottish army finally arrived. Warwick, still in command of the Yorkist forces, declined to offer battle. According to Warkworth it was an almost farcical situation: Warwick was frightened of the Scots but the Scots feared a trap. The commander of Alnwick, Lord Hungerford, was allowed to march out of the castle while Warwick's army looked on. The account in *Annales* suggests the English were outnumbered by the Scots, which is surprising given that Edward had raised such a large army. Is it possible, therefore, that Edward had now dismissed some of his troops, or at least had allowed them to leave? For John Warkworth, though, Warwick's problem was not one of numbers but morale: the English troops were reluctant to fight because they had 'lain there so long in the field, and were grieved with cold and rain'.[29] Both Warkworth and *Annales* agree that the Scots missed a chance to strike a significant blow against the English. According to *Annales*, 'if the Scots had been bold and wise, they could have destroyed all the nobility of England'.[30] But the Scots withdrew across the border and on the next day Alnwick surrendered. All the northern castles were now under Yorkist control, although one clerical chronicler remained unimpressed:

> And in all this long time, when almost all the knighthood of England was assembled against our enemies, what, I ask, what action memorable or deserving of praise was done, except the capture of the aforesaid three castles?[31]

This is surely a harsh judgement. The chronicler underestimates the logistical difficulties of conducting a winter campaign, and Margaret had declined to meet Edward in battle when their troops were fresh. All of the northern castles – some of the strongest in England – had been effectively garrisoned on this occasion. Veteran soldiers were present in the garrisons of each of the castles, led by experienced commanders. To take all these castles without major losses was no small achievement. Furthermore, it must be stressed that much medieval warfare was 'Vegetian' in that it hinged on the capture and control of strongpoints and supplies.[32] Vegetius advised commanders to avoid battle whenever possible, because of the great risks entailed, and instead to pursue other means to victory. The Wars of the Roses represent a special case because *both* sides usually sought a decisive encounter – even if there was more variation within the various generals' strategy than is usually allowed.[33] The Lancastrians' strategy in this campaign was therefore very unusual within the context of the Wars of the Roses, possibly because of the presence of so many foreign troops in their army. The Yorkists adapted their own strategy accordingly.

Nevertheless, the chronicler was surely writing with the benefit of hindsight, in the knowledge that all the good work of the winter was undone shortly afterwards. Warwick had remained in the north after Edward left, to consolidate the Yorkist position, but as soon as he returned south, in March, Sir Ralph Percy once again switched sides. He opened the gates of Bamburgh and Dunstanburgh to a Franco-Scottish force. In May, Alnwick Castle was betrayed by the constable, Sir Ralph Grey, hitherto a committed Yorkist, who was disillusioned because he had been passed over for the command.[34] Naturally these events gave Margaret renewed hope and she persuaded the Scots once more to invade England. Again it fell to the Nevilles to conduct the war in the north. On 26 May Montagu was appointed Warden of the East March in his own right, and he was shortly afterwards in the field. He was quickly joined by his brother, Warwick, who retained the wardenship in the west. In early July the Scots invaded England and laid siege to Norham Castle. Margaret, her son Prince Edward, Mary, Brézé and the young James III were all present. But the Scots appear to have had little stomach for a fight. Warwick had recruited troops in Yorkshire and the Nevilles had raised a substantial army. When the Nevilles appeared at Norham, the Scottish army withdrew in panic. The Nevilles took the opportunity to launch a major raid into Southern Scotland, while the Earl of Douglas was active in the West March. Dispirited by this latest failure, Margaret once again sought refuge on the Continent. She was accompanied by her son and Brézé, although her husband remained in Bishop Kennedy's care. Although she would continue to fight tenaciously on his behalf, Margaret would never see Henry again.

Brézé was embittered by his experience of fighting with the Scots.[35] Unsurprisingly, English writers were also scornful of their performance at Norham. According to 'Gregory', only one of the Scots had emerged with any credit:

> And at the departing of Sir Pierre de Brézé and his fellowship was one manly man that purposed to meet with my Lord of Warwick, that was a taborette, and he stood upon a hill with his tabor and his pipe, taboring and piping as merrily as any

man might, standing by himself. Till my lord come unto him
he would not lease [release] his ground. And there he became
my lord's man, and yet [still] he is with him full good and to
his lord.[36]

Obviously this passage reflects well on Warwick too, because he is deemed
an appropriate lord for such a 'manly man'. In a letter to the French
diplomat Jean de Lannoy, Lord Hastings also praised the deeds of
the 'noble and valiant' Warwick.[37] Edward, on the other hand, wrote
Hastings, had continued to pursue the pleasures of the chase. This is
often interpreted as implicit criticism of Edward but it seems unlikely.
The point Hastings wished to make was that Edward had not *needed* to
concern himself. Hastings notes that Edward's subjects were also able
to go about their business undisturbed, which suggests the Scots were
not able to threaten Edward's position in a significant way. Yet a major
expedition against the Scots was then being prepared, in which Edward
had promised to take a leading role. On this understanding Edward had
received a major taxation grant from Parliament of £37,000, together with
a substantial subsidy from the Church. Once Edward himself took the
field, Hastings implied, the Scots would 'repent until the day of judgement' for their support of the Lancastrian exiles. However, although
Edward had reached York in early September, he proceeded no further.

Once again, there was much criticism: 'Shame and confusion was the
wretched outcome of it all.'[38] This was understandable. Edward's subjects
had been taxed heavily to pay for his 'campaign', although much of the
money was used to pay off existing debts. Edward later felt obliged to give
his assent to a reduction of the burden. Yet as Edward appeared to be
inactive at York, events elsewhere were moving in his favour. Louis XI's
eyes were now fixed on Burgundy, so he was willing to reach a temporary
accord with Edward. Duke Philip, who was genuinely committed to
the ideal of a crusade against the Turks, was always willing to promote
peace. He therefore suggested that diplomats from England, France and
Burgundy should convene at St Omer. Although Edward remained
suspicious of Louis' motives, this was agreed. Margaret of Anjou, in
desperation, gained an interview with Philip of Burgundy to solicit his
support. Duke Philip took pains to protect his chivalrous reputation, and
Margaret was treated with courtesy. She received a small sum of money to
maintain herself and her household but that was all. Margaret's worst
fears would soon be realised. The conference made little progress at
St Omer but when the delegates moved to Hesdin a breakthrough was

quickly achieved. On 8 October the English and French agreed to a year's truce (except at sea) and Edward and Louis were bound not to support each other's enemies during this time. Louis had separately achieved his main aim – the recovery of the Somme towns, ceded to Burgundy in 1435 – and was in an uncharacteristically generous mood. He is even said to have offered Edward help with the conquest of Scotland.

Crucially, therefore, Edward's diplomats had isolated the Scots, who had been shaken by Warwick's recent exploits and were alarmed by Edward's presence in the north. They now had no alternative but to negotiate. The death of Mary of Guelders, on 1 December 1463, made no difference to the direction of Scottish policy. Envoys were despatched by Bishop Kennedy to meet Edward at York, and on 9 December the terms of a truce were agreed. There was to be peace between England and Scotland until 31 October 1464, and further talks were scheduled to bring about a more lasting treaty. Most significantly, Edward agreed that he would offer no further assistance to the Earl of Douglas. In return the Scots agreed to abandon their support for the Lancastrian exiles. Henry VI was duly removed from the safety of St Andrews and sent to Bamburgh. The Lancastrian cause was now hanging by a thread.

What gave the Lancastrians hope was an astonishing *volte face* by Henry Duke of Somerset. Somerset had been restored to his lands and appeared to be in favour at the Yorkist court. But in late December 1463 Somerset suddenly appeared in Northumberland at the head of yet another Lancastrian rising. Edward's relationship with Somerset therefore deserves greater scrutiny.

Henry Duke of Somerset is one of the most intriguing characters of the period. Contemporaries accorded him the ability to influence others and, by implication, to influence events. On the Continent he was regarded, like Warwick, as a 'prince'. When Somerset was in exile he was able to hold his own with the cultured courtiers of Burgundy. Charles Count of Charolais, the Duke of Burgundy's son, fell completely under Somerset's spell. Somerset's *élan* was acknowledged by the court chronicler Chastelain, even though he was concerned about Somerset's influence over Charolais: 'he was a very great lord, and one of the [most] handsome young knights who came from the realm of England'.[39] Even hostile writers acknowledged his military prowess: both 'Gregory' and the author of *Annales* describe his conduct in the field as 'manly'.[40] But it would appear that to trust Somerset was dangerous. At Calais, Somerset had sworn that he would never take up arms against Warwick again, but quickly reneged on the promise.[41] Edward has been criticised for his decision to pardon Somerset.[42] It has been argued that Edward was reckless, that he blithely believed he could charm Somerset into loyalty. However, Somerset's subsequent attainder implies that his pardon was a carefully considered act: Edward had 'laboured himself into forgetfulness'.[43] It was not easy to forgive the deaths of his father and brother. It was a calculated risk, but Somerset's reputation was such that his defection offered great benefits to the Yorkist cause. Surely Edward also wished to end the blood feud that had claimed so many lives? Nevertheless, Somerset's rehabilitation proceeded in stages,[44] and there is no evidence to suggest that Edward's policy was not supported by the Yorkist hierarchy. Oddly enough, it was to *Warwick* that Somerset first intimated he would be willing to come to terms. This was as early as September 1462.[45]

Yet Edward's treatment of Somerset appears to have gone far beyond *realpolitik*. According to 'Gregory' Edward and Somerset became inseparable.[46] The two men rode out 'a-hunting' accompanied only by a small group of attendants, and Somerset 'lodged with the king in his own bed many nights'. Edward, inspired by his 'great love' for the Duke, organised a tournament at Westminster in Somerset's honour. In fact, there is nothing here to provide certain evidence of a truly intimate relationship, although it was surely hoped that these acts would *lead* to a closer relationship. This was an example of what the historian Stephen Jaeger has called 'ennobling love'.[47] An act of sharing, whether this was sharing food, a horse, or even a bed, was a public symbol of reconciliation during the Middle Ages.[48] Presumably the tournament referred to by 'Gregory' was also symbolic. Like many other medieval kings, although most notably Edward III, Edward consciously sought to imitate King Arthur's court. For example, membership of the Order of the Garter, with its explicitly Arthurian overtones, was restricted to a select few.[49] Edward also sponsored a revival of the tournament.[50] Edward's courtiers began to follow the example of their contemporaries across the Channel, fighting in outlandish disguises like the heroes of romance.[51] The tournament organised for Somerset, therefore, is likely to have been a heavily ritualised occasion designed to establish him within Edward's own 'circle of honour'. 'Gregory' tells us that Somerset jousted in a 'sorry hat of straw'. The straw hat was probably part of a costume or disguise with allegorical connotations that were missed by the chronicler.[52] 'Gregory' does go on to say that Somerset was reluctant to joust (or feigned reluctance) until he was persuaded by Edward. But 'then he [Somerset] ran full justly and merrily [...] and then every man marked him well'.

Tensions quickly appeared, however. At Northampton the common people attempted to lynch Somerset, and only Edward's personal intervention (aided by a barrel of free wine for the people) saved the duke's life. Somerset was sent to his castle of Chirk, in North Wales, for his own protection. But the problem now was that Somerset's isolation from court meant that it was easier for Lancastrian sympathisers to approach him, and to draw Somerset back towards his former allegiance. They would have stressed not only Somerset's prior obligations to Henry VI, but also his ties to Margaret of Anjou and to the men with whom he had fought as brothers in arms. Eventually, we must assume, Somerset was unable to deny the strength of their arguments.[53] Presumably Sir Ralph Percy had been placed under similar pressure in Northumberland.[54] Jean de Wavrin draws attention to Somerset's impossible dilemma. Wavrin implies that, even as he became a traitor, Somerset was motivated by honour:

> I have learned that he [Somerset] knew well that the said party of King Henry did not have the necessary strength or vigour to oppose the power of King Edward, who had done him great honour. Nevertheless he deserted him to return to King Henry and to join with those who had no power.[55]

What Somerset's 'treachery' reveals most clearly, therefore, is not Edward's failure as a statesman, but rather the incredible tenacity of the Lancastrian nobles and, paradoxically, their deep commitment to principle.[56]

There were also risings in Wales, and disturbances throughout the south, but the Lancastrian plans always hinged on success in the north. Their first aim was control of Newcastle, which would have given them access to a market and supplies. Here, some of Somerset's most trusted men were members of the garrison, and they had intended to hand over the city to the duke. Fortunately for Edward's cause, the plot was discovered shortly before Somerset arrived. Most of the conspirators were captured and executed. Somerset himself narrowly avoided capture at Durham, escaping 'in his shirt and barefoot'.[57] Somerset made his way to Bamburgh, where he rejoined Henry VI and his remaining supporters. But on this occasion, the Lancastrians were not prepared to shelter passively behind castle walls. In the early months of 1464 the Lancastrians gained control of much of Northumberland. Further Anglo–Scottish talks had been planned to take place at Newcastle in early March but in the circumstances had to be postponed. The conference was re-scheduled to take place at York on 20 April. Montagu was sent north from York in mid April, to provide an escort for the Scottish delegation but the Lancastrians were waiting for him. On his way to Newcastle he narrowly escaped an ambush laid by Sir Humphrey Neville of Brancepeth. At Newcastle Montagu gathered more troops before continuing north. This did not deter the Lancastrians, however, who were understandably determined to disrupt the Anglo–Scottish negotiations. At Hedgeley Moor, north of Alnwick, Montagu was attacked by a strong Lancastrian force that included Somerset, Percy, Roos, Hungerford and Grey. Initially there was fierce fighting, although the Lancastrians are said to have become dispirited by the death of Sir Ralph Percy.[58] They took to flight. Montagu's mission was completed without further incident and the Scottish envoys were safely conveyed to York.

The Lancastrian rebels were now in a desperate position as the *détente* between England and Scotland ensured they would receive no support from north of the border. They would also have been aware that Edward was raising a large army at Leicester. Commissions of array had been sent to the sheriffs of thirty counties; the royal ordnance had been mobilised on 16 April for the journey north. The Lancastrians had little left to lose. In early May they decided upon a bold strategy, marching south into the Tyne valley. As John Gillingham explains, 'their only hope lay in swift and aggressive action before they were crushed by the sheer weight of Edward's men, carts and guns'.[59] Henry VI accompanied his army and was established at Bywell Castle. Once again, the Lancastrians threatened Newcastle, where Montagu was currently based. By now Montagu must have known that support was on its way, but he displayed a verve and decision worthy of Edward himself. He did not wait for the King to reinforce him. On 15 May Montagu fell upon Somerset at Hexham and his forces comprehensively defeated the smaller Lancastrian army. To the evident satisfaction of the chronicler 'Gregory':

> Lo, so manly a man is this good Earl [*sic*] Montagu, for he spared not their malice, not their falseness, not guile, nor treason, and took many of men and slew many one [*sic*] in that journey [battle].[60]

Somerset was captured immediately after the battle and summarily executed. On the next day Lords Hungerford and Roos were caught hiding in a wood, and Sir William Tailboys was later discovered in a coalpit. £2,000 was found in Tailboys' possession, which had been intended to pay the Lancastrian army's wages. Montagu shared this money between his troops. The captured nobles quickly followed Somerset to their deaths: over thirty prominent Lancastrians were executed at this time. The Lancastrian outposts in the Tyne valley fell rapidly, including Bywell, although Henry VI escaped into the Pennines. Henry would survive as a fugitive for another year, but it was only a matter of time before he fell into Yorkist hands.

Edward expressed his gratitude towards Montagu in a way that was truly profound. At York, on 27 May, Edward invested Montagu with the earldom of Northumberland. Now one of the greatest men in England, John Neville rode out of York followed by a formidable host, which included his brother, Warwick, and the royal artillery. The three northern castles that had caused Edward so much trouble were still in Lancastrian hands, but the new Earl of Northumberland was determined to have them at his will. Alnwick, the seat of the Percys, surrendered without a fight, as did Dunstanburgh. But the Lancastrians' surviving leaders, Sir Ralph Grey and Sir Humphrey Neville, had taken refuge at Bamburgh. The Yorkist army appeared before the castle on 25 June. Heralds were once again despatched to treat with the Lancastrian commanders, although their message was stern:

> The king, our most dread sovereign lord, specially desires to have this jewel [Bamburgh] whole and unbroken by artillery, particularly because it stands so close to his ancient enemies the Scots, and if you are the cause that great guns have to be fired against its walls, then it will cost you your head, and for every shot that has to be fired another head, down to the humblest person within the place.[61]

The heralds offered the garrison a pardon, but it conspicuously excluded Grey and Neville. The Lancastrians defied the royal army to do their worst. And so Edward's 'great guns' – *Dijon, London* and *Newcastle* – unleashed their terrible power against Bamburgh's walls.[62] Grey was badly wounded when a cannonball smashed into his chamber, and he was left for dead. As the Yorkists made ready to storm the battered fortress the garrison surrendered to Nevilles' mercy. Humphrey Neville somehow managed to gain clemency, perhaps by appealing to kinship, and his life was spared. But for Sir Ralph Grey there would now be a reckoning.

Edward's treatment of Somerset, Percy and others had been that of a merciful and chivalrous prince. Edward, the victor of Mortimer's Cross and Towton, possessed the 'dread' that Henry VI conspicuously lacked, but he also understood the need to temper his justice with 'love'. He had treated all the Lancastrians who submitted as men of honour, whose oath was their bond. The implication was that he considered them to have been worthy adversaries who deserved respect. But Edward gave scant consideration to their subsequent dilemmas. Thus it was according to the chivalric code that the Lancastrians would now be condemned, even beyond the grave. Edward's anger comes across strongly in contemporary documents. Somerset's treachery, we are told, was against the nature of 'gentleness [nobility] and all humanity'.[63] More anger was reserved for Sir Ralph Grey, who, wounded as he was, was dragged to Doncaster to hear Edward's terrible judgement.[64] Sentence was pronounced by the Constable of England, John Tiptoft Earl of Worcester. First, Grey was to be degraded from the order of knighthood: 'thy spurs struck off by the hard heels with the hand of the master cook'. Then his coat of arms – the most important symbol of his noble lineage and 'worship' – was to be publicly torn from him. It would be replaced by 'another coat, of thine arms reversed', as a sign of Grey's disgrace. Then Grey was to be drawn through the streets to a 'scaffold made for thee'. Only then, finally, would he meet his death. For a medieval aristocrat, this was a peculiarly shameful way to die. In fact, even in this case Edward's ferocity had its limits, and Grey was spared the degradation from all his honours. But he was not spared execution, and his death marked the end of Lancastrian resistance in the north.

Edward had proved himself a formidable soldier, but since Towton he had done none of the fighting himself. However, as argued by Gillingham, Edward's main role in the years immediately after Towton was to 'create the political, financial, administrative and diplomatic circumstances which virtually guaranteed victory in the field'.[65] The most crucial military operations were delegated to able lieutenants. Both Montagu and Herbert fully repaid Edward's trust, notwithstanding the betrayals by others. Warwick was also active in Edward's service, and at this time all his ambitions were complementary to Edward's own. There is no doubt that Edward actively pursued pleasures of many kinds – Edward's personal motto, indeed, was 'comfort and joy'! – but he also applied himself diligently to the problems of government. Moreover, whether this was by nature or nurture, evidently Edward preferred to operate in the mould of rulers such as Charles V of France. As Christine de Pisan sagely observed, Charles V won victories against the English without leaving his palace.[66] At Towton, where everything was at stake, Edward's presence inspired his men, but it was not politic for a king to risk his life in battle unless absolutely necessary. Having proved himself as a warrior, there could be no suggestion that Edward lacked courage or ability in the field. Now that his throne was secure, doubtless Edward's subjects hoped that he would turn to other pressing issues, notably the maintenance of law and order. More security would come with an heir, although for this, of course, Edward needed a wife. In early 1464 Edward must have appeared the most eligible bachelor in Europe. The Earl of Warwick, who was growing increasingly close to Louis XI, was keen to promote an Anglo-French alliance. Louis suggested that Edward could marry Louis' sister-in-law, Bona of Savoy. But Warwick was soon to discover there was a glaring impediment to the match: Edward was already married.

Chapter 5

Reading, September 1464

Edward's bride was Elizabeth Grey, née Woodville, the widow of Sir John Grey of Groby. This was an extraordinary choice. Elizabeth had many qualities – she was beautiful, intelligent and cultured – but contemporaries were shocked. Elizabeth, we might assume, would have been regarded as an ideal mistress for Edward but certainly not an ideal queen. Elizabeth's background was unusual. Her mother, Jacquetta de Luxembourg, was of the highest European nobility, claiming descent from Charlemagne. Jacquetta was also the widow of John, Duke of Bedford. But Elizabeth's father, Sir Richard Woodville, now Lord Rivers, came from more modest origins: his marriage to Duchess Jacquetta had been controversial.[1] Richard Woodville had carved out an impressive career in France, but his family were no more than county gentry. A king was expected to marry a princess, ideally one who was a virgin: what was Edward thinking? Edward has gained a reputation as a man driven by lust, which has some basis in contemporary sources. To some extent, though, Edward's sexual reputation is derived from the retrospective criticisms of his brother, Richard.[2] Yet it seems difficult not to conclude that Edward's marriage was motivated purely by 'love', as the chronicler 'Gregory' tells us.[3] Understandably the marriage caused consternation, which explains why Edward kept it secret for over four months. Edward had married Elizabeth on 1 May, slipping away from his attendants early in the morning. But by September, when he was pressed to make a decision about the proposed French marriage, he could no longer remain silent. The members of Edward's council, which had convened at Reading, were furious, not least because they had not been consulted about such a great matter of state. The Earl of Warwick, who had been the chief advocate of the French marriage, was dismayed.

Traditionally Edward's marriage has been seen as the cause of the ensuing breach with Warwick. However, the King's marriage in itself cannot explain the breakdown in their relationship, although it certainly marked a turning point. How did things change? Naturally Warwick had benefited from Edward's patronage after Towton, although Michael Hicks has argued the extent of Warwick's rewards should not be overstated.[4] Certainly Warwick did not receive everything he desired. He did not become a duke, for example, because Edward reserved this title for his immediate family. He initially received important offices in Wales, which had been a focus of his ambitions in the 1450s, although after reflection Edward decided these should be given to Lord Herbert instead. Nevertheless, Warwick was indisputably the greatest man after the King. On the basis of his lands alone his income dwarfed most of his peers',[5] although his agglomeration of offices could not have continued without Edward's consent. Warwick's brothers were also well rewarded. John, as we have seen, became Earl of Northumberland; George, who became Archbishop of York in 1465, was Edward's Chancellor. Now, though, Edward needed to provide for his new wife's family, as well as for the Queen herself. Elizabeth had no fewer than five brothers and six sisters, most of whom were unmarried, as well as two sons from her first marriage. Edward no longer had major resources of patronage at his disposal, so he sponsored marriages between the Woodvilles and members of the English nobility. One of these marriages may have particularly frustrated Warwick. In 1465 the Queen's sister, Katherine, married the young Duke of Buckingham, Henry Stafford. Warwick had two daughters – Isabel and Anne, his only children – who were now approaching marriageable age: Buckingham would have provided an appropriate match for one of the girls. In some ways, though, the Woodville marriages did not really threaten Warwick's position. His many lands and offices ensured that he would remain England's premier earl. But was the tide turning against him?

Personal factors also need to be considered. Closeness to the King was always one of the most important keys to power during the Middle Ages, but Edward and Warwick began to grow apart. Significantly, the Woodvilles became prominent members of the new courtly society that surrounded Edward. As we have seen, there was a renewed emphasis on chivalric display, which was inspired by the world of romance. In April 1467 Edward himself took part in a tournament at Eltham, which was described by Sir John Paston as 'the goodliest sight that was seen in England these forty years'.[6] Queen Elizabeth's eldest brother, Anthony Lord Scales, had already begun to forge a reputation in the sporadic tournaments of the late 1450s, but now he came increasingly to the fore. In April 1465 Scales was surprised by the Queen's ladies, who fastened a golden collar to his thigh, exhorting him to carry out a great deed of arms. The result, eventually, was Scales' famous combat with Anthony, Bastard of Burgundy, which took place in June 1467. Warwick took no part in any of this. As A.J. Pollard observes, 'Warwick had no time for the new Camelot. And perhaps the new Camelot had little time for him.'[7] But Warwick must have understood that politics were not distinct from the courtly rituals from which he held aloof. The Woodvilles were also prominent in the council chamber. Queen Elizabeth's father, recently promoted to Earl Rivers and Treasurer by 1466, became one of Edward's closest advisors. Men such as Lords Herbert and Stafford, and Sir John Fogge, sometimes referred to as the 'new' Yorkists, also consolidated their position, both at court and in the provinces.

There can be no doubt that Warwick resented the increasing influence of the Woodvilles, as well as the power of others he considered *parvenus*. Lord Herbert was a particular focus of Warwick's ire. In the 1450s Herbert had served Warwick in Wales, as well as the Duke of York, but now, at court at least, his influence rivalled Warwick's own. However, according to the well-informed second Crowland Continuator, a disagreement about the direction of foreign policy was the main cause of Warwick's growing disaffection.[8] Warwick leaned towards a pro-French policy, whereas Edward began to adopt a more hostile attitude towards his 'ancient enemy'. The background to diplomatic affairs in this period therefore requires some explanation. To some extent, Edward's attitudes reflected his changed circumstances. When Edward was seeking to consolidate his position his diplomacy was necessarily defensive, but now that his throne was secure he could begin to contemplate a more aggressive stance. Edward's position was further strengthened in July 1465 when Henry VI was finally captured and confined in the Tower.[9] Margaret of Anjou, with her young son, had established a modest court in Lorraine, although the meagre support offered by Louis XI gave her little cause for hope. Louis, indeed, had his own problems. In 1465 Louis faced a serious rebellion, led by his own brother, Charles. The rebel confederation, the so called 'League of the Public Weal', included some of the greatest noblemen in France. It was supported by Louis' nominal vassals Francis, Duke of Brittany, and Charles, Count of Charolais. Charolais commanded the forces of the League at the Battle of Montlhéry (16 July), in which Pierre de Brézé was killed fighting for King Louis. This battle was inconclusive, although Louis was compelled to make concessions to his enemies. Their price included, once again, the surrender of the Somme towns to Burgundy.

Relations with Count Charles became increasingly important to the English. Throughout the 1460s Edward made alliances with a host of European powers, but the key to an anti-French policy, of course, was Burgundy. By the mid 1460s power within the duchy increasingly lay with Count Charles, because the ageing Duke Philip was growing frail. Charles of Burgundy was a very different man from his father. According to contemporary chroniclers, he hated Louis XI with a passion that went far beyond political rivalry.[10] Moreover, although Duke Philip continued to think of himself as a Frenchman, despite his long political struggle with the French kings, his son actively sought to downplay his French lineage. On at least one occasion he referred to himself as *Portuguese*, drawing attention to his mother's origins.[11] Through his mother, however, Charles was also related to the House of Lancaster. He took this kinship equally seriously. As we have seen, Charles had forged a particularly close relationship with Henry Duke of Somerset, and for much of the 1460s he sheltered Duke Henry's younger brother, Edmund. Edmund fought with Charles in his campaigns and he was showered with favours. Understandably, Beaufort preferred life in Burgundy to the threadbare existence at Margaret's court in France. After he became duke in 1467 Charles continued to support other Lancastrian exiles in Burgundy, notably the Duke of Exeter.[12] Nevertheless, Charles understood that an alliance with Edward offered him the best chance of protection from the King of France, and hopefully also a chance to damage his great enemy.

A crucial opportunity arose in September 1465 when Charles's wife, Isabella, died. This raised the possibility of a marriage between Charolais and Edward's sister, Margaret. For most princes marriage was a matter of state, and the initial overtures came from Charles himself. But the situation was complicated by an ongoing trade war between England and Burgundy. Duke Philip remained obdurate, despite his long-standing friendship with the House of York, which ensured that Edward was not yet fully committed to an anti-French policy. In the spring of 1466 Warwick was sent with powers to treat with Burgundy *and* France, although little was achieved. Relations with Burgundy were scarcely improved because Warwick and Charolais conceived a violent dislike of each other.[13] Nevertheless, as the year progressed it became clear that Edward favoured a Burgundian alliance, whereas Warwick became ever more closely associated with the French. Warwick was no longer trusted to conduct diplomacy with Burgundy. Now Earl Rivers, whose links to the Burgundian court through his wife proved invaluable, took the lead. In October Edward and Charles put their seals to a secret treaty of friendship. In public, Edward continued to play France and Burgundy off against each other. In May 1467 Warwick was sent to France, where he was splendidly received by King Louis, while a separate embassy was despatched to the Burgundian court at Bruges. The combat between Lord Scales and the Bastard of Burgundy provided an opportunity for further discussions behind the scenes, although these were abruptly halted by the news of Duke Philip's death on 15 June. Charles was now Duke of Burgundy.

On 24 June 1467 Warwick returned to England, accompanied by a high-powered French delegation. He discovered that, in his absence, his brother, the Archbishop of York, had been dismissed as Chancellor. On 8 June Edward rode in person to demand the great seal from Archbishop Neville, who was then ill. This must have been a shock to Warwick, although worse was to come. Edward treated the French delegation with contempt. The French ambassadors were virtually ignored. At Rouen Louis had presented the English envoys with gold and silver cups; Edward reciprocated with hunting horns and leather pouches.[14] It was clear to all that Warwick had lost the argument over foreign policy. If people at the French court had continued to believe that Warwick was the real master of England, now they learned the truth. Louis XI bitterly reproached Warwick for his failure to bring about the treaty he had promised. By the end of September the trade dispute between England and Burgundy was over, the pact between Edward and Charles made public, and the impending marriage of Charles and Margaret formally announced. A further alliance against France was made with the Duke of Brittany, who was already bound to Duke Charles by a treaty of mutual aid. Although the author conflates all these events with Edward's own marriage, *Warkworth's Chronicle* is probably correct to suggest this marked the point of no return: 'And yet [Edward and Warwick] were accorded divers times: but they never loved together after.'[15]

Warwick retired to the north in fury. Reports reached the Continent of Warwick's anger towards 'traitors' whom he believed were now directing the King's policy.[16] By the autumn of 1467 diplomatic sources in France recorded incredible rumours: it was alleged that Warwick had reached an understanding with the Lancastrians.[17] A plot between Warwick and the Lancastrian exiles seems far-fetched, at least during this period, although it is clear that the earl had started to look for new allies closer to home. Warwick reached out to Edward's younger brother, George, now Duke of Clarence, who had achieved his majority in 1466. Clarence had been well provided for by Edward, but his head was turned. Contemporary accounts describe Clarence as handsome and intelligent – he was not without ability – but he was also volatile and dangerously ambitious.[18] At present he was the heir to the throne because, as yet, Edward and Elizabeth had no sons.[19] But this state of affairs could not have been expected to endure. Warwick offered Clarence the prospect of marriage to his eldest daughter, Isabel. This, considered Clarence, would make him the heir to the greatest landowner in the country – and perhaps more. Edward vetoed the match, although he soon discovered that Archbishop Neville had continued to seek a dispensation for the marriage.[20] Infuriated by these intrigues, Edward cruelly mocked Archbishop Neville's ambitions for a cardinal's hat. In September Edward forwarded a letter from the Pope confirming that Archbishop Bourchier had instead been selected for promotion.

In October 1467 Herbert captured a messenger who was *en route* to Harlech, where a small force of Lancastrians, under Dafydd ap Eynon, continued to defy Edward.[21] Under interrogation, the messenger implicated Warwick in Lancastrian plots. Herbert, who sensed an opportunity to damage or perhaps even destroy Warwick, sent the messenger to the King. Although Edward may have been happy to dismiss earlier rumours of Warwick's treason, this news appeared to give them greater weight. Edward summoned Warwick to answer the charges. But Warwick refused, even when he was offered safe conduct. Warwick, perhaps recalling the attempts on his life during the 1450s, may have genuinely feared for his safety at court. As king, Edward had the right to decide his own foreign policy – Warwick could not dispute this – but the *manner* of Edward's decision had deeply humiliated the earl. Edward's treatment of the Archbishop of York had been uncharacteristically harsh, even vindictive. Now, however, Edward realised he had pushed the Nevilles too far. He wisely decided not to provoke Warwick any further. Instead he sent the prisoner to his 'right entirely beloved cousin' at Sheriff Hutton.[22] Edward accepted Warwick's denials and his protestations of loyalty.

At the beginning of 1468 relations between Edward and Warwick were still strained. In January Warwick again refused a summons to court. Soon, though, there was a thaw in their relationship. This was brought about by the agency of Archbishop Neville and Earl Rivers. Warwick was persuaded to return to court, where Edward gave him an honourable reception. Warwick was publicly reconciled with a number of the 'new' Yorkists, including Lord Herbert. But all was not well. Warwick continued to oppose the anti-French policy, and he refused to contribute to Princess Margaret's extravagant dowry. Edward pressed on regardless. On 17 May his new Chancellor, Bishop Robert Stillington of Bath and

Wells, announced Edward's intention to make war on his 'ancient enemy' of France.[23] An enthusiastic Parliament granted Edward a substantial grant of taxation. In June Princess Margaret crossed the North Sea to marry Duke Charles of Burgundy at Bruges – Warwick condescended to escort her to the coast – where she was greeted with great ceremony. John Paston III, a member of Margaret's entourage, was awestruck by the nobility of Burgundy. He compared the Burgundian court, naturally, to Camelot.[24]

Unsurprisingly, Louis XI retaliated. In June 1468, Louis agreed to support a modest Lancastrian invasion fleet under Jasper Tudor. In truth Louis invested very little in this enterprise, but Tudor still had many friends in Wales. Tudor enjoyed some initial success but Lord Herbert's resources were much greater. Tudor was once again put to flight. In the wake of Tudor's defeat, on 14 August 1468, Lord Herbert finally captured Harlech. This was the culmination of a determined and brutal campaign. Some of the Welsh bards were strong supporters of Herbert throughout the 1460s. Writing of Herbert's exploits in the north of England, for example, Lewis Glyn Cothi describes 'his frame ablaze on prancing steed, and his eyes glistening like glowing embers'.[25] Yet others lamented Herbert's cruelty. Traditional stories survive of an old woman of Anglesey who cursed him during the Harlech campaign.[26] Despite her entreaties to spare at least one of her boys, Herbert had ordered that all seven of her sons should be put to death. Edward, however, was greatly impressed by Herbert's achievements. As a reward for his capture of Harlech, the last Lancastrian stronghold in the British Isles, Herbert was created Earl of Pembroke.

By the autumn of 1468 plans for war with France were well advanced, although it is again uncertain that Edward planned to campaign in person. However, by 10 September preparations were being made for a force of 3,000 men to go to the aid of Brittany, which was then under attack from France. This force was to be commanded by Sir Walter Blount, now Lord Mountjoy. It was intended that an equally strong force, under Lord Scales, was to land in southern France. The problem was that Brittany had been under considerable pressure since mid July. Duke Francis, never the most resolute of men, felt compelled to come to terms with Louis. He agreed to abandon his allies in return for a truce. Although he continued to maintain close ties with England, Charles of Burgundy was also unwilling to engage in full-scale war with France at this time. On 14 October he and Louis XI signed a treaty at Péronne. The English fleet had put to sea nonetheless, under the command of Lord Scales. There were rumours that Margaret of Anjou had assembled an invasion force at Harfleur, although this fleet failed to materialise. With few enemies to fight except the weather, there was little for Scales to achieve. The English did manage to recapture Jersey, although this was a paltry return for the money expended. Edward had raised and spent £18,000, which was a considerable sum.[27]

If *Warkworth's Chronicle* can be trusted, many of the common people became disillusioned with Edward's rule.[28] They had been subjected to heavy taxation and they felt Edward had failed to provide the peace and order he had promised. Towards the end of 1468 there was widespread disaffection throughout the country, which gave fresh hope to Lancastrian sympathisers. In November Edward's spies uncovered a conspiracy involving Henry Courtenay, the heir to the Earl of Devon, and Thomas Hungerford, the heir of Lord Hungerford. John de Vere, Earl of Oxford, also came under suspicion; his father and brother had been executed in 1462 for their part in a Lancastrian plot. Oxford was committed to the Tower, where he disclosed the names of a number of Lancastrian agents. Oxford managed to convince Edward's men of his own innocence, although Courtenay and Hungerford were found guilty of treason. On 12 January 1469, in Edward's presence, they endured the full horrors of a traitor's death. There was no indication that Warwick was involved in any of the Lancastrian plans, although several people had been implicated who were very close to the earl. Oxford was Warwick's brother-in-law, and he had become closely associated with the Nevilles. Earlier in the year a captured Lancastrian agent, John Cornelius, had implicated Warwick's deputy in Calais, Lord Wenlock. Warwick's complicity cannot be proved, although he cannot have failed to contrast his own continued popularity with Edward's unpopularity. By the spring of 1469 Warwick was ready to move against Edward. He had resolved to put forward his own policies by force of arms.

The crisis began in April, when there were two local risings in Yorkshire. The leaders of the revolts were shadowy figures who were known, respectively, as 'Robin of Redesdale' and 'Robin of Holderness'. Initially, Robin of Holderness appeared the more dangerous: his rising was aimed at the restoration of the Percy family. But both rebellions were quickly suppressed by the Earl of Northumberland. Robin of Redesdale slipped the net, although Robin of Holderness was captured and executed.[29] It appeared that John Neville, whose service was as valuable to Edward as ever, had restored order. In June Edward set out on a pilgrimage to East Anglia. He was accompanied by his youngest brother Richard, now Duke of

Gloucester, and many others. Edward planned to visit the shrines at Bury St Edmunds and Walsingham. By 18 June, though, Edward's devotions were interrupted when he was informed of new disturbances in Yorkshire, which were again instigated by 'Robin of Redesdale'. This time Edward resolved to go north in person.[30] From Norwich he commanded that coat armour, livery jackets and banners, 'together with such other stuff for the field', should be made ready for the coming campaign. Two days later orders were sent to mobilise the royal artillery. Edward also sent word to the Earl of Pembroke and to Humphrey Stafford, whom he had recently promoted to Earl of Devon, instructing them to raise troops in Wales and the West Country. Evidently Edward did not feel under great pressure, because his progress north was slow. From Walsingham, now accompanied by the Dukes of Norfolk and Suffolk, Edward moved on to his ancestral castle of Fotheringhay, where he spent a week with his wife. On 5 July Edward had only reached Stamford, where he wrote to the burghers of Coventry, asking the city to send 100 archers to join his army.

From Stamford Edward rode north to Newark, via Grantham and Nottingham. By 9 July disturbing rumours of Warwick and Clarence's treachery had been brought to his attention, although even now Edward was reluctant to believe it. He wrote to Warwick and Clarence, calling on them to show they were not 'of any such disposition towards us, as the rumour here runs'. But on the next day Edward learned the truth, together with other alarming news. Edward wrote again to Coventry, this time with more urgency. Edward called again for the hundred archers, although 'with more if you goodly may [...] without failing, all expenses laid apart, upon the faith and liegance you owe us'. Edward now understood that Robin of Redesdale's rising was something much more dangerous than a local disturbance; Robin was currently marching south at the head of a great host. The rebel army was vast, estimated at more than three times the King's strength. Edward must also have realised that the rebels were no mere rabble. Although many commoners had joined the rising, motivated by a wide range of factors, its core was provided by Warwick's northern affinity: Warwick had shown his hand. There can be no doubt that Warwick had instigated this latest rising. On this occasion 'Robin of Redesdale' is generally accepted to have been a member of the Conyers family, important members of Warwick's affinity in Yorkshire.[31] The head of the family, Sir John Conyers, was steward of the lordship of Middleham, the centre of Warwick's power in the north. Other rebel leaders were Warwick's kinsmen, including his nephew, Sir Henry FitzHugh, and a cousin, Sir Henry Neville, who was the son of Lord

Latimer. Manifestos that were issued by the rebels matched all of Warwick's own grievances.

Meanwhile, as Robin of Redesdale raised the men of the north, Warwick and Clarence had been active in the south. On 13 May Warwick attended the annual Garter Ceremony at Windsor, where the order was conferred on Duke Charles of Burgundy. From here he moved to Sandwich, where he supervised the refitting of his most formidable ship, the *Trinity*. His brother, George, joined him by 12 June, on the pretext that the Archbishop was to bless the refurbished ship. By the end of the month Warwick had returned to London, where he was joined by Clarence. Warwick now began to make his intentions clear.

On 28 June he wrote to his supporters in Coventry, announcing the imminent marriage between Clarence and his daughter Isabel, for which Archbishop Neville had now secretly obtained a dispensation. On 4 July they were joined by the Earl of Oxford at Sandwich, and from here the party crossed to Calais. On 11 July Clarence and Isabel were married by Archbishop Neville.[32] On 12 July Warwick and Clarence openly embraced rebellion. They issued a manifesto, designed for a wide audience, which set out their grievances in full.[33] They deplored the exclusion of the true nobility from Edward's secret council in favour of 'certain seducious persons'. These were revealed to be Earl Rivers and his wife, Lord Scales and his brothers, the Earls of Pembroke and Devon, Lord Audley, and Sir John Fogge. This, according to the manifesto, had caused the 'realm to fall in great poverty and misery', because Edward's advisors were concerned only for their 'own promotion and enriching'. Warwick and Clarence called on their supporters to join them at Canterbury on 16 July, in order to seek a 'remedy and reformation'. The rebels received a rapturous reception in Kent, and from Canterbury they marched towards London, raising troops *en route*. The rebels were given a reluctant and nervous reception in London, however, where the City Fathers were induced to grant them a loan. From London Warwick and Clarence set out towards Coventry, where they hoped to join with Robin of Redesdale.[34]

Edward retreated to Nottingham in the face of the northern rebels' advance, where presumably he hoped to join with Pembroke and Devon. Soon, though, Edward was cut off from support. Redesdale outflanked the royal army, speeding south towards a rendezvous with Warwick and Clarence. But near Banbury, at Edgecote, Redesdale's forces encountered the army raised by the Earls of Pembroke and Devon. The royalists were probably several thousand strong. All sources agree that Pembroke and Devon became separated: Pembroke's forces were compelled to face the northerners alone. According to *Warkworth's Chronicle* and *Hearne's Fragment*, Pembroke and Devon 'fell to variance over lodgings', although Wavrin tells us that poor reconnaissance was to blame.[35] According to Wavrin the two armies first became aware of each other late on 25 July. They camped for the night on opposite sides of a river, presumably the Cherwell. Next morning there was a fierce struggle to secure the river crossing, in which the northerners were worsted. Although the bards may have later coloured their exploits, it is clear that Pembroke's Welshmen fought hard. The northerners experienced heavy casualties. Of the nobility and gentry, Sir Henry Neville and Sir John Conyers' son, also called John, were killed; Robert Lord Ogle, died later of his wounds.[36] Their morale was shaken, but late in the day the northerners were reinforced by an advance party from the Earl of Warwick's army. Sir Geoffrey Gate and Sir William Parr persuaded the northerners to attack again. Now Pembroke was outnumbered and his forces overwhelmed. Devon, either through fear or spite, left Pembroke and his Welshmen to their fate. Pembroke and his brother, Richard, were both captured. The following day they were taken to Northampton, where Warwick presided over their summary execution.

On 29 July Edward moved south from Nottingham. It is clear that Edward suffered from faulty sources of intelligence during this campaign, because he remained blissfully unaware of the disaster that had overtaken his supporters. Edward walked into a trap. At Olney, in Buckinghamshire, Edward was taken captive by Archbishop Neville. Presumably Warwick sent his brother because he wished to avoid the impression of using force, although the Archbishop must have been supported by an armed escort. But what happened to Edward's army? Earlier in the campaign he had been supported by at least two peers, Suffolk and Norfolk, as well as his brother Richard, although the Woodvilles are said to have been sent away to safety. Most historians have accepted without question the testimony of *Warkworth's Chronicle*, which tells us that 'all his people raised were fled from him'.[37] But it is also possible that Edward's men were scattered throughout the surrounding villages and he was taken by surprise.[38] Edward's enemies had avoided a direct confrontation with him on the battlefield, but, on this occasion, he had been comprehensively out-thought.

Edward was taken first to Warwick Castle, where he encountered the Earl of Warwick himself. We may assume that Warwick knelt before Edward and offered him formal respect as king, just as Edward had knelt before Henry VI almost a decade before. In mid August Edward was taken north, to Middleham. What were Warwick's plans, now that Edward was in his power? For the moment, Warwick ruled in Edward's name; Edward appeared to accept his constricted role. As the historian Paul Kendall plausibly suggests, he gave his captors 'fair words, he smiled, he signed whatever they put before him'.[39] While Edward was powerless to resist, Warwick continued to strike against Edward's supporters. Earl Rivers and his son Sir John Woodville were captured and executed; the Earl of Devon was lynched by a mob at Bridgwater. Although Queen Elizabeth and her daughters were left in peace, her mother was charged with sorcery. Yet Edward could not be content as a puppet king and he would not give in to despair. As Kendall puts it, the lion would become a fox.[40] But Edward's time was short. Warwick had called a Parliament to convene at York, where the government of the realm was to be discussed.

Was Edward's deposition to be on the agenda of the planned Parliament? The rebels' manifesto from Calais had ominously compared Edward's policies to those of Edward II, Richard II and Henry VI. These were all kings, of course, who had been deposed. Rumours were also now circulating, probably encouraged by Warwick, that Edward was illegitimate, the son of an archer called 'Blancborgne'.[41] Edward's effective removal caused chaos, however, and Warwick found it was impossible to restore order. In East Anglia, for example, the Duke of Norfolk took advantage of the opportunity to wrest control of Caister Castle from the Paston family. More seriously, Sir Humphrey and Charles Neville, from the Lancastrian branch of the family, took the opportunity to raise rebellion in the name of Henry VI. Men refused to follow orders to join a royal army until they could be sure the orders really came from Edward himself. Warwick was therefore compelled to let Edward appear in public. An army was now quickly raised and the Lancastrian revolt was quashed. Edward witnessed the execution of the leaders at York, and this gave him his chance to act. He sent word to his brother, Richard, and to other noble supporters, and they quickly came to his side. The Earl of Northumberland, who had held aloof from his brother's rebellion, also answered Edward's call. Edward announced his intention to travel south. Warwick had continued to maintain the fiction of loyalty to Edward in public, and so he could no longer prevent Edward from carrying out his own wishes. Edward proceeded in state to London, where he resumed the rule of the kingdom.

For a while there was a curious standoff. Oxford and George Neville were near London, at the Archbishop's palace at the Moor, although Edward brusquely refused to grant them an audience. Presumably Warwick and Clarence remained in the Midlands. But then, remarkably, there was a reconciliation:

> There were frequent missions and embassies going between the King and the disaffected lords. Eventually, on the appointed day, in the great chamber of Parliament, the Duke of Clarence, the Earl of Warwick and their supporters appeared before a Great Council of all the lords of the realm where peace was made and it was agreed that all disagreements should be abandoned.[42]

Once again, Edward had forgiven his enemies, but had he forgotten? Sir John Paston was not convinced:

> The king himself hath good language of the lords of Clarence, of Warwick, saying they be his best friends. But his household men have other language.[43]

Similarly, the second Crowland Continuator considered that 'there probably remained, however, a sense of outraged majesty, deep in the heart, on the one side, and, on the other, a guilty mind conscious of an over-daring deed'.[44]

Edward's true feelings cannot be known. It must be said that he negotiated from a position of strength, and not all of the decisions could have been to Warwick's liking. Although the Earl of Pembroke had been removed, Warwick was forced to accept a check to his ambitions in Wales. The king's own brother, Richard, was to be groomed as a successor to William Herbert. More significantly, Edward had resolved there must be a counterweight to the Nevilles' power in the north. He therefore resolved to restore the Percy heir, Henry, to the earldom of Northumberland.[45] Of course, this would entail the dispossession of John Neville, who had remained loyal to Edward during his brother Warwick's rebellion. John therefore needed to receive compensation and evidently Edward gave this serious thought. John Neville was to lose an earldom, although he was promoted to Marquess Montagu. For the loss of some of his lands in the north he was to be compensated with lands forfeited by the Courtenays in the south-west. Finally – and this was surely a major concession to Neville pride – John's young son, George, was betrothed to Edward's eldest daughter, Elizabeth. George was given the title Duke of Bedford.

A fragile peace had been achieved, although shortly afterwards a new crisis arose. Once again local events took on national significance. In early 1470 there were serious disturbances in Lincolnshire. These had their

origin in a feud between Sir Thomas Burgh, a member of Edward's household, and Lord Welles. Edward learned from his mistakes. No longer
willing to tolerate local disorder in the north, Edward's reaction was quick
and decisive. Lord Welles and his associate Sir Thomas Dymmock were
summoned to court to account for their transgressions; they obediently
obeyed. By early March Edward was moving north in person to restore
order; an army had been summoned to join him at Grantham on
12 March. Ironically, however, Edward's actions caused an escalation.
Rumours arose that Edward's intention was not to restore peace but
rather to seek vengeance on the commons for the risings of the previous
year. On Sunday 4 March Sir Robert Welles, the eldest son of Lord
Welles, declared himself 'great captain of the commons of Lincolnshire',
claiming that Edward was coming to 'destroy the commons', and called
for supporters to join him two days later at Ranby Hawe near Lincoln.[46]
Sir Robert stated his actions were motivated purely in self-defence,
although by now he was part of a much larger conspiracy. Possibly Sir
Robert had taken the initiative to contact Warwick or Clarence, although
the two magnates quickly resolved to manipulate the disaffection in
Lincolnshire to their own ends. Their hastily planned strategy was similar
to that of the previous year. Warwick would instigate another rising in the
north, while Clarence encouraged rebellion in the south-west. Edward
was to be diverted and confused by the various risings. Warwick and
Clarence would maintain a fiction of loyalty until the time was right to
strike.

At Fotheringhay, on 11 March, Edward was informed that the Lincolnshire rebels, now several thousand strong, had bypassed Grantham and
were heading for Leicester. Here, according to Sir Robert Welles' later
confession, they planned to join with Warwick and Clarence.[47] Apparently
Edward was still not aware of the involvement of Warwick and Clarence
in the rebellion, because they had both been trusted (albeit belatedly) to
raise troops. The two nobles had both sent Edward comforting messages
of support, saying they would join him soon. But the curious movements
of the Lincolnshire rebels, which echoed those of Robin of Redesdale,
must have aroused Edward's suspicions. Even so, Edward had resolved not
to wait passively on events. He maintained his focus on the suppression
of the Lincolnshire rising. Two days earlier the captive Lord Welles had
been forced to send a message to his son: if the rebels did not submit Lord
Welles and Dymmock would be executed. In response the rebels suddenly
changed direction and marched towards the King. Sir Robert had
resolved to rescue his father. Welles' decision was as rash as it was brave.

Ludlow Castle, Shropshire, where Edward IV spent his youth. (*Geoffrey Wheeler*)

Micklegate Bar, York, where the heads of defeated commanders were displayed. (*Rae Tan, Heritage Image Studio*)

Facsimile by Geoffrey Wheeler from British Library MS Harley 7353. Edward IV witnesses the trip[le] sun phenomenon before the Battle of Mortimer's Cross. Edward speaks the words *'Domine quid wi[s] me facere'*: 'Lord, what would you have me do?' (*Geoffrey Wheeler*)

The *Coventry Sallet*, c. 1480. (*Geoffrey Wheeler*)

A view across North Acres, from the monument to commemorate the Battle of Towton. The tree on the horizon marks the extent of the Yorkist lines. (*Rae Tan, Heritage Image Studio*)

The infamous Cock Beck. It is difficult to imagine this was a scene of slaughter in March 1461. (*Rae Tan, Heritage Image Studio*)

Edward IV, adapted from a representation in the
Rous Roll (British Library). (*Geoffrey Wheeler*)

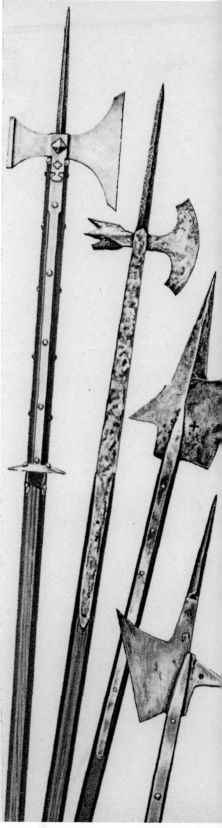

Late medieval polearms. (*Geoffrey Wheeler*)

Edward IV. Detail from fifteenth-century glass in the 'Royal' Window, Canterbury Cathedral. (*Geoffrey Wheeler*)

Bamburgh Castle, Northumberland. (*Rae Tan, Heritage Image Studio*)

Middleham Castle, Yorkshire. The Earl of Warwick's most favoured northern residence. (*The Richard III Foundation, Inc.*)

The palatial home of Louis de Gruuthuse, where Edward stayed during his exile of 1470–1. (*The Richard III Foundation, Inc.*)

The Battle of Barnet. Fifteenth-century illumination from Ghent MS 236. (*Geoffrey Wheeler*)

The Gastons. View from the Duke of Somerset's lines at the Battle of Tewkesbury. (*Steven Goodchild*)

Lincoln Green Lane, the 'secret way' used by the Duke of Somerset at the Battle of Tewkesbury. (*Steven Goodchild*)

Tewkesbury Abbey. (*Steven Goodchild*)

Presumably his plan was to surprise the royal army at Stamford, but Edward was alert and ready for battle. On 12 March Edward reached Stamford, where he discovered the rebel army was only 5 miles away at Empingham. Edward immediately advanced on the rebels, who were hastily drawn up into battle array. As noted by Anthony Goodman, 'Edward's generalship is seen at its best in his determination to force the issue that day, after a hard march.'[48] Before the battle began, Edward showed he could match the ruthlessness shown by his enemies, and he ordered the execution of Lord Welles and Sir Thomas Dymmock.

The Battle of Empingham was scarcely a battle at all. According to *Warkworth's Chronicle* the encounter commenced with a barrage from Edward's artillery, which may have forced the rebels to attack.[49] But little else is known except that the rebels were quickly put to flight.[50] Strategically, Edward's victory ensured control of the south and east, but its real significance was political. According to the *Chronicle of the Rebellion of Lincolnshire*, the battle provided certain evidence of Warwick and Clarence's treachery.[51] It tell us that as the two armies closed the rebels cried out 'A Clarence! A Clarence! A Warwick!' A 'casket' [helmet] was found on the battlefield, apparently, which contained incriminating letters from Warwick and Clarence. Sir Robert Welles, who was captured shortly afterwards, is said to have been wearing Clarence's livery. Welles confessed the role of Warwick and Clarence under interrogation. He swore their aim was to make Clarence king. But the most detailed sources for this series of events, including the *Chronicle of the Rebellion*, are 'official' productions, produced shortly afterwards by Edward's clerks. Some modern writers have argued, therefore, that Warwick and Clarence were not really involved in the Lincolnshire rising at all: did Edward, with an army at his back, seize the opportunity to destroy Warwick and Clarence? He would not have been the only medieval king to act in such an arbitrary manner, although the 'conspiracy theories' are ultimately unconvincing.[52] Edward had again 'laboured himself into forgetfulness', or at least he had tried. But sadly for Yorkist England, the bond of trust between Edward and Warwick had been irreparably broken. It is possible, on this occasion, that Clarence was the driving force behind the rebels' plans, such as they were, and that Warwick was reluctantly drawn in. Nevertheless, ultimately the disturbances in Lincolnshire gave Warwick another opportunity, which he decided he must take.

Edward allowed his men some rest, although by now he was aware of the rising in Yorkshire, under the leadership of Lord Scrope of Bolton and Sir John Conyers. Edward marched north: by 16 March his army had reached Newark. Here Edward received messages from Warwick and Clarence, who were now in arms to his west. Edward ordered Warwick and Clarence to dismiss their army and summoned them to his presence.[53] Warwick and Clarence replied that they would agree to come if Edward provided safe-conducts, as well as full pardons for themselves and 'all the lords and others that had taken their part'. Now convinced of their guilt, Edward responded with kingly anger. Warwick and Clarence could expect treatment only, he said, 'as a sovereign lord ought to use and entreat his subjects, for his ancient enemies of France would not desire so large a surety for their coming to his royal presence'. Edward had pardoned many rebels in the past, and he would do so again, but to give in to Warwick's demands would show dangerous weakness: 'it should be too perilous and too evil an example to all other subjects in like case'. The implications were clear: Warwick and Clarence would have to submit on Edward's terms. Otherwise he would pursue them and destroy them.

Warwick and Clarence decided to run. On 19 March Edward was at Doncaster, where he presided over the execution of Sir Robert Welles and his lieutenant Richard Warren. The following day Edward advanced towards the rebels, whom he had learned were at Chesterfield. Edward's army was growing every day: it was said there 'were never seen in England so many goodly men, and so well arrayed a field'.[54] That evening Edward encountered the rebels' 'foreriders' at Rotherham. Perhaps Warwick and Clarence had considered making a stand, but their support, such as it was, was now crumbling.[55] Attempting to use the advance of their scouts as a feint, Warwick and Clarence retreated westwards towards Manchester. They made a desperate plea for help to Lord Stanley, but Stanley refused to commit himself to their cause. Doubtless Edward was inclined to continue the pursuit, but he was counselled by his lords to march towards York instead.[56] Here Edward would be able to replenish his supplies, because a full wagon train would be necessary if his army was to cross the Pennines. There was an additional advantage in that the royal army would be well placed to disrupt a junction between Warwick and his northern adherents. Edward concurred. In the event, however, the northern rising fizzled out. Scrope and Conyers submitted to Edward at York, where they were received into his grace. On 25 March Edward confirmed the restoration of Henry Percy to the earldom of Northumberland.

Now bereft of support in the north, Warwick and Clarence pinned their last hopes on the Courtenay affinity, who had risen in the south-west, although they may already have decided to take flight overseas. On 26 March Edward despatched commissions of array to the south-western counties, although these were not really effective because the rebels were moving south at speed. On 27 March Edward himself left York in pursuit, making equally rapid progress. By 25 April he was at Salisbury, having already gone as far south as Exeter. From Salisbury he released the names of fifty-three rebels who had not secured pardons, and ordered that their lands and property be seized.[57] The list shows that Warwick and Clarence's cause had once again failed to rouse much enthusiasm among the aristocracy. Their supporters included a substantial number of gentlemen, although many of them had long-standing connections with Warwick; others had Lancastrian ties. However, although there were question marks over the loyalty of Lord Stanley and the Earl of Shrewsbury, Lord Scrope was the only peer who had been active on the rebels' behalf. Evidently the Earl of Oxford feared he would be implicated in the rebellions, because he fled to France, but he had provided no active support. On the whole the nobility remained loyal to Edward, as they had done the previous year.

By now, though, Warwick and Clarence had made good their escape. Marching via Bristol, where Warwick abandoned his artillery train, the rebels had made their way to the Devon coast. Accompanied by the countess of Warwick and her two daughters – Duchess Isabel was heavily pregnant – Warwick and Clarence sailed for Calais. Warwick was able to gather a fleet at Dartmouth, although his flagship, the *Trinity*, was still berthed at Southampton. Warwick therefore attempted to repeat the exploits of 1460, when his men had captured much of the royal fleet at Sandwich. A number of ships were despatched under Sir Geoffrey Gate. But Anthony Woodville, now Earl Rivers, was in command at the port. He had not forgotten the events at Sandwich nor his subsequent humiliation at Calais. This time Rivers was ready and waiting, eager to avenge the deaths of his father and brother. Warwick's force was beaten off, losing both ships and men, and Gate himself was captured. Gate was spared, although some of his men were executed. Edward's constable, Worcester, now earned his soubriquet – 'the Butcher of England' – because their bodies were impaled.[58]

Repulsed from Southampton, the rebels pushed on towards Calais, but even here they could find no sanctuary. Warwick must have been counting on the loyalty of the garrison, but their commanders were divided. One of Warwick's lieutenants, the Gascon Lord Duras, remained staunchly loyal to Edward; his influence prevailed. To Warwick's consternation, the guns of Calais opened fire on the rebel fleet. Warwick withdrew out of range; a delegation from Calais, headed by Lord Wenlock, went out to speak with the earl. According to Commynes, who met him shortly afterwards, Wenlock remained true to the Earl of Warwick at heart.[59] Wenlock warned Warwick that Calais was a trap, and he implored the earl to look for safety in France instead. When the right time came, Wenlock assured Warwick, he would restore Calais to its captain. Wenlock was to be true to his word, but his promises offered Warwick little consolation now. The rebels were forced to depart, although not before Warwick and Clarence suffered a personal tragedy. Denied a refuge, Duchess Isabel was forced to give birth on board ship. Isabel recovered, but her son did not survive. Warwick's fleet put out to sea, where they began to terrorise merchant ships. They were joined by Warwick's nephew, Thomas Neville, the Bastard of Fauconberg. But Edward's naval commanders, Earl Rivers and Sir John Howard, were now also at sea and they were relentless in their pursuit of the rebels. Warwick lost fourteen ships to Rivers in one conflict, in which over 500 sailors are said to have been killed.[60] The rebels were compelled to seek shelter in the Seine estuary, in France, where Warwick resolved to seek further assistance.

Yet Warwick received a lukewarm reception. Apparently Louis XI was embarrassed by Warwick's presence; he encouraged him to depart as soon as possible. Eventually, though, Louis XI did agree to offer Warwick asylum and assistance, but at a price. Louis had displayed scant hospitality to his kinswoman, Margaret of Anjou, but now 'the universal spider' decided she could become a useful pawn. And so Warwick was forced to come to terms with Margaret, an extraordinary alliance that was as unpalatable to both parties as it was necessary. King Louis acted as an intermediary, although the negotiations were fraught. According to one contemporary account, Margaret was 'right difficult', although this is hardly surprising.[61] Warwick was scarcely more amenable: seeking to justify his earlier actions, when he had driven her husband from the throne, Warwick stated he had done nothing 'but that a noble man outraged and despaired [sic] ought to have done'. Eventually, however, terms were agreed, and both parties committed themselves to an aggressive alliance with Louis against Burgundy. Margaret and Warwick met at Angers, on 22 July. Warwick was forced to swallow his pride. He endured a humiliating ceremony in which he sued for Margaret's forgiveness on his knees. But Margaret also made concessions: the alliance was to be sealed by marriage. It was agreed that Warwick's younger daughter, Anne, would be betrothed to Prince Edward. Now seventeen years old, the Prince was an aggressive youth, anxious to reclaim his lost inheritance. Like a young Mordred, Prince Edward appears to have been raised with only one purpose in mind, to destroy the House of York by force of arms.[62] Nevertheless, Margaret was reluctant to release her precious son until success was assured. Warwick, therefore, would go ahead to conquer England on the Lancastrians' behalf. Accompanied by Jasper Tudor, Oxford and Clarence – who would now have to be content with the duchy of York – Warwick made ready to invade.

Warwick's preparations could not be kept secret, but on the Continent some writers believed that Edward was complacent and ill-prepared. According to Commynes, the Duke of Burgundy issued repeated warnings to Edward about Warwick's plans, but Edward 'paid no attention to him [Charles] and only continued his hunting'.[63] Chastelain's comments are more favourable towards Edward, but he makes essentially the same point:

> he [Edward] was a valiant prince, and he was always confident that he would be able to recover against him [Warwick] quickly enough [...] for he was certain that once he found himself on the field of battle with Warwick, the latter would not oppose him, for he was a faintheart and a coward.[64]

Perhaps it is true that Edward did not respect Warwick's abilities as a commander, although Chastelain's comments may be derived from Edward's bravado at the Burgundian court in the following year. Yet it is difficult to accept Commynes' conclusions.[65] For instance, Edward drew upon his own experience of exile in 1459–60, and his agents took steps to ensure that neither Calais or Ireland could be used as a rebel base. Furthermore, Edward made a personal visit to Sandwich and Dover, to ensure the defences were in good order and that his captains were alert. Edward also used Warwick's own methods against him. Some of the earl's ships, including the *Trinity*, became part of the royal fleet.[66] Edward's ships were supported by a substantial fleet from Burgundy, where Warwick's piracy had caused great anger. Warwick's ships had continued to engage in piracy, from their bases in the Seine, but the Anglo-Burgundian fleet achieved an effective blockade. This caused Warwick immense frustration. It took great tenacity on Warwick's part to persuade Louis' agents, and the French king himself, of the need to provide him with renewed financial support.[67] There were tensions between Warwick's men and the local people; a mutiny was narrowly averted.

In early August Edward was informed of yet another rising in the north, under the leadership of Lord FitzHugh, Warwick's brother-in-law. Presumably this rebellion was intended to create a diversion, in order to assist Warwick's invasion, although the earl remained confined to the Seine estuary. Edward, now ever conscious of the dangers of rebellion in the north, resolved to deal with the matter himself: 'the King has sent for his feedmen to come to him, for he will go to put them down'.[68] By 16 August Edward was at Ripon, and FitzHugh's rebellion crumbled in the face of the determined royal advance. FitzHugh fled to Scotland. To an extent, though, FitzHugh's rebellion succeeded, because Edward was still in the north when Warwick finally arrived. In early September storms broke up the Anglo–Burgundian blockade, meaning that Warwick's invasion fleet was finally able to sail. On 9 September Warwick and Clarence set out for England. Their journey was unopposed and they landed safely in Devon. Jasper Tudor made for Wales, as ever, although the rest of the army moved rapidly north–east. Warwick recovered his artillery at Bristol, and by the time they reached Coventry the invaders had raised a large army. This time they attracted some noble support, as the Earl of Shrewsbury and Lord Stanley appear to have joined their army. Should Edward be criticised for his decision to move north? Some contemporaries did suggest it was a mistake,[69] although most recent historians have appreciated Edward's dilemmas.[70] Edward's experience had taught him that a northern rebellion could not be allowed to grow unchecked, and how could he have known for certain where the invaders would land? It is not as though Edward was completely isolated. York was an important supply centre, on the Great North Road to London. Assuming that his rear was now secure, Edward was well placed to acquire provisions and then to move rapidly south towards a confrontation with the rebels. Ultimately Edward was to be defeated by treachery, not by his enemies' strategy.

Further north Edward had delegated the preparations for war to John Neville, Marquess Montagu, in whom he continued to have the utmost trust. As always, Montagu carried out Edward's instructions diligently and effectively. He raised a substantial force, estimated to be 6,000 strong.[71] But now Montagu faced a terrible dilemma. For the last ten years he had provided Edward with sterling service, and he had received many rewards in return. He had twice ignored his brother's appeal to blood kinship, but whether this was the result of a personal loyalty to Edward, ambition, or more abstract considerations, is unclear. Now, though, even if Edward had made a serious attempt to compensate him for his losses, he had his own grievances against the King. Montagu may indeed have considered the Courtenay lands to be a 'magpie's nest', as Warkworth claims.[72] Although these lands could have become a source of great wealth and power,

Montagu made no attempt to establish his presence in the south-west. What is more, to a northerner, the imported foreign title of 'Marquess' probably meant far less than the ancient title of Northumberland. Neville's possession of the Earldom of Northumberland had symbolised his family's triumph over their ancestral enemies, the Percys, who were now restored to power. A number of factors may have induced Montagu to betray Edward, although we cannot know which of these was the most important. Eventually Montagu resolved to join his brother, although contemporaries suggested that he did so with a heavy heart.[73]

Alexander Carlisle, Sergeant of the Minstrels, brought the awful news to Edward at Doncaster, where the King was hastily roused from sleep: Montagu was preparing to attack. Edward had never lost a battle, but for the second time in just over a year he tasted defeat. A small army was still at Edward's disposal, but he rapidly came to the conclusion that it would be impossible to make a stand. If Edward did not fear Warwick, evidently he had more respect for Montagu. He must also have understood that on this occasion, if he was captured, he would not be spared. Edward dismissed his levies. Now accompanied by a much smaller following, Edward took to flight. He made for the port of Lynn in Norfolk, by way of Lincolnshire and a hazardous crossing of the Wash. There was only one way for Edward to survive: exile.

Chapter 6

Texel, The Netherlands, October 1470

Edward pursued the best option available, to seek shelter at the court of Burgundy, but his voyage across the North Sea was alarming. Not only were his ships blown off course, but he was pursued by a small fleet belonging to the Hanseatic League. The Hansards nursed a grudge against Edward of several years' standing.[1] Forced to make use of the prevailing winds, Edward's ships made for the northern Netherlands, some way from the Duke of Burgundy's centre of power in Flanders. Edward's ships anchored off the island of Texel, but the harbour was shallow and the ships ran aground. The Hanse fleet gathered with menace, waiting for high tide when they planned to board Edward's ships. Fortunately for Edward, however, the local people helped the English ashore before the Hansards were able to reach them. According to Commynes, the English exiles were in a terrible state: 'there never was such a beggarly company'.[2] Doubtless they were wet, cold and hungry. They had no money or spare clothes, and Edward was forced to pay off the captain of his ship by giving up his fur-lined robe. But for now, at least, Edward was safe.

Edward was accompanied by a small but committed band of supporters.[3] The names of the most prominent exiles are recorded in a ducal letter of November 1470, in which Charles of Burgundy was later to grant Edward a modest allowance. They included Anthony Earl Rivers, William Lord Hastings, and William Lord Say and Sele. Four Knights of the Body were with Edward in Burgundy – Sir Robert Chamberlain, Sir Gilbert Debenham, Sir John Middleton and Sir Humphrey Talbot – all tough men who were willing and able to fight. Other exiles included Sir George Derrell, formerly Keeper of the Great Wardrobe, and Sir William Blount, the son of Lord Mountjoy. A notable name missing from this list is Edward's brother, Richard Duke of Gloucester, who appears to have followed Edward into exile some time later. Edward must have been particularly gratified by the loyalty of his younger brother, who had grown up in Warwick's household, and who had resisted the blandishments that were surely offered him by Warwick and Clarence. All of Edward's companions were to do him great service during the coming months; many of them were to give up their lives. Not all of Edward's company were soldiers, however. He was also accompanied, for example, by Thomas Norton, the famous alchemist and astrologer – although one wonders if Edward's confidence in Norton had been shaken by the reverses he had suffered![4] Another non-combatant, who offered more obviously practical support, was the Clerk of the Signet, Nicholas Harpisfield. He wrote some of Edward's correspondence during his exile, and was almost certainly the author of the *Arrivall*, a crucial source for the events following Edward's return to England.[5]

For the next two months Edward was the guest of Louis de Gruuthuse, the Governor of Northern Holland, who had hurried to greet Edward on hearing the news of his landing. While staying at Gruuthuse's house in Bruges, Edward took the opportunity to sample his host's impressive library.[6] Although Gruuthuse was an attentive host, however, Edward must have been disturbed by the apparent coldness of Duke Charles. Charles did not agree to meet Edward until 2 January 1471, when Edward was finally invited to court at Aire. Here, Commynes tells us that Edward 'strongly urged him [Charles] to assist his return, assuring him that he had much support in England, and, for God's sake, not to abandon him, seeing that he had married his sister and they were brothers in each other's Order [of chivalry]'.[7] Presumably Duchess Margaret lobbied hard on Edward's behalf. However, according to Commynes, Edward's presence placed Charles in a terrible quandary. Although aware of his obligations to Edward, Charles was still mindful of his kinship to the House of Lancaster, especially to the Beauforts. Edmund Beaufort, titular Duke of Somerset, remained a prominent member of Charles's court.[8] He argued passionately that Edward's case should be dismissed. Also, although Charles (justly) feared that Louis' support for Warwick had been won at the cost of a promise to assist the French against Burgundy, he was sceptical that the latest political developments in England could be overturned. Commynes tells us he was therefore despatched to Calais in an attempt to forestall war with England.[9] Lord Wenlock had kept his promise to Warwick, and the garrison had now declared for Henry VI. If successful, Commynes' mission would have left Edward high and dry. Commynes was charged to tell Wenlock that Charles was 'very happy and content' that his kinsman had regained his throne, and that Charles continued to desire peace and friendship with England – whoever was to be king.[10] But it has been argued that the extent of Charles's indecision has been exaggerated. Given his subsequent vacillations, Commynes' word cannot always be trusted.[11]

It must be stressed that concepts of honour – particularly with regard to kinship and other personal relationships – did matter deeply to medieval people. Nevertheless, beneath the elaborate façade of late-medieval diplomacy there remained a core of hard-headed pragmatism. In December Louis XI repudiated the treaty of Péronne and declared all of Charles's French lands to be forfeit: evidently this concentrated Charles's mind. Although nothing of great significance occurred in the resulting 'war' until 6 January, when the Burgundian town of St Quentin went over to the French, by the end of December Charles had already offered Edward clear support – even if Commynes is correct to say that this information was not made public. Edward must have been greatly relieved. On 31 December the duke granted Edward £20,000 to aid him in his 'departure from my lord the duke's lands to return to England'.[12] Troops – perhaps mercenaries – were also provided.[13] Edward himself had not passively waited on events, but had taken steps to prepare the ground politically for his return. Edward made contact with the Earl of Northumberland, the Duke of Norfolk, and many others. As we shall see, he also sought to build bridges with his errant brother, Clarence.

By 19 February Edward's preparations were almost complete, and his fleet made ready to sail from Flushing. It consisted of thirty-six ships painstakingly assembled – as secretly as possible – from a variety of sources. Ironically, fifteen of the vessels were provided by the Hanseatic League, who were now prepared to support Edward in return for a promise of future concessions. On his way to Flushing from Bruges, Edward displayed his usual panache, taking time to walk among the crowds who had gathered to watch him leave. From this point on, faced with a situation in which others might have crumbled, Edward reacted with poise and determination. Burgundian court poets compared Edward to Hercules.[14] Nevertheless, some observers gave his expedition little chance of success. In a famous passage one writer remarked that 'It is a difficult matter to go out by the door and then try to enter by the windows. They think he will leave his skin there.'[15]

Meanwhile, in England, Warwick had established control. In London, news of Edward's flight had caused panic. By early October 1470 a motley force of Kentishmen, shipmen and other lawless elements – albeit under the nominal command of Sir Geoffrey Gate – threatened the city. This caused Edward's queen, Elizabeth, who was heavily pregnant, to flee to sanctuary in Westminster. Other prominent Yorkists followed her lead and on 3 October the Tower was surrendered to the joint custody of Gate and the City Fathers. On 5 October Warwick's brother, Archbishop Neville, arrived in London: his right to take command of the Tower was not contested. Here, Neville would have found Henry VI, who had been abandoned by his frightened Yorkist attendants: he 'was not worshipfully arrayed as a prince, and not so cleanly kept as should seem a prince'.[16] The next day Warwick himself arrived, riding straight to the Tower. He knelt before Henry, who had been hastily clothed in more fitting garb, and acknowledged him as his king. On 13 October Henry was taken in procession to St Paul's – Oxford bore the sword of state and Warwick bore his train – where he once again wore the crown. Then he was taken to Westminster, where, doubtless thoroughly bemused, he was to begin a new reign as King Henry VI.

But Warwick was to rule. It must have seemed like a great triumph, although in truth Warwick was in a difficult position. If the so-called 'Readeption' of Henry VI was to be successful it would require a delicate balancing act. Of course Warwick could rely on his own supporters, and on committed Lancastrians such as Jasper Tudor, but he also needed to reach out to former supporters of Edward's regime. A number of prominent Yorkists, including the Duke of Norfolk, the Earl of Essex, Lord Mountjoy and Cardinal Bourchier were initially taken into custody, but they were soon released. Even Sir Richard Woodville, who had not joined his brother Anthony in exile, received a pardon within a few weeks. There were few reprisals against Edward's supporters. The only significant victim was the hated Earl of Worcester, who met his death in front of a baying crowd on 18 October. Warwick also gave clear orders, in King Henry's name, that the rights of sanctuaries were to be respected. Warwick chivalrously sent Lady Scrope to assist Queen Elizabeth during her coming labour. It is a mark of Warwick's restraint that when, on 2 November, Elizabeth gave birth to a son, Elizabeth and Edward's first, mother and child continued to be left in peace.

There are some indications that Warwick's regime was popular. Nevertheless, it must be said there were a number of supporters, like the Pastons, who had their own reasons to support the Readeption. The Pastons had been engaged in a long-running land dispute with the Yorkist Duke of Norfolk and others, connected with the ownership of Caister Castle. The return of the Earl of Oxford provided them with a valuable noble ally. It was local politics that ensured the Paston brothers would subsequently fight with Oxford at Barnet, rather than loyalty to Henry VI.

But perhaps the old king did retain some sympathy and respect. According to *Warkworth's Chronicle*, not only were his 'good lovers' 'full glad' at his restoration, but also 'the more part of the people'.[17] Warwick himself still enjoyed the support of the common people: once again crowds lined the roads, crying 'Warwick! Warwick!'[18]

Among the aristocracy, however, Warwick's conciliatory gestures did not achieve as much as he must have hoped. The main problem was that the political situation would remain unclear until Margaret and her son returned. Warwick had taken some rewards for himself,[19] but as yet there was little available to reward loyal Lancastrians who would expect to receive acknowledgement of their service. Warwick may have been genuinely willing to seek an accommodation with former Yorkists, but could Margaret and Prince Edward be expected to show the same attitude? The return of Somerset and Exeter – who sailed from Burgundy in February – cannot have helped to ease fears. Although he was associated with Warwick in government, and seems to have retained Warwick's trust, the Duke of Clarence must have felt especially vulnerable. Warwick's alliance with the House of Lancaster had shattered Clarence's dreams of becoming king, and the lands and titles he had received from his brother were now under threat. He was forced to give up some of his lands to Queen Margaret and her son, evidently under protest. The presence of the young Henry Tudor at court raised questions over his tenure of the honour of Richmond. According to the *Arrivall* Clarence was held in 'great suspicion, despite, disdain and hatred' and he was afraid, probably with reason, that there were many at court who were plotting to bring about the 'destruction of him and all his blood'.[20]

Warwick sent numerous messages to his allies in France. He promised to escort Margaret to England in person. Writing to King Louis, he also restated his personal commitment to war against Burgundy:

> As soon as I possibly can, I will come to you to serve you against this accursed Burgundian [Duke Charles] without any default, please God, to whom I pray to grant you all that your heart desires.[21]

Yet Warwick's true focus was on Edward's impending invasion, although his defensive measures reveal that he trusted few of the nobles. As Charles Ross points out, commissions of array had never before been entrusted to so few.[22] In the north, only Montagu received a commission – Northumberland was pointedly excluded – and in the rest of the country commissions were given only to Clarence, Oxford, Lord Scrope of Bolton and Warwick himself.

However, given his limited resources, Warwick deserves credit for the thoroughness of his preparations: his agents were active along the length of the east coast. As ever, Warwick relied heavily on sea power, and a powerful fleet under the Bastard of Fauconberg patrolled the Channel. Fauconberg was permitted to indulge in piracy in lieu of wages. He took a number of prizes, including Spanish, Breton and Dutch ships. Help might also have been expected from the French, as Louis XI had made naval preparations for war with Burgundy.

On 2 March 1471 Edward embarked on the *Antony*, a ship belonging to Henri de Borselle, the Lord of Veere, who was Gruuthuse's father-in-law. According to the *Arrivall* he had 2,000 men with him, but there may have been fewer.[23] It was but a small force to regain a kingdom! Edward's ships were kept in port by contrary winds for nine frustrating days, and it was not until 11 March that Edward's fleet finally set sail. Paradoxically, however, Edward was lucky, because the same bad weather kept Margaret of Anjou and her son from returning to England, and the French fleet remained in the mouth of the Seine. Moreover, the Bastard of Fauconberg's fleet was distracted by a Breton naval squadron, and the Calais garrison were not able to hinder Edward because they had troubles of their own. A lieutenant of the Woodvilles' kinsman Jacques de Luxembourg led a raiding party into the Calais Pale and caused serious damage. The turning of fortune's wheel allowed Edward to enjoy an uneventful journey across the North Sea. His fleet aimed for the coast of Norfolk, where Edward hoped to count on the support of the Dukes of Norfolk and Suffolk. Edward's ships dropped anchor off Cromer on 12 March. Sir Robert Chamberlain and Sir Gilbert Debenham, both men with local knowledge, were sent out to reconnoitre. But Chamberlain and Debenham quickly realised that the area was dangerous. Norfolk and other allies had once again been taken into custody, and the Earl of Oxford and his brother had been raising local troops. Edward therefore decided to sail north, making for Yorkshire, but the weather turned again: there were storms and the fleet was scattered. Edward eventually came ashore safely at Ravenspur, a now vanished port at the mouth of the Humber. Ironically, it was here that the first Lancastrian king, Henry IV, had landed when he invaded the country in order to depose Richard II in 1399.

In Yorkshire, Edward quickly discovered new dangers. Large bands of men were in arms and had been waiting for the Yorkists to land. There was a particularly strong force in the area under the command of Martin de la See, a gentleman from Holderness. Edward sought counsel, and various options were debated.[24] It was suggested, for example, that Edward should once again take to the water; that he and his army should cross the Humber into Lincolnshire, which would provide them with the shortest road south. This would take them closer to the heart of the kingdom, which was imperative if their enterprise was to succeed. But given their recent experience at sea, the soldiers were reluctant to return to their ships, while the leaders were concerned it would be assumed they had taken flight. It was therefore decided that the army should march inland, towards York. In order to appease the local levies that had been arrayed against them, Edward resorted to the gambit that had served Henry IV well in 1399. It was to be given out that Edward had not returned to claim the throne, but only his duchy of York. On this understanding, but also because Edward was able to show friendly letters from the Earl of Northumberland, Martin de la See's force allowed the Yorkist army to pass unhindered. The author of the *Arrivall* makes an interesting attempt to explain how Edward was able to employ this deception without incurring dishonour. The local levies had forgotten, of course, that Richard Duke of York, 'besides that he was Duke of York, he was also very true and rightwise inheritor to the realm and crown of England'.[25] Medieval writers relished arguments of this nature.

Edward's deception had averted disaster, but it brought him little in terms of active support. Moreover, his army was denied a chance to rest and gain supplies when the burghers of Hull refused to open their gates. Edward received more bad news as he approached York. The Recorder of York, Thomas Conyers, warned Edward that it would not be safe to enter the city. However, Edward had 'decreed in himself constantly to pursue that [*sic*] he had begun, and rather to abide what God and good fortune would give him, though it were to him uncertain'. Thus 'he kept boldly forth his journey'. York refused entry to Edward's army but agreed to admit Edward himself. Edward went into York with less than twenty attendants. It must have looked like a trap, but if the citizens of York did bear Edward any ill will they were quickly won over by his charm. Edward spent a convivial evening and by nightfall his whole army was admitted within the walls. The events at York provide us with an extraordinary example of Edward's personal charisma and force of character.[26]

From York, Edward moved to Sandal, via Wakefield, the castle of the dukes of York, from where his father had met his death.[27] Yet even here

Edward found little support. There 'came some folks to him, but not so many as he supposed would have come', as the *Arrivall* honestly states. Even so, this latest setback was not critical because everything would ultimately depend on the actions of the great magnates. If the two greatest lords in the region, the Earl of Northumberland and the Marquess of Montagu, had acted against Edward in concert then his army would surely have been destroyed. But neither made any effort to hinder Edward's progress. At the time Edward left York Montagu was based at Pontefract, well placed to intercept the Yorkist army, but he 'suffered Edward to pass in peaceful wise'. Why did Montagu fail to move? The author of the *Arrivall* seems uncertain: 'Whether it were with good will or no, men may judge at their pleasure; I deem yea.' As we have seen, Montagu may have been horribly torn between loyalty to Edward on the one hand, and loyalty to his brother on the other. However, Montagu's passivity can be explained in other ways and these are duly considered in the author's text. Chief among these is that the northerners were more inclined to follow the Earl of Northumberland, and they 'would not stir with any lord or noble man other than with the said earl, or at least by his commandment'. Nevertheless, although Northumberland himself would have preferred actively to support Edward – not least because he feared he was about to lose his earldom once again to Montagu – he was reluctant to push his followers too far. Even loyalty to the Percys had its limits, and many northerners refused to fight for Edward because they still remembered Towton, where so many of their kinsmen had been slain. But Northumberland's inactivity was considered 'politiquely done' and 'did the King [Edward] right good and notable service'.

The failure of Warwick's supporters to attack Edward when weak was crucial, because Edward now began, at last, to attract significant support. At Doncaster he was joined by a band of 160 men under William Dudley (later to become Dean of the Royal Chapel) and at Nottingham Sir William Parr and Sir James Harrington joined him with 600 men from Lancashire. But the enemy had not been idle. At Nottingham Edward learned that the Lancastrian peers Oxford, Exeter and Beaumont were at Newark with a growing army. The Yorkists made an aggressive move towards them. The Lancastrian lords were not prepared to meet Edward in battle, however, and they fled south in some panic. Edward returned to Nottingham. The events at Newark might have improved his army's morale, but he remained in a precarious situation. To the north Montagu was now, at last, moving south, Exeter and Oxford were to his flank and Warwick was to his south. He was virtually surrounded: could the 'Lancastrians' now have trapped him and destroyed him?[28] Perhaps Warwick missed an opportunity through caution, although it is also possible that he had listened to the counsel of Clarence. Clarence had apparently sent messages urging his father-in-law not to risk a battle with Edward until he arrived with his own forces. Edward was allowed to retain the initiative, marching directly towards the Earl of Warwick, who fell back from Leicester towards Coventry. At Leicester Edward received an enormous boost when Sir William Norris and Sir William Stanley rode in followed by 3,000 men.

Edward's army arrived at Coventry on 29 March, but Warwick withdrew within the walls. Edward repeatedly challenged him to come out and fight. This was a clear challenge to Warwick's 'manliness' but Warwick refused to leave the safety of the city. It was perhaps to goad Warwick further that Edward withdrew several miles to the town of Warwick and ensconced himself in the earl's own castle. At Warwick Edward was received as King, and proclamations were made to that effect from this point onwards. Remarkably, the *Arrivall* tells us that 'certain persons on the said Earl's behalf' now came to Edward to negotiate.[29] Even more remarkably, it is said that Edward 'granted the said Earl his life' on terms that seemed reasonable 'considering his [Warwick's] great and heinous offences'. But no deal could be agreed – if we can assume the representations on either side were genuine – so what happened next would depend on Clarence.

Using the commission of array that had been issued in the name of Henry VI, Clarence had raised 4,000 men,[30] but where did he intend to lead his army, and in whose interest? Clarence had been under pressure to reconcile with Edward for several months. He had received communications from a number of sources, including his mother Duchess Cecily, but 'most specially' his sister the Duchess of Burgundy. As we have seen, Clarence felt his position to be uncertain under the new regime, and by now he was inclined to return to the Yorkist fold. Nevertheless, Clarence did not want to back a hopeless cause. He kept his options open for as long as possible, but by the beginning of April his intelligence had convinced him that Edward's expedition had every chance of success.[31] On 3 April, Edward was informed that Clarence and his army were approaching from Banbury; Edward and his own forces marched towards him. When the armies were about half a mile apart Edward went forward accompanied only by Gloucester, Hastings and Rivers; Clarence went to meet him, also accompanied by only a few attendants. What followed was a spectacular piece of political theatre, which gave both Edward and

Clarence a chance to demonstrate their flair for drama.[32] As Edward approached, Clarence threw himself on his knees, but Edward hurried to raise up his brother and kissed him many times. Gloucester also embraced Clarence, and then 'the trumpets and minstrels blew up'. Clarence gave a speech to Edward's army 'in his best manner'; Edward spoke to Clarence's men and promised them his 'grace and good love'. And so Edward, Clarence and Gloucester 'made their peace [. . .] with banners displayed'. Thus reunited, the brothers of York made their way to Warwick.

At Coventry, the Earl of Warwick's position had now been strengthened by the arrival of Oxford, Exeter and Viscount Beaumont, although he must have been enraged by Clarence's *volte face*. Clarence was therefore a strange choice of emissary, but on the next day he appeared at the gates of Coventry. He offered himself, as a mediator, to negotiate a 'good accord'.[33] After all, if Edward was prepared to forgive his treacherous brother, then why not also Warwick? However, although Edward might have convinced himself that Clarence had been led astray, surely it would have been impossible to rebuild a mutual sense of trust with Warwick. This was the last chance of reconciliation. Following the failure of these talks Edward once again exhorted Warwick to meet him in the field. But the earl continued to refuse the challenge.

Edward could not remain in the field indefinitely. He lacked the artillery necessary to storm Coventry, and he must have feared that he would become trapped between superior forces. Moreover, Edward was short of supplies and Warwick must have been aware of this. Edward therefore decided that his success would depend, as it had in 1461, on control of the capital. On 5 April Edward's forces moved south. By Palm Sunday (7 April), Edward had reached Daventry. Here, it is said that God and St Anne showed Edward a 'fair miracle'.[34] Edward led a procession to the parish church, where he heard Mass. As it was Lent all the images in the church were covered, including a small statue of St Anne that was enclosed by wooden boards. Edward had prayed to St Anne in exile and now, as he knelt before the rood screen, there was a 'great crack'. The boards opened, revealing the image of St Anne for a time, before then closing again 'without any man's hand'. Although sceptical readers might discern the intervention of man during this episode,[35] once again we can see the power of the supernatural over the medieval mind. As at Mortimer's Cross, Edward immediately interpreted the 'miracle' as a sign of God's special favour, as did his men, and they left Daventry in good heart. Edward then moved on to Northampton, leaving a small force of archers and 'spears' to guard his rear, and continued his march towards London.

Warwick was not as passive as he appeared. Immediately alive to the danger posed by Edward's move towards London, he and his army set off in pursuit. He also wrote to his brother, Archbishop Neville, urging him to hold London until he could join him. George Neville, a cleric, intellectual and politician – but obviously no soldier – did his best. He summoned anybody who remained loyal to the House of Lancaster to join him at St Paul's, 'with as many men in harness of their servants and other as they could make'.[36] Between 600 and 700 men answered his appeal. This was surely fewer than he might have wished, but Neville was determined to stage a martial display. Henry's 'army' marched through the city, with the old king himself in their midst. Lord Sudeley, an elderly but distinguished veteran of the Hundred Years' War, bore Henry's sword. A horseman rode before him, flourishing the famous foxtail standard of Henry V. Yet Henry had always been a pale shadow of his illustrious father, and now he was a broken man. Neville held his hand all the way. Henry had also reverted to wearing an old blue gown that he had worn previously in the Tower; perhaps Henry would have preferred to return to the solitude and quiet of his cell. What Archbishop Neville had intended to act as a call to arms had the opposite effect. As the author of the *Great Chronicle* notes, the sight of King Henry had 'pleased the citizens as a fire painted on a wall warmed the old woman'.[37] With a true warrior king almost at their gates, the London citizens were now even more reluctant to do battle on Henry's behalf. Indeed, a number of prominent Lancastrians had already concluded that the city could not be held.[38] On hearing of the imminent arrival of the Lancastrians' true leader, Margaret of Anjou, the Duke of Somerset and the Earl of Devon had left London on 8 April. They made for the south coast, taking with them a commission that appointed Prince Edward Lieutenant of the Realm. Henry was abandoned to his fate.

The city council quickly came to the conclusion that 'as Edward late king of England was hastening towards the city with a powerful army, and as the inhabitants were not sufficiently versed in arms to withstand so large a force, no attempt should be made to resist him'.[39] On 11 April Edward and his army swept into London. The army was led by Burgundian troops: a force of 'black and smoky gunners', which one chronicler estimated at 500 strong.[40] Presumably they were armed with the latest version of the matchlock *arquebus*. After giving thanks at St Paul's, Edward's next priority was to secure the person of Henry VI, who he found at the bishop's palace. The historian Cora Scofield offers an evocative and convincing reconstruction of their meeting:

> to the rival, frail in body and in mind, whose crown he was about to take from him for the second time, Edward extended his hand with cold civility; but Henry, not content with such a greeting, half trustingly, half fearfully offered an embrace with the words: 'My cousin of York, you are very welcome. I know that in your hands my life will not be in danger.' Surprised, and perhaps touched, Edward assured Henry that he had nothing to fear . . .[41]

Henry was sent back to the Tower; he was joined by Archbishop Neville, who had already submitted to Edward in writing.

Understandably, Edward's thoughts now turned to his family, from whom he had been separated for nearly six months. From the bishop's palace Edward hurried to Westminster and, after paying his respects at the Abbey, he was able to enjoy a happy reunion with his wife and daughters. Here, too, Edward was able to meet his newborn son, also called Edward, for the first time. Edward and his family spent the night with his mother at Baynard's Castle. This was a pleasant interlude, but on the next morning Edward turned his focus back to war. Indeed, London quickly became ablaze with activity, as Yorkists emerged from sanctuary. Commynes, perhaps with some exaggeration, claims that more than 2,000 Yorkists had been in sanctuary during the Readeption, including 300–400 knights and esquires.[42] Other supporters came to London from elsewhere. On Good Friday, 12 April, Edward was joined by Sir John, now Lord Howard, and Lord Hastings' brother, Sir Ralph, who had taken sanctuary in Colchester, and also by Sir Humphrey Bourchier and his brother, Lord Berners' sons, who brought with them a large number of Kentishmen.

On the same day, Edward learned that Warwick was now approaching London; he had reached St Albans.[43] The *Arrivall* suggests that Warwick hoped to catch the Yorkists unawares, assuming they would be preoccupied with the celebration of Easter. However, Edward reacted immediately. The next day, following a hasty muster, the Yorkist army set out towards St Albans on the Great North Road. Edward arrived at Barnet as darkness was falling, having scattered some of Warwick's foreriders, and here he learned that Warwick was now camped about half a mile to the north. Von Wesel reports that Warwick had taken up a position 'just beside the highway to St Albans on a broad green plot'.[44] Edward was conscious of the disasters that had befallen the defenders at both battles of St Albans, and did not wish to fight within the town, but he was determined to force a battle on the following day. It was also easier to maintain discipline when the army was camped in the open, under the watchful eyes of their commanders.[45] Edward therefore advanced just outside Barnet, towards the Lancastrian position. But in the gathering gloom it became difficult to see clearly. This meant that '[Edward] took not his ground so even in the front afore them as he would have done if he might better have seen them [the Lancastrians], but somewhat asidehand'. Von Wesel tells us similarly that Warwick and Edward made camp on opposite sides of the road (with Warwick's army camped on the left of the road coming from Barnet and Edward to the right). This would have serious implications on the next day, but Edward had achieved his main objective: a battle was now certain to occur. Edward and Warwick had spent the last two years fighting through proxies, but now, at last, they would face each other on the field.

It was a strange course of events that had brought Edward and Warwick here, one that must have been unthinkable ten years earlier. There was little time for introspection, however, because, according to Von Wesel, 'Warwick set up his ordonnance of arquebuses and serpentines up the way towards Barnet and the arquebuses carried over all night long.' But the bombardment did Edward's army no harm, and Warwick's ammunition was expended in vain. Some of Warwick's guns may have been firing into thin air, although the *Arrivall* tells us that Warwick's guns 'overshot' Edward's forces, because they were 'nearer than they deemed'. Edward ordered silence throughout his army, so as not to give away its true position.[46]

With the two armies lying so close to each other, their dispositions would have been arranged during the night before battle. But none of the fullest and most contemporary sources – the *Arrivall*, *Warkworth's Chronicle* and Von Wesel's newsletter – provide any information about how the armies were organised. The *Great Chronicle* does give details about the various commands, but, as it is reported that the Duke of Somerset was in command of the Lancastrian centre – he cannot have been present – in this case its testimony is dubious.[47] We have more information about the numbers involved, although as usual the chroniclers do not agree. The *Arrivall* tells us that Edward was outnumbered, even after the boost he received from Clarence's defection. According to this source Edward had 9,000 men, whereas Warwick's forces 'numbered themselves' at 30,000. Other sources give the Yorkists more and the Lancastrians fewer.[48] What does seem clear is that both armies were large by the standards of the time.

On the whole, the armies at Barnet would have resembled those deployed in previous battles of the Wars of the Roses. However, an intriguing feature of the battle is the presence of the Burgundian handgunners in Edward's army. It has been plausibly suggested that the performance of the Burgundians may have encouraged Edward to make further investments in gunpowder technology.[49] Apparently Warwick had already used 'arquebuses', albeit to little effect, but how might Edward's handgunners have been deployed on the day of battle? Bert Hall explains why small arms were most effective in defence. The main problem, for a general on the offensive, was the handgun's slow rate of fire:

> soldiers armed with small arms are extremely vulnerable during their reloading cycle; they must be protected either by sufficient numbers of their own kind to maintain a continuous volley of fire or by troops with very different kinds of weapons.[50]

Even so, it may be interesting to consider the possibility that the handguns were employed in an offensive manner at Barnet, because the arquebus could be devastating at short range. Emerging out of the mist that was to fall, accompanied by the usual war cries, this would have been a terrifying way for Edward's troops to announce their presence close at hand.

Next morning, 14 April, was Easter Sunday, but Edward showed no reluctance to shed blood on this holiest of days.[51] He launched the attack at dawn, around 4am. Dawn attacks are often successful because the aggressor catches his enemies at their worst, hastily aroused from sleep.[52] But Warwick knew Edward's character and we must assume that he had considered the possibility of an early attack. Most likely Warwick and his men were ready and waiting; Warwick may not have slept at all. Indeed, Warwick's bombardment must have ensured that both armies were deprived of sleep, which can induce erratic behaviour and impair decision-making.[53] This was surely a significant factor during the battle, not least because both armies were hampered by mistrust within their ranks. How did the Duke of Exeter feel, for example? He had been Warwick's sworn enemy for over ten years. Even the behaviour of Warwick's own brother, Montagu, had recently been ambiguous, to say the least. The Yorkist force was more cohesive, but here too there may have been tensions. Could Clarence really be trusted? Another crucial factor was, once again, the weather:

> at daybreak, around four o' clock they [the two armies] became aware of each other, but a thick fog came down as it did, too,

in London so that neither side was able to see the other.
[Von Wesel, p. 68.]

As we have seen, the two armies were 'not front to front', but the fog made this obscure. This meant the Yorkist attackers outflanked the Lancastrians on their right, but their left wing was itself outflanked. Archers and artillery were, of course, employed by both sides – Von Wesel claims 10,000 arrows were expended – but with both sides firing blind the two armies quickly came 'to hands'. On the right, naturally the Yorkists had some success, but their left wing was shattered. Most of the survivors fled in panic.[54] Paradoxically, however, the fog now helped the Yorkist cause, because it shielded the remainder of Edward's army from certain knowledge of the disaster that had engulfed their left flank.[55] Yet fighting in the fog must have been a terrifying and confusing experience. We may imagine the Yorkist troops bunching together, peering at ghostly figures ahead of them, trying to determine whether they were friends or foes, straining to interpret horrifying sounds made by men they could not see.

Ignorance of their comrades' fate therefore cannot solely explain why the Yorkist line did not break; there was another reason why the Yorkists maintained their resolve. At the very heart of the Yorkist 'battle' their leader was fighting heroically, in the midst of his household:

> he manly, vigorously and valiantly assailed them [Warwick's army], in the midst and strongest of their battle, where he, with great violence, beat and bore down afore him all that stood in his way, and, then, turned to the range, first on that one hand, and then on that other hand, so that nothing might stand in the sight of him and the well assured fellowship that attended truly on him. [*Arrivall*, p. 20.]

There is no reason to doubt that Edward was heavily involved in the fighting; it is clear that most of the Yorkist leaders fought 'manly'. The fighting was fierce and there were many casualties. Lords Cromwell and Say were killed on the field, as was Sir Humphrey Bourchier, and Sir William Blount was later to die of his wounds. Richard of Gloucester, fighting in his first battle, acquitted himself well and was also 'severely wounded'.[56] But Gloucester quickly recovered: he was fit enough to fight at Tewkesbury three weeks later. As we shall see, Edward was to take note of his brother's now proven courage.

Let us assume that Oxford did lead the Lancastrian van, on the right wing, as the *Great Chronicle* tells us. If so, Oxford had broken the Yorkist left and pursued the survivors for some distance. He now rallied his men and returned to the battlefield, probably hoping to smash into the Yorkist rear. However, either because Oxford's men had found it difficult to navigate in the fog, or because the lines of battle had shifted, Oxford found himself confronting not Edward, but Warwick. Warkworth tells us that in the fog Warwick's men mistook Oxford's personal emblem of the 'star with streams' for Edward's emblem of the 'sun with streams'.[57] Warwick moved to the attack, causing Oxford and his men to flee the field, crying 'Treason! Treason!'[58] It is said that the Lancastrians had been on the verge of victory several times, during three or four hours of savage fighting, but these events gave the advantage, irrevocably, to the Yorkists. It may even be that barely concealed tensions within the 'Lancastrian' army now exploded, and they began to fight amongst themselves. Their leaders fell one by one. Montagu is said to have fought bravely – according to Wavrin he had been cutting off arms and heads like a hero of romance – but he was now overwhelmed and killed. Exeter, too, who also 'fought manly', was badly wounded and left for dead.[59] And then, finally, the shout went up that Warwick himself had been slain.

How Warwick died is not clear; the *Arrivall* tells us he was killed 'somewhat fleeing'. This is not the only time the author glosses over a controversial subject, although the implication of cowardice was seized on with relish by chroniclers in Burgundy, where Warwick was unpopular because of his close connections with King Louis of France.[60] But in truth it would be difficult to argue that Warwick was a coward; although he was a cautious commander he had demonstrated personal courage on numerous occasions. What is certain is that Warwick's death made Edward's victory complete. Warkworth tells us that Edward tried to save Warwick, although it is impossible to believe there could have been a further reconciliation. If Warwick had survived the battle he would surely have ended his life on the block. Yet, for many, perhaps including Edward, Warwick's death must have provoked ambivalent feelings. Warwick was an extraordinary man, whose passing would create a great void in English politics. The historian A.J. Pollard has noted that Warwick's emergence as a great man coincided with sightings of Halley's Comet; the comet heralded the arrival of another glittering star.[61] Perhaps contemporaries drew the same analogy. But this star had now fallen to earth.

Chapter 7

London, April 1471

So passed Richard Neville, Earl of Warwick, the so-called 'Kingmaker'. On the Continent, it was probably considered that the apprentice had bested the master. Edward's own thoughts were surely more complex. If Warwick had never truly been a mentor he had once been a valuable ally, and many of Edward's closest supporters would have been sorry to see Warwick die. Yet, in darker moments, Edward must have felt he had removed a parasite: Warwick had restricted Edward's freedom of movement for most of his adult life, and had finally revealed himself to be malign. But Edward spent little time in reflection now. After much-needed rest, Edward and his army returned to London, where they were 'welcomed and received with much joy and gladness'.[1] He went straight to St Paul's Cathedral, where he was received by Cardinal Bourchier and a thanksgiving Mass took place. The following day Edward commanded that the bodies of the two Neville brothers should be brought to St Paul's and exposed to the common gaze. The citizens of London would, of course, have been used to seeing the grisly remains of defeated noblemen, but Edward did not see the corpses as trophies; nor was the display intended to act as a deterrent. The bodies were treated with respect – they were not mutilated – and the display was presumably to confirm that Warwick and his brother were really dead. After two days the bodies were released to be buried at Bisham Abbey, where they were laid to rest alongside their father, the Earl of Salisbury.

Doubtless Edward's badge of the 'rose-en-soleil' was much in evidence on the streets of London at this time. And yet, in the West Country, storm clouds were gathering. On the very day of Edward's victory at Barnet, on Easter Sunday, Margaret of Anjou had landed at Weymouth, accompanied by her son Edward, his wife Anne, John Langstrother the Prior of St John, and Lord Wenlock. Her arrival had been imminently expected since January, when she and her party had reached Dieppe. However,

Margaret did not attempt a crossing until 24 March, embarking at Honfleur, although bad weather forced her to turn back. A successful crossing was not possible until 13 April. One can only speculate as to what might have happened differently had Margaret arrived in England earlier. Although bad weather obviously played a part, we have seen that Margaret was reluctant to risk the life of her son until the country was secured – even though Prince Edward himself might well have been eager to return to England as soon as possible.

The following day Margaret lodged at Cerne Abbey, and here she received the Duke of Somerset and the Earl of Devon.[2] Somerset and Devon may have brought the news of Warwick's catastrophic defeat, which must have hit Margaret hard; but Somerset and Devon argued that, paradoxically, 'for that loss, their party was never the feebler, but rather the stronger'. According to the *Arrivall* the nobles promised Margaret that 'they should assemble so great puissance of people in divers parts of England, truly assured unto their party, that it should not more lie in the King's power to resist them'. Naturally, the author of the *Arrivall* was not privy to these discussions, but it is plausible to assume that Somerset thought in these terms, even if Margaret did not. For men like Somerset, who were hoping to achieve their 'rightful' place – both in terms of land and office – as well as vengeance for dead relatives, Warwick's demise had simplified matters greatly. Indeed, a report from Bruges to the court of Milan (dated, ironically, 7 May), based on the testimony of a Spaniard who had left London on 24 April, related that

> there are many who consider the Queen's prospects favourable,
> *chiefly because of the death of the Earl of Warwick*, because it
> is reckoned she ought to have many lords in her favour, who
> intended to resist her because they were enemies of Warwick.[3]

Edmund Duke of Somerset is invariably characterised as a 'die-hard' Lancastrian, although we have seen that he preferred Burgundy to life at the Lancastrian court in exile. However, even if any tensions had existed between them earlier, Margaret was surely now grateful to have the service of this bellicose, experienced and determined man. From this point Somerset took a prominent role. He threw himself into recruiting men throughout the West Country, and appears to have been highly successful. Although Warwick's agents had already been busy in the area, the presence of Somerset, as well as Devon, seems to have concentrated the local gentry's minds. This was possibly because they 'reputed them old inheritors of the country'.[4] The Lancastrian army mustered at Exeter, where Margaret stayed for two weeks, and there she was joined by local notables such as Sir Hugh Courtenay of Bocconoc and Sir John Arundel of Lanherne. According to the *Arrivall* the Lancastrians 'raised the whole might of Devon and Cornwall'.[5] From Exeter the Lancastrians marched on the Glastonbury road to Taunton, and then on to Wells. By 30 April the Lancastrians had reached Bath. Margaret's army continued to attract new recruits, even though, at Wells, the Lancastrians' behaviour must have alarmed the local inhabitants: they sacked the Bishop's Palace and stormed the prison, releasing all the prisoners.[6]

Yet everything did not go the Lancastrians' way in the West. For instance, the powerful Sir Nicholas Latimer, who had previously fought with Henry Duke of Somerset, and was appointed Sheriff of Somerset and Dorset under the Readeption government, chose to follow the lead of his new lord, Clarence, and ignored his former Lancastrian ties. As ever, men everywhere faced hard choices. Shortly after the Battle of Barnet Sir John Paston – doubtless still nursing his wounds – wrote to his mother that:

> The world I assure you is right queasy, as you shall know within this month; the people here fear it sore. God has shown Himself marvellously like Him that made all and can undo again when Him list [*sic*] and I can think that by all likelihood shall show Himself as marvellous again, and that in short time.[7]

The Battle of Barnet was a great triumph for Edward, but everyone knew there would be further struggles to come: the ultimate outcome remained in God's hands. Paston was an optimist, even in adversity, although he may soon have received news to bolster his faith. As Margaret's army grew daily in the West, Jasper Tudor was gathering troops in Wales, and Edward received disturbing news of Lancastrian risings in the north. However, as Malcolm Mercer has shown in a recent article, the extent of gentry support for the Lancastrian cause must not be overstated, even in the West Country.[8] As usual many men, if they had not already committed themselves, lay low, waiting for the crisis to pass. But even if they did not flock to Edward's banner, it seems increasing numbers of Englishmen concluded that God would remain with the Yorkists. Edward's victory over Warwick had fully restored his reputation and many people must have castigated themselves for having underestimated their former King. The City of Salisbury pledged forty men to join Somerset, but ultimately sent the men to fight for Edward instead; as early as 16 April the city recorded that Edward was 'both *de facto* and *de jure* King of England'.[9] On the road to Exeter, at Chard, Prince Edward had despatched a message to the burghers of Coventry, the city that had been the virtual capital of Lancastrian England during the late 1450s and, more latterly, a powerbase for Warwick. Nevertheless, the city now decided to back the cause of York, and sent both the message and its messenger to King Edward at Abingdon. Such victories were small, but they must have buoyed Edward immensely.

In London, Edward had learned of Margaret's landing by 16 April, and he reacted to the new threat with the same sense of decision and vigour that was the hallmark of all his actions since his return to England. Barnet had been one of the most hard-fought of all the battles of the Wars of the Roses, and Yorkist casualties must have been heavy. Both armies had been fully engaged, and one of the Yorkist 'battles' had been routed. The *Arrivall* talks of Edward making provision for the sick and wounded – 'right many in number' – and implies the army had been largely disbanded.[10] Von Wesel paints a harrowing picture of the Yorkists' return to London:

> Those who had set out with good horses and sound bodies returned home with sorry nags and bandaged faces, some without noses.[11]

Messengers were therefore sent out throughout the kingdom calling for fresh troops.[12] Proclamations declared Margaret and her adherents to be traitors, and set out Edward's own claim to the throne. Above all Edward needed able-bodied men, but his army also needed new military equipment. Although time was short, Edward's preparations seem to have been thorough: 'purveyed he artillery, and ordnance, guns and other, for the field great plenty'.[13] John Warley was given responsibility for the equipment of Edward's army; such men are the unsung heroes of the Wars of the Roses. On April 17 he was given license

> to take wheelers, cartwrights and other carpenters, stone-cutters, plumbers and other workmen for the works of the King's ordnance, bombards, culverines, fowlers, serpentines and other cannons and powder, sulphur, saltpeter, stone, iron, lead, and other necessaries for them, crossbows and bolts, bows, arrows, bowstrings, *langdebeves*, lances, glaives and hammers and other necessaries and carriage for the same and horses called hackneys.[14]

The passage quoted is particularly interesting because it makes clear the extent of the support network needed to maintain artillery. Edward probably acquired some of his guns from Warwick's defeated army.

Edward sent out word that his army was to muster at Windsor, where he prepared to celebrate the Feast of St George and the annual Garter Ceremony. As we have seen, during Edward's reign the Order of the Garter took on renewed significance, and Edward maintained a great affection for Windsor.[15] Although membership of the Garter was sometimes granted for political reasons, it was also a symbol of personal closeness to Edward, and in this instance he would surely have used the Garter Ceremony as a means to create an 'esprit de corps' amongst his chief captains. The army that joined Edward at Windsor is generally estimated to have been around 5,000 strong. This was not an inconsiderable force by contemporary standards, although it was probably smaller than most armies that fought during the Wars of the Roses.[16] Before leaving Windsor, Edward needed to wait for the reports of his scouts, because he was unsure of the Lancastrians' immediate intentions. As the *Arrivall* puts it, the Lancastrians, in the West Country, were in 'an angle of the land'.[17] They had two choices. First, the Lancastrians could move towards London, either by way of the south coast, which would allow them to join with Warwick's partisans in Kent, or more directly by way of Salisbury. Second, they could move north, crossing the Severn in order to join with Jasper Tudor, who had now landed in South Wales. The second option would also allow them to recruit in Cheshire, traditionally the home of skilled archers and a former source of support for the Lancastrian cause.

Edward's dilemma shows, once again, that the notion both sides in the Wars of the Roses always adopted 'battle-seeking' strategies needs to be nuanced somewhat. It is worth briefly considering previous strategies, as they must have been in the opposing commanders' minds as they formulated their plans. In the winter campaign of 1460–1 the Lancastrians had, for the most part, pursued a quasi-Vegetian strategy. They avoided set-piece battles and preferred to make use of ruses (as at Wakefield) and surprise attacks (as at St Albans II). Only at Towton, after the Yorkists may have thwarted a surprise attack at Ferrybridge, did their leaders totally commit their forces to the hazards of the field. Yet Edward's greatest strength as a commander lay in his ability to fight and win offensive engagements on ground that was not of his own choosing. In the campaigns of 1461 and 1471 Edward aggressively sought open battle, regardless of terrain, weather or any other circumstances. The Lancastrians must have been aware that on this occasion Edward would be relentless in his pursuit of an engagement, and this would have been a powerful psychological weapon on Edward's behalf.

Although as tacticians the Lancastrian leaders were to show considerable flair, unlike Edward they lacked the boldness or confidence to march on London. As in 1461, the Lancastrian leaders made the fateful decision to eschew the advance on London and instead to move north. However, they made an attempt to sow confusion within the Yorkist ranks, sending out foreriders from Exeter to Salisbury via Shaftesbury, and from Wells to Brunton and Yeovil. The intention was surely to persuade Edward that the Lancastrians would move on London via Reading. The gambit failed, although whether this was due to the strength of Edward's intelligence system or astute calculation is unclear. Edward moved north-west, leaving Windsor on 24 April, making for Cirencester, where he arrived on Monday 29 April, via Abingdon. Here, Edward learned that the Lancastrians were approaching Bath and intending to offer battle. But the following day Edward's scouts brought no news of the Lancastrians so the Yorkists advanced a few miles to Malmesbury. Here Edward received frustrating news. Although the Lancastrians had indeed been at Bath on 30 April, they had now moved: not north-east towards Malmesbury but west. On Wednesday 1 May the Lancastrians were welcomed into the City of Bristol.

Evidently Edward had been deliberately misinformed of the Lancastrians' intentions, although the extent to which the Lancastrian manoeuvres constituted a grand strategy is not certain. Certainly Bristol offered considerable advantages. Here the Lancastrians gained 'money, men and artillery'.[18] Bristol was noted as a centre for the manufacture of artillery, and at least one prominent citizen joined the Lancastrian army in person; Nicholas Hervey, the city's recorder, was later to be killed in action. However, assuming the Lancastrians were still reluctant to meet Edward in battle, the diversion to Bristol made their position precarious, because the Yorkists were now in a position to cut them off from the Severn crossings. Even so, if the Lancastrians had placed themselves in a trap, they now extricated themselves with considerable skill. Once again they employed deception. As before, they offered battle, on 2 May, this time naming a specific place. This was 'Sodbury Hill', probably to the east of modern Chipping Sodbury. However, although the Lancastrians did indeed leave Bristol on 2 May, marching towards the Yorkists, they quickly turned north, now aiming to cross the Severn at Gloucester. It is difficult to understand why Edward should have been taken in by the same ruse as before, although the Lancastrian 'cover story' was given credence when their foreriders 'distressed' their Yorkist counterparts in Sodbury itself. Edward's army arrived at 'Sodbury Hill' by noon. Edward himself initially took position on the 'hill' itself, presumably at the site of the Iron Age fort, which offers superb views of the surrounding countryside. In the absence of other certain news, Edward waited here for the rest of the day, although doubtless scouring the horizon with increasing trepidation.

At 3am the following morning Edward received the news he must have dreaded. Now that he realised the Lancastrians' intention was to cross the river at Gloucester, he sent messengers to Richard Beauchamp, the governor of the town and castle, warning him of the Lancastrians' approach and commanding him to hold the town until Edward's army could relieve him (during the Middle Ages, in order to cross the Severn bridge from the English side, one had to pass through the City of Gloucester itself, which was strongly fortified). Edward's messengers must have arrived just in time. The Lancastrians, who had rested briefly at Berkeley, were aware of the need to maintain their advantage, and had decided on a night march to Gloucester. They reached the city at around 10 o' clock in the morning but found the gates barred against them. Beauchamp's garrison must have been small, and the Lancastrians made a show of besieging the town. Nevertheless, Beauchamp was resolute and the Lancastrians were forced to the next crossing, at Tewkesbury. Here they hoped to ford the Severn at the Lower Lode. But as the Lancastrians wearily resumed their march Beauchamp may have done Edward further service: Hall recounts a story that Beauchamp sallied out, attacked the Lancastrian rear, and captured some of their guns. Edward himself was now on the road to Tewkesbury, following the less onerous and more direct route across the Cotswolds, in furious pursuit of the Lancastrians.

The Lancastrians reached Tewkesbury at about four o' clock. They were, understandably, 'right weary for travelling, for by that time they had travelled 36 long miles [day and night], in a foul country, all in lanes and stony ways, betwixt woods, without any good refreshing'.[19] In the previous three days the Lancastrians had in fact covered nearly 60 miles, a remarkable achievement, and their leaders had displayed determination and cunning. But Edward and his army had matched them all the way: on 3 May the Yorkists covered an astonishing 35 miles, a great distance for a medieval army.[20] The foot soldiers must have been pushed extremely hard.[21] Ultimately, however, the army could only move as fast as its supply train – as well as the carts carrying the precious Yorkist artillery. The animals that pulled the Yorkist carts and wagons must have been driven even harder than the men. Nevertheless, the main challenge facing the Yorkists must have been lack of water. The Yorkists' route – across the 'champain' [champagne] country' of the Cotswolds – would have been much easier than the one followed by the Lancastrians, although the weather was hot, and here too there was a lack of good 'refreshing':

> [Edward's] people could not find horse meat, nor man's meat, nor so much as drink for their horses, save in one little brook, where was full little relief it was so soon troubled with the carriages that had passed [through] it.[22]

Disappointingly, the *Arrivall* tells us nothing about Edward's own conduct during the march, although his personal role must have been considerable. As General A.P. Wavell explains,

> in sustained pursuit, mobility is dependent mainly on the personal will and determination of the commander-in-chief, which alone can keep alive the impetus of the troops.[23]

Other evidence suggests Edward possessed the kind of charisma that can persuade, as well as command, and he would surely have given his troops his own version of a 'little touch of Harry in the night'. According to Mancini, 'if [Edward] saw a newcomer bewildered at his appearance and royal magnificence [...] he would give him courage to speak by laying a kindly hand on his shoulder'.[24] We have seen that Edward was happy to walk among the crowds of common people in Burgundy. On the road to Tewkesbury Edward asked much of his troops, but they responded to his call.

At Tewkesbury, the Lancastrians now had to accept they had lost the race. To their horror, they discovered the ford at the Lower Lode was not passable. Even if they had been able to continue – the author of the *Arrivall* believed the footmen could go no further – they would now have faced another series of challenges. The next crossing of the Severn was at Upton upon Severn, although to reach Upton would have first meant crossing the Avon north of Tewkesbury, using a complicated system of bridges. The way to the bridges was through the cramped streets of Tewkesbury, and the bridges themselves were narrow and in a poor state of repair. To navigate this series of obstacles would have been a logistical nightmare, and the Lancastrian leaders were acutely aware that Edward and his army were now only a few miles away. They were rightly concerned that, if they had continued, Edward would have 'fallen upon them [...]

to their most disadvantage'.[25] Brought to bay at last, the Lancastrians resolved to fight.

The Lancastrians had failed in their objective to cross the Severn, and were forced to give battle against their will. There could be no hope of reinforcements – by the time they heard news of the battle, Jasper Tudor and his Welshmen had only reached Chepstow.[26] But the Lancastrians still had one considerable advantage – they had the choice of ground. Although Queen Margaret may have rested for the evening at Gupshill Manor, or perhaps in Tewkesbury Abbey's lodging house, the rest of the army seems to have camped for the night in an enclosed field, or 'close', called the Gaston, to the south of the Abbey.[27] Here, too, the Lancastrians decided they would make their stand. The Lancastrians took up a strong defensive position, 'a marvellous strong ground':

> In front of their field were so evil lanes, and deep dykes, so many trees and bushes, that it was right hard to approach them near.[28]

It is not clear whether the Lancastrians had fortified their 'field' in the manner of Ludford Bridge or Northampton, although the existing natural defences might have seemed formidable enough. The River Swilgate would have provided additional protection to the rear and their left flank. The Lancastrians' right flank was bounded by the Southwick Brook; beyond this stream was a heavily wooded area, which was then a deer park.

Any fortifications would have taken time to prepare, and the Lancastrian commanders must have been worried about the possibility of a surprise attack. Doubtless the Lancastrians passed yet another restless night. The Yorkists' evening is likely to have been more relaxing, insofar as the night before a battle could ever be. Edward had reached Cheltenham when he heard of the Lancastrians' arrival at Tewkesbury, and their decision to offer battle. Edward halted the march, and 'somewhat comforted himself, and his people'. He allowed his army to rest, and to eat and drink, finally using up the supplies that had been so carefully husbanded. After eating and drinking their fill, the Yorkists pushed on towards Tewkesbury. The Yorkist army camped for the night within 3 miles of the Lancastrian position, probably at Tredington. Although he might have slept little, Edward surely rested content, secure in the knowledge that his enemies could no longer escape him. As Goodchild perceptively notes, 'though they had not chosen the place, [the Yorkists] had full control of the time'.[29]

On the morning of the battle the Yorkists made the usual preparations, including the familiar rituals before battle was joined:

> Edward [...] displayed his banners, did blow up the trumpets, committed his cause and quarrel to almighty God, to our most blessed lady his mother, the Virgin Mary, the glorious martyr Saint George, and all the saints; and advanced, directly upon his enemies.[30]

Presumably the Yorkist battle plan was formulated in advance at Tredington, using the reports of scouts. However, as his soldiers slowly made their way onto the field, Edward must have taken advantage of an elevated position to survey the battlefield for himself. Following the *Arrivall*'s account, it seems Edward drew upon his experience of previous battles in order to adjust his plans. As we have seen, the Lancastrians had previously employed deception in their tactics. Edward, when making his own final dispositions, was determined that the Yorkists would not, on this occasion, be taken unawares. He noticed the wooded area covered by the deer park, to the west of his position, and was concerned that it could conceal enemy units – presumably cavalry – which would be in a position to attack the flanks and rear of his army once battle was joined. He therefore despatched a 'plomp' of 200 mounted 'spears' to investigate the area,

> giving them charge to have a good eye on that corner of the wood, if case that any need were, and to put themselves in 'devoure' [service], and, if they saw none such, as they thought most behovefull for time and space, to employ themselves in the best wise as they could.[31]

It is unfortunate that we do not know the name of the man who commanded the 'plomp' because he was later to do Edward great service.

We know little else for certain about the rest of Edward's dispositions. The *Arrivall* tells us that Edward deployed the rest of his army in the traditional three 'battles'. Richard Duke of Gloucester led the vanguard (perhaps as an acknowledgement of his prowess at Barnet), Edward himself commanded the centre, and the rearguard was entrusted to William Lord Hastings. But historians have struggled to make sense of the two armies' deployment. The *Arrivall* has Edward's 'vaward', under Gloucester, starting the battle, with Somerset's division (which formed the Lancastrians' vanguard) taking the brunt of the Yorkist assault. When medieval armies deployed with their 'battles' abreast, the vanguard was usually deployed on the right, which means that Gloucester should have faced Devon, not Somerset. It has been suggested that Edward, taking note of Hastings' failure at Barnet, and Gloucester's relative success, revised his formation accordingly, so that Hastings would face Devon, whereas Gloucester would have to deal with the more warlike and experienced Somerset.[32] But the simplest solution, as James Bennett suggested many years ago,[33] is that the three 'battles' went into action in column, which would make sense if the Lancastrians had taken up a fortified position with a fairly narrow front.

As we have seen, late-medieval tactics were much more flexible than historians of the period often suppose. Many of the Yorkist archers seem to have been concentrated in Gloucester's 'vaward', although they would have surely been supported by men with staff weapons and a select group of men-at-arms under the personal command of the duke himself. Much of Edward's strength would have lain in his main 'battle'. As ever, Edward himself, with many of his nobles and their retinues, would have taken position in the centre, with the levies deployed on the flanks. In this instance, Hastings' rearguard might have consisted of a reserve of light cavalry, from which were drawn the 200 spears of the 'plomp'. Battle dispositions in the Middle Ages can only ever be speculative, although this formation shares common elements with the battle plans described above.[34] The Lancastrians may also have deployed in column, with their most reliable troops in the van. But from what we know of the course of the battle, it seems likely that the Lancastrian army was arranged in a more 'traditional' defensive formation. This could have entailed three 'battles' of footmen abreast, with such archers as the Lancastrians had initially deployed to the front, and perhaps also to the flanks.

What of Edward's ordnance, of which we are told he now had 'great plenty'? In the fog at Barnet presumably any field pieces were of little use, but at Tewkesbury guns were to play a greater role. The artillery would probably have been deployed on the flanks. If there is any truth in Hall's account of the Yorkists capturing some of the Lancastrians' guns at Gloucester, then to see their own artillery ranged against them cannot have helped the Lancastrians' morale. There may also have been scope at Tewkesbury for Edward's 'black and smoky sort of gunners' to do him good service once again. In this instance the handgunners may have been effectively employed by Edward as skirmishers.[35] Assuming Edward did obtain crossbows, crossbowmen may also have been used in this role. The crossbowmen and handgunners – who would also have been protected by pavises – would have used the natural cover available in order to get close enough to harass the Lancastrian line, although they would surely have been ready to fall back quickly if necessary.

The Lancastrians were outgunned. The Yorkists also held the advantage in terms of archers, and their missile assault must have been fearsome:

> the King's ordnance was so conveniently laid afore them, and his vanward sore oppressed them, with shot of arrows, that they gave them right-a-sharp shower. Also they did again-ward to them, both with shot of arrows and guns, whereof they had not so great plenty as had the King.[36]

The Yorkist attack must have taken a terrible toll, and in an 'archery duel' – with the Yorkists well supported by gunpowder weapons – there could be only one winner. But the Duke of Somerset now made a daring move that could have changed the outcome of the battle:

> Edmund, called Duke of Somerset, having that day the vaward, whither it were for that he and his fellowship were sore annoyed in the place were they were, as well with gunshot, as with shot of arrows, which they neither would nor durst abide, or else, of great heart and courage, knightly and manly advanced himself, with his fellowship, somewhat aside-hand the King's vaward, and by certain paths and ways therefore afore purveyed, and to the King's party unknown, he departed out of the field, passed a lane, and came into a fair place, or close, even afore the King where he was embattled, and, from the hill that was in one of the closes, he set right fiercely on the end of the King's battle.[37]

This passage has caused the most debate among historians of the battle. The 'lane' is likely to have been Lincoln Green Lane, which was then a road leading to Deerhurst and, eventually, to Gloucester. At least some of the Lancastrian soldiers are likely to have followed this road on their way to Tewkesbury, which would explain how it had been 'purveyed' in advance. The road followed the bottom of the valley, which was uncultivated, and it is therefore likely to have been obscured by trees and bushes. The 'hill' is likely to have been the hillock in Southwick Park, only a few hundred yards down Lincoln Green Lane. So the road Somerset took seems fairly clear, although his *intentions* are less certain.

Was Somerset a hothead, like the French nobles at Agincourt, or was the Yorkist bombardment simply too much to be borne? Or was this manoeuvre pre-arranged? Ingenious arguments have been produced to explain how Edward could have been taken by surprise. There is the suggestion, for example, that Somerset left a screen of men to mask his advance.[38] Yet, as Chris Gravett notes, there is no real indication Edward was *completely* taken by surprise.[39] The *Arrivall* says that the path was unknown to the Yorkists, although this does not suggest, of course, that Somerset's advance was entirely hidden until he arrived in the close 'afore the King'. Goodchild tentatively suggests Somerset's 'fellowship' may have been a small group of mounted men, which would have allowed them to move at speed, and this is plausible from a tactical point of view.[40] However, the *Arrivall*'s account of the ensuing struggle does seem to imply that Somerset attacked in force, and so presumably dismounted. Moreover, the trees and bushes that may have obscured the road would have provided Somerset with much-needed cover from Gloucester's archers, but a group on foot, including heavily armoured men-at-arms, presumably several hundred strong, could scarcely have moved in silence, completely out of sight. Ultimately, it is most likely that Gloucester's vanguard had succeeded in its primary objective, which was to draw the Lancastrians out of their fortified position, and that Somerset's manoeuvre was indeed a spontaneous reaction to the Yorkist assault. Whereas the *Arrivall*'s account is ambivalent, the chronicler Warkworth is unequivocal: Somerset 'went out of the field, by the which the field was broken'.[41]

Watching events unfold in front of him, Richard of Gloucester must nonetheless have been deeply concerned. As Somerset's 'fellowship' moved, the Yorkist 'skirmishers' – the crossbows and Burgundian hand-gunners – probably made a hurried withdrawal, expecting to be the target of the Lancastrian attack. To the left, Yorkist archers are also likely to have fallen back, reluctant at this early stage to 'come to hands' with the Lancastrians' elite troops. Ideally, Gloucester must have hoped the Lancastrians would make a direct frontal assault. The Lancastrians would have walked into the 'arrow storm', assuming his archers still had arrows in reserve,[42] and Gloucester would have been confident that his men-at-arms could hold off any survivors, at least long enough to be reinforced by Edward's main 'battle'. But Somerset's oblique line of advance meant Gloucester now faced a dilemma. With the Lancastrian vanguard now 'aside hand', and the other Lancastrian 'battles' now facing him, although still yet to move, Gloucester faced the possibility of being caught in a pincer movement. It must have been tempting to retreat, yet to fall back could have led to panic. Presumably Gloucester tried to rally his men and grimly held his ground.

Reaching the crest of the hillock, Somerset prepared to attack. Somerset, with his own banner of the portcullis floating above him, would have been able to see Edward's banner, now only a few hundred yards away. He would have pointed out the Yorkist leader to his men, telling them the end of the war was within their grasp. With a great shout, the Lancastrians charged down the slope. This was the crucial point of the battle. Whatever the origin of Somerset's decision to attack, he had now adopted the 'decapitation strategy' that had served numerous armies well during the Wars of the Roses. His engagement with the Yorkists' centre 'battle' was surely no accident. If Edward was killed, or if his division routed, the whole army is likely to have disintegrated. Edward, not for the first time, rose to the challenge magnificently:

> The King, full manly, set forth even upon them, entered and won the dyke, and hedge, upon them, into the close, and, with great violence, put them up towards the hill, and, so also, the King's vaward, being in the rule of the Duke of Gloucester.[43]

Like all generals in the 'heroic' mould, from Alexander the Great onwards, once Edward was in the line fighting with his men he could only be aware of what was directly in front of him and could only react to that. As we have seen, the conduct of a leader in combat is crucial. But in a very interesting passage, the fifteenth-century writer Du Bueil suggests a leader needed the same qualities in the heat of battle as when formulating his strategy:

> often things happen so suddenly that there is no time to think of anything. But a good man of war should always be thinking about what he may be faced with; and, when the moment comes, he should act with ardour. But this ardour comes from coolness; for everything should be thought through in cold blood before-hand, how to act when the situation comes up, so that it will be a deliberate, calculated plan.[44]

A split second of uncertainty could have been fatal. But Edward, as ever, did not hesitate.

Fighting generals also need to choose worthy captains, capable of exercising independent command and in this, too, Edward was successful. If Gloucester had been initially perplexed by Somerset's manoeuvre, his speed and decision now vindicated Edward's trust in him. The morale of the Yorkist army must have been buoyed greatly by seeing their leaders fighting in their midst. Their initial attack repulsed, it appears the Lancastrians fell back upon the natural defences of the dykes and hedges – and here the fighting must have been bitterly contested. But the

Lancastrians must have been heavily outnumbered, and ultimately their line could not hold in the face of the Yorkists' ferocious assault. The Tudor writer Vergil relates, at a critical point in the battle, that Somerset drew his men back to their standards, so that 'being close together, they might more easily resist'.[45] Vergil's account of the later Battle of Bosworth is excellent, almost certainly based on the recollections of veteran soldiers, and here, too, his account provides plausible detail. It would make sense if Somerset drew his men back from the grim struggle around the dykes, with the Yorkists now breaking through, attempting to rally them on higher ground. But it was at this moment that the commander of the Yorkist 'plomp' saw his chance to act. Emerging from the trees, the Yorkist light cavalry smashed into the Lancastrians' flank. Now assailed on all sides, the Lancastrian 'fellowship' disintegrated. There was no chance of a fighting retreat, and the Lancastrians ran for their lives, hotly pursued by Yorkist horsemen.

Somerset himself escaped, eventually seeking shelter in the Abbey, but Hall claims he first returned to the Lancastrian lines. When he encountered Lord Wenlock, still 'stood looking on',[46] Somerset is said to have called him a traitor – presumably for failing to support the attack – then struck him dead with one blow of an axe to the head. What should we make of this extraordinary story? Certainly, Wenlock was killed in the battle, but, as we have seen, the sources of many of Hall's anecdotes are unclear. In the absence of more contemporary supporting evidence, Hall's account must once again be used with great caution. Nevertheless, Hall's use of anecdote was carefully selective, and here he draws attention to a crucial point. *Should* Wenlock have supported Somerset? Although he was a veteran soldier, Wenlock was by inclination a politician, and he had now changed sides several times. It would be understandable, in a civil war, for his inactivity to be interpreted as treachery; similar accusations were to be levelled at the Earl of Northumberland after the Battle of Bosworth. But there are numerous parallels for this scenario where a commander's loyalty was not in question. For example, at Formigny in 1450, a division of English archers sallied out in an attempt to silence the French artillery.[47] Although the attack was initially successful, it was not supported by the English commander, Sir Thomas Kyriel. The French were able to bring up reinforcements and the English were ultimately overwhelmed. Wenlock must almost certainly be absolved of treachery, although the Lancastrians' failure to advance in support of Somerset must remain a puzzle. There is too much we cannot ever know about the

Lancastrian leaders on the day of the battle – particularly with regard to their state of mind – and about the men they commanded.

Back in the 'close', perhaps seeing Somerset himself take to flight, Edward and Gloucester realised the Lancastrian vanguard was finished as a viable fighting force. They successfully restrained their men from pursuit, which was probably now left to the Yorkist cavalry. Edward now launched a general assault on the remaining Lancastrians, who – for reasons that are now obscure – had continued to trust in their defensive position. There may have been a direct frontal attack, although some of the Yorkists probably followed the paths and lanes recently used by Somerset. This would have allowed Yorkist men-at-arms – perhaps including Edward himself – to smash into the Lancastrian flank, rolling up their line. Possibly a group of Lancastrian nobles and their retinues made a desperate last stand – the Earl of Devon was killed on the field, among others – although Yorkist casualties were light, which suggests the Lancastrians quickly broke and fled. But with the rivers Avon, Severn and Swilgate barring their way to safety, the Lancastrian 'field' had become a deathtrap and the Yorkists gave no quarter. Many must have died on or near the narrow bridge near the Abbey; others seem to have drowned in a mill race. Still others must have tried to reach the ford at the Lower Lode, but many of these – perhaps including the survivors of Somerset's vanguard – were caught and killed in a narrow field that is still known today as 'Bloody Meadow'. Lord Hastings' role in the battle is obscure, although he may now have organised the pursuit; Yorkist horsemen seem to have chased Lancastrian fugitives for several miles. At Didbrook, near Winchcombe (about 10 miles from Tewkesbury), some Lancastrian survivors appear to have been killed in the church.[48]

Somewhere amidst the carnage of the rout, the Lancastrians' greatest fear was realised: Prince Edward of Lancaster was killed. Later writers produced imaginative reconstructions of the Prince's death. Vergil, for example, has Prince Edward taken captive and then brought to face the Yorkist leaders.[49] After a sharp exchange, where the Prince displays his 'bold mind', Edward IV thrusts him into the arms of his commanders, and the latter waste no time killing young Edward in cold blood. But according to the *Arrivall* Prince Edward was 'taken fleeing toward the town wards and slain in the field'.[50] Warkworth – who lacked any motive to be circumspect about controversial details – concurs, but adds the imaginative detail that the desperate prince called out to the Duke of Clarence for mercy.[51] Nevertheless, although Clarence was, of course, still the Prince's brother-in-law, he was as stone. Once Prince Edward fell into the hands of the Yorkists his fate was sealed, although the manner of his death remains uncertain.

Edward himself pursued the Lancastrians as far as the Abbey, where many of the fugitives – including Somerset and Langstrother – had fled. According to Warkworth, Edward entered the Abbey with a drawn sword; the *Chronicle of Tewkesbury Abbey* goes further.[52] According to this source the Yorkists entered the Abbey in arms, plundered it, and even killed some of the Lancastrian fugitives on consecrated ground. Warkworth claims Edward was only restrained from more bloodshed when a priest – perhaps Abbot Strensham himself? – bravely confronted the King with the sacrament in his hands. There is a rather formulaic element to this story – a pious man of God calms a warrior who is still in the heat of battle – but there does appear to have been some sort of standoff between Edward and the Abbot. According to the *Arrivall*, Edward refused to accept the Abbey could grant sanctuary to traitors but agreed to grant a general pardon to the rebels. Nevertheless, the Lancastrian leaders were taken into custody. Warkworth alleges the leaders were included in the pardon but Edward then broke his word. This is a grave charge and the *Arrivall* rather evades the issue. In this text the prisoners captured in the Abbey were grouped together with others taken 'in other places of the town'. By doing this the author appears to have deliberately shifted the emphasis away from the disturbing events that occurred on consecrated ground.[53] It seems inconceivable, however, that Edward would have granted Somerset a pardon. Perhaps he had offered a selective pardon, which excluded Somerset and several others, although this was initially misunderstood. But for now Edward considered there should be no more bloodshed, and it was time to mark his victory. Forty men who had distinguished themselves were knighted on the field of battle; this was followed by a thanksgiving Mass in the Abbey.

Two days later, Somerset, Langstrother, Hugh Courtenay and several others were tried according to the Law of Arms, with Gloucester acting as judge in his capacity as Constable; alongside him was the Duke of Norfolk, as Marshal. Predictably found guilty, the captives were publicly beheaded in Tewkesbury's market square. Yet Edward's summary justice was tempered by discretion. He consciously eschewed the savagery that had followed earlier battles of the Wars of the Roses, or the barbarities of his former constable, Worcester. There was no further mutilation or 'setting up', and his enemies' bodies were treated with respect. Langstrother's body, for example, was encased in lead and taken to London for burial; other Lancastrian nobles, including Prince Edward, were buried in the

Abbey. It should also be noted that nearly all those executed had, at some stage, accepted Edward's rule. Several who had consistently followed the cause of Lancaster were pardoned. These included non-combatants such as Sir John Fortescue, but also soldiers such as Sir Henry Roos.

Edward left Tewkesbury – the site of yet another brilliant victory – on 7 May. Although he had been informed of risings in Kent as early as 3 May, his army marched north, towards Coventry via Worcester. Edward was most concerned about the Northern risings – given the events of the previous year, this was surely understandable. Moreover, Margaret of Anjou – who of course had not been on the battlefield in person – was still at large. Although much of her power had always been predicated on her status as the mother of the Prince of Wales, if she was allowed to escape to Wales or to the north, she could still conceivably act as a rallying point for the Lancastrian cause. However, on the road to Coventry, and shortly after his arrival in the city, Edward received two good pieces of news. First, he learned Margaret of Anjou had been captured, hiding in a 'poor religious house', and was now 'at his commandment', along with Anne Neville and several other members of her entourage.[54] Margaret was now almost certainly a broken woman – her long and tenacious struggle on behalf of Lancaster was finally at an end – although Edward would surely have wanted to see this with his own eyes. Second, on 13 May Edward received the Earl of Northumberland, who informed him that, as a result of the Yorkist victory at Tewkesbury, the Northern rising had collapsed. Some of the leaders were now in Northumberland's custody and the City of York, a centre of unrest, had put itself at the mercy of the King.

However, the news from the south was disturbing. Thomas Neville, the Bastard of Fauconberg – who had previously been involved in piracy and now commanded a large fleet – had raised the men of Kent, Essex and Surrey, and was threatening to invest the City of London by land and sea. Clearly, his main aim was to rescue Henry VI from his captivity in the Tower. Ominously, Fauconberg's army was much more than a rabble; at its core were members of the Calais garrison, England's most professional soldiers. They were well supplied with firearms from the garrison's arsenal.[55] Nevertheless, Edward seems to have been confident that the defences of London would hold. Certainly he would have expected the presence of several noblemen in the city, including Earl Rivers and the Earl of Essex, to stiffen the city's resolve. Although Edward must have known of the threat posed by Fauconberg several days earlier, he did not set out for London in person until 16 May (however, a strong advance guard of 1,500 men was sent on 14 May). His calculations proved correct.

On the road, Edward would have been informed that Fauconberg had assaulted the city in force on the 14th, but that the city had been success-fully defended. He would have learned that Rivers, in particular, had distinguished himself, and that the citizens were also fighting stoutly on his behalf. After this reverse Fauconberg seems to have lost the stomach for further confrontation: his fleet sailed the same night, doubtless pre-paring his retreat. Although his army remained at Blackheath for three more days, it made no further attacks. On 18 May, with Edward's arrival now imminent, Fauconberg left, accompanied only by his soldiers from Calais (the remaining troops were obliged to fend for themselves). Perhaps Fauconberg had already negotiated a pardon, because, while his companions took ship for Calais from Sandwich, he decided to remain. As Edward approached London on 20 May, he must have felt the war was almost at an end.

On 21 May, Edward entered London like a Roman Emperor. His army marched into the city with banners displayed and trumpets blaring. Gloucester, undisputedly one of the heroes of the campaign, was given the honour of leading the procession. In the rear was a carriage in which sat the humbled Margaret of Anjou – a powerful symbol of Edward's victory.[56] The same night, Henry VI died in the Tower. Although the author of the *Arrivall* would have us believe Henry passed away due to 'pure displeasure and melancholy',[57] there can be no doubt that Henry met his death on Edward's orders. As one foreign observer put it: 'King Edward has chosen not to have the custody of King Henry any longer [...] He has in short chosen to crush the seed.'[58] Oliver Cromwell described the execution of Charles I as a 'cruel necessity'; Edward surely thought of Henry's death in similar terms. Edward's position was now secure, yet still he did not rest. Gloucester was sent to receive the surrender of Fauconberg (who was later executed for new, unspecified treasons), whereas Edward himself led his army into Kent. It was, in effect, a punitive expedition; as Warkworth put it, he returned to London 'with much good[s] and little love'.[59] Edward took the liberties of the Cinque Ports into his own hands, exacted large fines, and there were numerous executions.[60] Certainly, Edward's treatment of the Kentish rebels was uncharacteristically harsh, although his commissioners in Essex and Surrey, the Earl of Essex and Sir William Bourchier, appear to have been even more severe.

The last embers of the Lancastrian resistance flickered in South Wales. Incredibly, Jasper Tudor – elusive and resourceful as ever – continued to trouble the local Yorkist commanders until September, when he finally surrendered Pembroke Castle. Tudor fled to exile in Brittany, where he was to remain for the rest of Edward's reign. He was accompanied by his nephew, Henry Earl of Richmond, the son of Margaret Beaufort, a hitherto obscure young nobleman who was now the last surviving hope of the Lancastrian cause. In the autumn of 1471, Henry Tudor's chances of success must have seemed very slim indeed. Edward was now the undisputed master of England. His right to rule would never be seriously challenged again. Although he could not have known it, Edward, still not thirty years old, had fought his last battle.

Chapter 8

Epilogue

King Edward IV ruled for almost twelve more years, for the most part in peace and prosperity. Christine Carpenter has concluded, in her recent survey of Edward's 'second' reign, that he was 'one of the greatest of medieval kings'.[1] Mancini, who was writing shortly after Edward's death, suggested that he perfected the crucial balance between 'dread' and 'love':

> Edward was of a gentle nature and cheerful aspect: nevertheless should he assume an angry countenance he should appear very terrible to beholders.[2]

For Carpenter, this sense of balance was an essential aspect of Edward's management of the nobility and gentry, in which he excelled.[3] Edward was willing to be flexible, to act impartially, and he continued to delegate to able lieutenants. His brother, Richard of Gloucester, following his sterling service in 1471, became the greatest man after the King.[4] Gloucester married Warwick's daughter, Anne, in the teeth of resistance from Clarence, which allowed him to succeed to Warwick's power and influence in the north. Richard also led an English invasion of Scotland in 1482 which resulted in the recapture of Berwick.[5] Edward's relationship with George of Clarence was very different though, and ultimately showed Edward at his most ruthless. In 1478 Clarence's loyalty was again called into question. Edward ordered his brother's execution. Was this another cruel necessity?[6] The second Crowland Continuator believed that Edward afterwards 'repented of the deed', although he also notes that 'thereafter [...] he appeared to be feared by all his subjects while he himself stood in fear of no one'.[7] Perhaps something of this fear lingered even after Edward's death, although some chroniclers did express reservations about Edward's character. Mancini, for example, was scandalised by Edward's decadent lifestyle, notwithstanding his acknowledgement of

Edward's strengths. He also notes Edward's growing reputation for avarice, although he adds a subtle nuance:

> Though not rapacious for other men's goods, he was yet so eager for money that in pursuing it he acquired a reputation for avarice.[8]

Most of Mancini's comments are echoed by the second Crowland Continuator, including the criticisms of Edward's personal morality, although the latter's overall assessment of Edward is positive.

Of course, Edward's reign will always be overshadowed by the events that followed his sudden death in April 1483. It is unclear why Edward died. Mancini believed his fatal illness originated in a chill that Edward caught on the river, although other possibilities, including poison, have been put forward.[9] Edward IV's heir was his son, Prince Edward, still only twelve years old but a youth of great promise.[10] He was briefly acknowledged as King Edward V. However, the young King was quickly deposed, on the grounds that Edward IV's marriage to Elizabeth Woodville was invalid, and Richard of Gloucester took the throne in his stead. Edward V and his younger brother, Richard Duke of York, were last seen shooting in the grounds of the Tower: their subsequent fate is unknown. On 22 August 1485, on the field of Bosworth, barely two years after Edward IV's death, the Yorkist dynasty came to an end. Some historians have held Edward to be personally responsible for all these events, through a lack of foresight, although he can scarcely have expected to die aged barely forty.[11] It is my own view that Richard of Gloucester was a brave, charismatic and intelligent man, but his actions in 1483 defy easy analysis. There are more questions than answers – which lie beyond the scope of this book – and readers are encouraged to explore the debate for themselves.[12]

But there is one aspect of Edward IV's later reign that cannot be so easily passed over, in a study of his military career, and that is his expedition to France in 1475.[13] Edward himself took ship from England on 4 July, landing at Calais. Calais was to be the base for the invasion. Preparations had been thorough, although not without some frustrations. In particular, although Parliament had reacted enthusiastically to Edward's appeal for support, the taxes granted were hedged around with caveats and proved difficult to collect. Nevertheless, Edward managed to raise a substantial army. The expedition was well supported by the peerage, including Edward's two brothers. Clarence brought 120 men-at-arms and 1,200 archers; Gloucester brought even more. Edward's army, of at least 11,451 men, was probably the largest medieval English army ever to invade France, although such a size was not impressive by Continental standards. Opinions were also divided about the quality of Edward's army. Serious efforts had been made, however, to ensure that a formidable artillery train would be available, which demonstrates the seriousness of Edward's intent.[14] William Rosse was charged with the task of modernising the royal ordnance. A foundry was established at Calais, where old and damaged guns were melted down and new ones forged. The most impressive new gun was the *Great Edward of Calais*, an iron bombard made in 1474. Rosse also commissioned guns from specialists in Flanders, including a 'long iron serpentine' that was made by John van Meighlyn of Brussels.[15] Vast sums were expended, although Rosse carried out his duties effectively. Writing in March 1475, an impressed Italian observer considered Edward's artillery train more impressive than the Duke of Burgundy's. Another Italian noted Edward's interest in artillery and his personal supervision of its production and maintenance.[16]

Yet of course Edward did not expect to fight alone. Once again the ground had been prepared by careful diplomacy. The Dukes of Brittany and Burgundy were expected to provide support, as was the count of St Pol. But in the event, the Duke of Brittany did not stir, the count of St Pol betrayed Edward, and even the Duke of Burgundy let Edward down. Naturally the actions of Duke Charles were most crucial, but they are hard to explain. Obviously Charles was privy to all Edward's plans, but instead of preparing for war with France Charles allowed himself to become embroiled in a minor war in Germany. Charles attempted to gain control of the archbishopric of Cologne, in the Rhineland, and in July 1474 Charles laid siege to the town of Neuss. Matters quickly escalated and Charles found himself opposed by a formidable coalition including the Emperor Frederick III, the Duke of Lorraine and the Swiss. The Swiss defeated a Burgundian army in November, and the siege of Neuss continued into the winter months. As the year 1475 progressed Charles stubbornly persisted with the siege, while Edward began to grow alarmed. Charles was still at Neuss in April, when English preparations were nearing completion. Earl Rivers was sent to implore the Burgundians to abandon the siege, but Charles did not agree to raise the siege until June, when Louis XI launched raids into Burgundy – even then, his army moved slowly. When Charles eventually joined Edward at Calais, in mid July, he was accompanied by a small bodyguard only: the Burgundian army remained to the east in distant Lorraine.

Charles's arrival without his army caused consternation, and some of the English leaders counselled Edward to withdraw immediately. But

Edward consented to Duke Charles's proposal that the English should march east towards Péronne, and then into France proper. It had been agreed that the Count of St Pol would provide a base at St Quentin. Louis had been expecting an attack on Normandy, and so he had concentrated most of his own forces in that area. Charles counselled Edward that St Quentin would therefore allow control of Champagne, and hence of Rheims, where Edward would be crowned. Then, argued Charles, Edward would surely be accepted as King of France. But in the event the plan failed, notably through the treachery of St Pol. When the English reached St Quentin they were greeted with gunfire and some English soldiers were killed. Charles of Burgundy inexplicably barred the gates of his own towns to the English. Louis was now aware of the Anglo-Burgundian strategy, and French troops were burning Picardy and Artois to the English rear. This was designed to deny Edward's army supplies. The French commanders of towns in Champagne were now ready and pre-pared. What was Edward to do? It seemed clear that Edward would be left to fight the French alone. By the middle of August Edward was still denied access to the bases he had been promised, and the English position was becoming precarious. Without active support from his 'allies' Edward's forces were heavily outnumbered by the French. Edward took counsel with his lords, and the decision was taken to make peace. Much to the chagrin of Charles of Burgundy, Louis was happy to accept. According to the terms of the Treaty of Picquigny (29 August 1475) Edward and Louis agreed to a truce for seven years. Louis was to pay Edward 75,000 crowns immediately, followed by an annual pension of 50,000 crowns (the English referred to this as tribute). It was also agreed that a marriage would take place between the Dauphin Charles and Edward's eldest daughter Elizabeth, as soon as both parties reached marriageable age (if Elizabeth died then Edward's next daughter, Mary, would take her place).

The second Crowland Continuator tells us that Edward returned home 'with honourable terms of peace'.[17] For Commynes, however, Edward's policy was the result of physical decline and moral degeneracy, not political or military calculation.[18] Apparently Edward was still 'a very good-looking, tall prince', but 'he was beginning to get fat'. Louis XI, it is said, astutely realised that 'the King of England was more inclined to make peace and to take his gifts' than to fight.[19] This was because Edward 'was addicted to his pleasures. He had not known how to endure the rigours of war in this country [France], and having seen himself escape from great difficulties he had no wish to return to them'. Did others share this view? Indeed, David Grummitt and Michael K. Jones have recently written eloquently of the disappointment of 'chivalric expectation' during Edward's last years. It is well known, for example, that Louis de Bretelles, a Gascon in the retinue of Earl Rivers, told Commynes that the peace at Picquigny was shameful; the shame had outweighed the honour Edward had won by all his victories.[20] Some Englishmen might well have echoed such sentiments,[21] perhaps even members of Edward's inner circle. Notable 'hawks' at the English court included William Lord Hastings and possibly Duke Richard of Gloucester. Grummitt and Jones both offer persuasive ideas, based on thorough study of the mentality of late medieval warriors. Grummitt cites the letters of Sir John Paston and the modern work of Catherine Nall to suggest that 'chivalric expectation' was relatively widespread throughout Yorkist England.[22] Nevertheless, it would be something of a leap to argue that this evidence completely validates Commynes' criticisms of Edward, because it is possible to offer a more positive interpretation of Edward's policy.

Edward was justly proud of his victories but he does not appear to have been driven by the pursuit of martial glory. Although by no means a saint, he was indeed a man who was temperamentally inclined to peace. His capacity for forgiveness was remarkable, even though he did not always forget – as Clarence discovered to his cost. This book has shown much of Edward's 'dread', although there were times when Edward would seek 'comfort and joy' in simple, quiet pleasures.[23] But Edward's nature was not always 'gentle'. A common feature of medieval thought was that peace at home, within the realm, depended on foreign war: Edward was no less competitive and aggressive in foreign relations than the other princes of his age. J.R. Lander's argument that Edward's campaign in 1475 was 'defensive' is unconvincing, but the flexibility that was an essential part of his nature allowed Edward to adapt his strategy. Edward understood better than most men how important is the role of chance in warfare. Although Edward was clearly prepared to fight when he invaded France, the peculiar circumstances of the 1475 campaign quickly appeared in-auspicious. Perhaps, like Malory's King Arthur, Edward concluded that he had already spilt enough blood:

> enough is as good as a feast, for to attempt God overmuch I hold it not wisdom.[24]

King Arthur had already conquered Rome though, in Malory's reworking of the legend, whereas Edward did not conquer France. Circumstantial evidence exists, however, to suggest that Edward regarded the bloodless

French campaign as a great achievement. The Treaty of Picquigny was commemorated on the misericord of the King's personal stall in St George's Chapel.[25] Clearly this was not 'propaganda' designed for a public audience: does this offer a brief glimpse into Edward's private world?

The Treaty of Picquigny was not the only example of Edward's willingness to eschew violence in favour of more peaceful achievements, although it was not ultimately successful. In 1477 Charles the Bold was killed in battle against the Swiss. The death of his heir, Mary, in 1482, shifted the balance of power inexorably towards the French. Mary's husband, Maximilian, was unpopular in Burgundy and unable to assert active leadership. The estates of Flanders and Brabant gained custody of Mary's infant daughter, Margaret, and opened negotiations with Louis. The Dauphin was betrothed to Margaret – in contempt of the Treaty of Picquigny – and Louis swallowed up much of Burgundy. No further instalments of Edward's pension were ever paid. Naturally Commynes, who considered Edward dissolute and indolent, felt that Edward only had himself to blame. He interpreted Edward's response as melancholy, which hastened his early death,[26] although English sources describe Edward's response as rage. When his blood was truly stirred, Edward would fight like a lion to assert his rights. In 1461 and 1471 Edward waged two ferocious campaigns. Perhaps it was fortunate for France, and for Louis XI's reputation, that Louis outlived Edward. At a distance of over 500 years it is impossible to read Edward's character with certainty, although Commynes surely underestimated him.

Edward was a courageous and talented soldier, but his reluctance to fight in France has denied him a place in history as one of England's greatest warrior kings. Edward IV's military reputation will always be overshadowed by that of Edward III and Henry V. For an Englishman, at least, the names Barnet, Tewkesbury and (above all) Towton will call to mind the tragedies of civil war. In contrast, the names Crécy, Poitiers and Agincourt may provide inspiration and evoke national pride. Although the second Crowland Continuator, for one, understood and approved of Edward's decision, which was soundly based, it is clear the Treaty of Picquigny disappointed some of Edward's subjects. War with France, the 'ancient enemy', had popular appeal. The chivalric code encouraged men to seek honour eagerly on the battlefield, to seize every opportunity to demonstrate their prowess. Yet perhaps there were still others, whose voices remain unheard, who were grateful that Edward was not such a man.

Abbreviations

Arrivall:	Historie of the Arrivall of Edward IV in England and the Finall Recouerye of his Kingdomes from Henry VI. A.D. M.CCCC.LXXI. ed. J. Bruce (Camden Society, 1838).
Annales:	'Annales Rerum Anglicarum' in *The Wars of the English in France* ed. J. Stevenson, vol. II, part 2 (Rolls Series, 1864).
Blood Red Roses:	V. Fiorato, A. Boylston and C. Knüssel (eds.), *Blood Red Roses: The Archaeology of a Mass Grave from the Battle of Towton AD 1461* (Oxford, 2000).
CCR:	*Calendar of the Close Rolls.*
Chastelain:	G. Chastelain, *Oeuvres* ed. K. de Lettenhove, 8 vols. (Brussels, 1863–6).
Commynes:	P. de Commynes, *Memoirs: The Reign of Louis XI 1461–83* tr. and ed. M.C.E. Jones (Harmondsworth, 1972).
CPR:	*Calendar of the Patent Rolls.*
Crowland Chronicle:	*The Crowland Chronicle Continuations 1459–86* ed. N. Pronay and J.C. Cox (Gloucester, 1986).
CSPM:	*Calendar of State Papers and Manuscripts ... of Milan*, ed. A.B. Hinds, vol. I (London, 1912).
English Chronicle:	*An English chronicle, 1377–1461* ed. W. Marx (Woodbridge, 2003).
Gillingham:	J. Gillingham, *The Wars of the Roses* (London, 1981).
Goodman, *Military Activity*:	A.E. Goodman, *The Wars of the Roses: Military Activity and English Society, 1452–97* (London, 1981).
Goodman, *Soldiers' Experience*:	A.E. Goodman, *The Wars of the Roses: The Soldiers' Experience* (Stroud, 2005).
The Great Warbow:	M.J. Strickland and R. Hardy, *The Great Warbow: From Hastings to the Mary Rose* (Stroud, 2005).
Great Chronicle:	*The Great Chronicle of London* ed. A.H. Thomas and I.D. Thornley (London, 1938).
Gregory:	'Gregory's Chronicle' in *Historical Collections of a Citizen of London* ed. J. Gairdner (Camden Society, 1876).

Grummitt,   D. Grummitt, 'The Defence of Calais and the
  'Defence of Calais':   Development of Gunpowder Weaponry in England in
                         the Late Fifteenth Century', *War in History* 7 (2000).
Hall: E. Hall, *Hall's Chronicle* ed. H. Ellis (London, 1809).
Hicks, *Warwick*:   M.A. Hicks, *Warwick the Kingmaker* (Oxford, 1998).
Holmes, *Acts of War*:   R. Holmes, *Acts of War: The Behaviour of Men in Battle*
                         (London, 2003, *c*.1985).
Hughes, *Alchemy*:   J. Hughes, *Arthurian Myths and Alchemy: The Kingship
                         of Edward IV* (Stroud, 2002).
Ingulph: *Ingulph's Chronicle of Croyland Abbey* ed. H.T. Riley
                         (London, 1854).
Jones, *Bosworth*:   M.K. Jones, *Bosworth 1485: Psychology of a Battle*
                         (Stroud, 2002).
Mancini: D. Mancini, *The Usurpation of Richard III* ed. and tr.
                         C.A.J. Armstrong (London, 1969).
PL: *The Paston Letters* ed. J. Gairdner, 6 vols. in 1
                         (Gloucester, 1993, *c*.1904).
Pollard, *Warwick*:   A.J. Pollard, *Warwick the Kingmaker: Politics, Power and
                         Fame* (London, 2007).
Ross, *Edward IV*:   C.D. Ross, *Edward IV* (London, 1974).
Scofield: C.L. Scofield, *The Life and Reign of Edward IV*, 2 vols
                         (London, 1923).
Three Fifteenth   Three Fifteenth Century Chronicles ed. J. Gairdner
  Century Chronicles*:   (Camden Society, 1880).
Warkworth's Chronicle: *A Chronicle of the First Thirteen Years of the Reign of
                         Edward IV, by John Warkworth* ed. J.O. Halliwell
                         (Camden Society, 1839).
Wavrin: J. de Wavrin, *Receuil des Croniques et Anchiennes Istoires
                         de la Grant Bretaigne* ed. W. Hardy, vol. V (Rolls Series,
                         1864–91).
Whethamstede: *Registrum Abbatiae Johannis Whethamstede Abbatis
                         Monasterii Sancti Albani* ed. H.T. Riley, vol. I
                         (Rolls Series, 1872–3).

Notes

References are given in full on the first occasion in which they appear in each chapter but in shortened form thereafter. English spelling has been modernised. Quotations from Latin and French have been translated into English. Translations are my own unless otherwise specified.

Introduction

1. E.g. Gillingham, pp. 15–8, pp. 27–9, p. 123, pp. 254–7.
2. J.L. Watts, *Henry VI and the Politics of Kingship* (Cambridge, 1996), p. 366.
3. For the next two paragraphs see: Goodman, *Military Activity*, pp. 119–52; *Idem, The Soldiers' Experience*, pp. 78–125; M.A. Hicks, 'Bastard Feudalism, Overmighty Subjects and Idols of the Multitude during the Wars of the Roses', *History* 85 (2000), esp. pp. 389–91; R.E. Horrox, 'Service', in *eadem, Fifteenth-Century Attitudes: Perceptions of Society in late medieval England* (Cambridge, 1994), pp. 61–78.
4. Gentlemen frequently offered various types of service, including military service, in return for a less clearly defined promise of 'good lordship'. 'Good lordship' could include, for example, support in the interminable title disputes which plagued landed society at this time.
5. Captains, including magnates such as York, would sign indentures with the crown, offering service for specified periods (although payments from the exchequer were often unreliable, as York, for one, discovered to his cost).
6. Bands of men seem to have come together almost spontaneously to resist Edward IV's invasion in 1471, for example; Jack Cade's rebels also appear to have made use of existing administrative structures in 1450.
7. A famous case concerns Sir Henry Vernon, who, in 1470, repeatedly ignored requests for military support from both the Earl of Warwick and Edward's brother, George Duke of Clarence (although Vernon did provide Clarence with useful information. See below p. 172, n. 31).
8. For discussion of motivations see R.E. Horrox, 'Personalities and Politics' in A.J. Pollard (ed), *The Wars of the Roses* (Basingstoke, 1995), pp. 89–109 and M.A. Hicks, 'Idealism and politics', in *eadem, Richard III and his Rivals: Magnates and their Motives in the Wars of the Roses* (London, 1991), pp. 41–60.

9. Chivalry has been succinctly described by Maurice Keen as 'an ethos in which martial, aristocratic and Christian elements were fused together'. M.H. Keen, *Chivalry* (Yale, 1984), p.16. However, as Professor Keen makes clear, 'chivalry' defies easy analysis, because each of these elements could come to the fore in different contexts, without the others being completely excluded. For a wide-ranging study of the 'ambivalent force of chivalry', see R.W. Kaeuper, *Chivalry and Violence in Medieval Europe* (Oxford, 1999).

10. The Earl of Warwick, in particular, was described as an 'idol', who held a genuinely popular appeal. *Crowland Chronicle*, p.147; Hicks, 'Idols of the Multitude', esp. pp.399–402; I.M.W. Harvey, 'Was there Popular Politics in Fifteenth-Century England', R.H. Britnell and A.J. Pollard (eds.), *The McFarlane Legacy: Studies in Late Medieval Politics and Society* (Stroud, 1995), pp.155–75.

11. For further information on arms and armour at this time see the articles by Thom Richardson ('Armour'), Graeme Rimmer ('Weapons') and John Waller ('Combat techniques' and 'Archery') in *Blood Red Roses*.

12. Moreover, the armour used for tourneying was generally heavier than that used in the field. For knights leaping see S. Anglo, 'How to Win at Tournaments: The Technique of Chivalric Combat', *Antiquaries' Journal* 68 (1988), p.251.

13. Mancini, p.98.

14. English yew tends to be twisted and knotty, whereas the hot summers and cold winters of central Europe are more likely to produce yew trees which are straight and fine-grained – ideal for use as bowstaves.

15. It has been argued that the 'killing power' of the longbow has been much exaggerated. However, Clifford Rogers notes, first, that *all* weapons are psychological weapons, and that an army does not need to be entirely obliterated to acknowledge defeat. He then goes on to marshal a large body of evidence to demonstrate, *contra* Kelly DeVries, that arrows did in fact inflict large numbers of casualties. C.J. Rogers, 'The Efficacy of the English Longbow: A Reply to Kelly DeVries', *War in History* 5 (1998), pp.233–42.

16. *Langdebeve* is derived from the French *Langue de Boeve* or ox tongue. The langdebeve was so-called because its two-headed blade resembled an ox tongue.

17. For developments in gunpowder weapons at this time see B.S. Hall, *Weapons and Warfare in Renaissance Europe: Gunpowder, Technology and Tactics* (Baltimore, 1997), esp. chapters 3 and 4, pp.67–133.

18. All of the named sources in the next three paragraphs are cited extensively below.

19. Most of the chronicles named in the next two paragraphs are discussed in more detail in A. Gransden *Historical Writing in England II, c. 1307 to the Early Sixteenth Century* (London, 1982); for a guide to the mentality of chroniclers see C. Given-Wilson, *Chronicles: The Writing of History in Medieval England* (London, 2004).

20. See below, p.21.

21. See my unpublished paper ' "Fighting fulle manly": The Wars of the Roses in *Gregory's Chronicle*'.

22. See A.H. Burne, *The Battlefields of England* (Barnsley, 2006, *c.* 1950), pp. xix–xx.

23. For example, in his account of the second Battle of St Albans, when he speculates that Margaret of Anjou was personally responsible for the Lancastrians' daring tactics, perhaps inspired by her countrywoman Joan of Arc. Burne, *Battlefields*, p. 234.

24. For a forceful critique of Burne's approach see M.K. Jones, 'The Battle of Verneuil (17 August 1424): Towards a History of Courage', *War in History* 9 (2002), esp. pp. 375–6.

25. The implications for the study of medieval military history are summarised in C. Knüsel and A. Boylston, 'How has the Towton Project Contributed to Our Knowledge of Medieval and Later Warfare?' in *Blood Red Roses*, pp. 169–88.

26. A.W. Boardman, *The Battle of Towton* (Stroud, 1994), p. vii.

27. K. Dockray, 'Edward IV: Playboy or Politician?' *The Ricardian*, 10 (1995), pp. 306–25. See also M.A. Hicks, *Edward IV* (London, 2004), pp. 81–102.

28. T. More, *The History of King Richard III*, ed. R.S. Sylvester (Yale, 1963), p. 4.

Chapter 1 – Rouen, April 1442

1. See below, p. 94. The allegations of illegitimacy, and their implications, have been discussed by Michael K. Jones, whose work has caused much controversy. Jones's arguments are not followed here, although I believe his ideas have often been misunderstood. By taking it as a premise that Edward *was* illegitimate, this allows him imaginatively to explore themes that mattered deeply to medieval people – and to Richard III in particular – notably concepts of family honour and the possibility of redemption through military action. As Jones himself puts it: 'it is a story I offer here, and a quite sensational one. Whether in an academic sense it is "true" or not is not ultimately important'. Jones, *Bosworth*, p. 7.

2. The kings of England held lands in France since the Norman Conquest. Technically, therefore, the King of England owed allegiance to the King of France for his French lands, and this was understandably a cause of friction. However, the direct cause of the Hundred Years' War was Edward III's claim to the French throne, through his mother Isabella, which he first advanced in the 1330s. Edward III and his eldest son, the famous Black Prince, won a series of victories. Yet by the turn of the fifteenth century most of England's French possessions, with the exceptions of Calais and Gascony, had been lost.

3. Charles VI had died in October 1422.

4. Although Burgundy remained neutral in the conflict thereafter. Duke Philip and his son, Charles, were to rule in a state of autonomy until 1477, when Charles was killed at the Battle of Nancy.

5. In his youth Charles appeared to be a weak character. He was dogged by allegations of illegitimacy and he had been badly affected when a floor had collapsed beneath him, sending him falling to the level below. See Jones, *Bosworth*, p. 49.

6. For the Pontoise campaign see Jones, *Bosworth*, pp. 49–51, quoting *A Parisian Journal, 1405–1449* at p. 51. A planned epitaph on York's planned tomb at Fotheringhay was to refer to his prowess at this time.

7. For this, and the subsequent military operations in Normandy, see R.A. Griffiths, *The Reign of King Henry VI* (Stroud, 1998, *c.* 1981), pp. 504–22.

8. See M.K. Jones, 'Somerset, York and the Wars of the Roses', *English Historical Review*, 104 (1989), pp. 285–307.

9. Edmund Mortimer was descended from Edward III's second son Lionel Duke of Clarence; Clarence's only child, Philippa, had married Edmund Mortimer's father. Henry IV's father, John Duke of Lancaster, was Edward III's third son. Mortimer's claim was therefore transmitted through the female line, although this, of course, was the basis on which the English kings claimed the French throne. For the competing claims of Lancaster and York see I. Mortimer, 'York or Lancaster: who was the rightful heir to the throne in 1460?', *Ricardian Bulletin* (Autumn, 2008), pp. 20–4.

10. The last Earl of March had died without issue in 1425. York was the son of March's sister, Anne, and Richard Earl of Cambridge.

11. However, York may have wished Henry to nominate him officially as his heir, because Henry and Margaret had no children yet. This was possibly because Henry's confessor, Bishop Aysgough of Salisbury, had counselled Henry not to go 'nigh' Margaret, although of course this is uncertain. Griffiths, *Henry VI*, p. 256.

12. For good introductions to the structures of politics, governance and society at this time see C. Carpenter, *The Wars of the Roses: Politics and the Constitution in England, c.* 1437–1509 (Cambridge, 1997), esp. pp. 27–66; M.A. Hicks, *English Political Culture in the Fifteenth Century* (London, 2002); R.E. Horrox (ed), *Fifteenth-Century Attitudes: Perceptions of Society in Late Medieval England* (Cambridge, 1994).

13. The two were not always intrinsically linked. The Beaufort family, for example, had little landed base, but derived their power from their kinship to the royal family.

14. For a concise discussion of Henry's character, and excerpts from the relevant sources, see K. Dockray (ed.), *Henry VI, Margaret of Anjou and the Wars of the Roses: A Sourcebook* (Stroud, 2000), pp. 1–10. See also Griffiths, *Henry VI*, pp. 248–54.

15. In 1472 Ludlow became a royal borough, meaning the town was freed from the authority of the lord's steward, and Edward also conferred the privilege to return two burgesses to Parliament. Thus Edward acknowledged 'the laudable and gratuitous [sic] services which our beloved and faithful subjects the burgesses of Ludlow had rendered unto us in the obtaining of our right to our crown of England'. See M.A. Hicks, *Edward V* (Stroud, 2003), p. 100.

16. For York's oath see *The Politics of Fifteenth-Century England: John Vale's Book*, eds. M.L. Kekewich *et al* (Stroud, 1995), pp. 193–4.

17. *Chronicles of London*, ed. C.L. Kingsford (Oxford, 1905), p. 163.

18. Henry's subsequent illness has been described, for instance, as catatonic schizophrenia, but we should be wary of retrospective diagnosis. Similarly, although it is clear that his grandfather (Charles VI of France) also suffered from mental illness, it is uncertain that genetic factors were to blame. See Griffiths, *Henry VI*, pp. 715–7.

19. Thomas Percy, the second son of the Earl of Northumberland.

20. See C. Rawcliffe, 'Richard, Duke of York, the King's "obessant liegeman": a new source for the protectorate of 1454 and 1455', *Historical Research*, 60 (1987), pp. 232–9. York's letter to Edward is printed at pp. 238–9.

21. *PL*, I, p. 265.

22. It is striking that when Edward wrote to his father in June he made no mention of raising troops, nor did he refer to his father's anger. Edward was almost entirely preoccupied with the minutiae of his life at Ludlow. See below, p. 18.

23. John Talbot, Earl of Shrewsbury, was similarly present, on the Lancastrian side, at the Battle of Towton. At this time Shrewsbury was also thirteen. See C.F. Richmond, 'The Nobility and the Wars of the Roses', *Nottingham Medieval Studies* 21 (1977), p. 73. For further examples see Goodman, *Soldiers' Experience*, pp. 128–40.

24. For the Battle of St Albans see C.A.J. Armstrong, 'Politics and the Battle of St Albans', *Bulletin of the Institute of Historical Research* 33 (1960), pp. 1–72; P. Burley, M. Elliot and H. Watson, *The Battles of St Albans* (Barnsley, 2007), esp. pp. 17–42.

25. It is unclear at which point the royal banner was raised. See Burley *et al*, *The Battles of St Albans*, pp. 27–8.

26. *PL*, III, p. 30.

27. Bibliotheque Nationale, Paris, MS Fr. 1996, cited in S. Anglo, 'How to Win at Tournaments: The Technique of Chivalric Combat', *Antiquaries' Journal* 68 (1988), p. 250.

28. *Le livre des faicts du Mareschal de Boucicaut* in *Nouvelle collections des Mémoires pour server a l'histoire de France*, eds. Michaud and Poujoulat, 32 vols (Paris, 1836–9), II, pp. 219–20.

29. Quoted in C.T. Allmand (ed), *Society at War* (Woodbridge, 1998), p. 100.
30. For the context, see P. Caudrey, 'William Worcester, *The Boke of Noblesse*, and Military Society in East Anglia', *Nottingham Medieval Studies*, 52 (2008), pp. 191–211.
31. In one of two surviving letters from their boyhood Edward and his brother complained to their father about the 'odious rule and demeaning of Richard Croft and his brother'. Quoted in Scofield, I, p. 21.
32. *PL*, I, p. 149.
33. Commynes, p. 258.
34. See Hughes, *Alchemy*, pp. 80–1.
35. A.R. Myers, *The Royal Household of Edward IV*, pp. 126–7.
36. Mancini, 71.
37. Henry VII's son, Prince Arthur, had an expensive bow bought for him when he was only five years old. English noblemen continued to shoot throughout their lives, and sometimes laid bets on the outcomes of shooting competitions; Henry VII and Sir John Howard lost large sums. See N. Orme, *Childhood to Chivalry*, pp. 200–4. The last recorded sighting of Edward IV's sons, then aged twelve and ten respectively, refers to them shooting at targets in the Tower of London. *Great Chronicle*, p. 234.
38. Edward's great-grandfather, Edward Duke of York, translated into English a famous hunting treatise written by Gaston de Foix. See N. Orme, *From childhood to chivalry: the education of the English kings and aristocracy 1066–1530* (London, 1984), p. 197.
39. J. Hardyng, *The Chronicle of John Hardyng*, ed. H. Ellis (London, 1811), i–ii.
40. *PL*, III, p. 75.
41. See J.L. Laynesmith, 'Constructing Queenship at Coventry: Pageantry and Politics at Margaret of Anjou's "Secret Harbour"',' in L.S. Clark, ed., *The Fifteenth Century, III, Authority and Subversion* (Woodbridge, 2003), pp. 137–148.
42. Most of the nobility remained tenaciously loyal to Henry himself at this time, even though it must have appeared unlikely that he would ever be able to provide effective rule.
43. Cheapside, in London. *Six Town Chronicles*, ed. R. Flenley (Oxford, 1911), p. 159.
44. For example, on 19 May 1457 Judde received payment for providing twenty-six serpentines, together with apparatus for the field, a culverin, and a mortar, as well as sulphur and saltpetre to make gunpowder. See Goodman, *Military Activity*, p. 160. Judde remained industrious in royal service until he was murdered near London in 1460.
45. See C.F. Richmond, 'The Earl of Warwick's Domination of the Channel and the Naval Dimension to the Wars of the Roses, 1456–1460', *Southern History* 20/21 (1987–9), pp. 1–19.
46. Quoted in Pollard, *Warwick*, p. 167.

47. Pollard, *Warwick*, p. 181; L. Visser-Fuchs, ' "Warwick, by himself": Richard Neville, Earl of Warwick, "the Kingmaker", in the *Receuil des Croniques D'Engleterre* of Jean de Wavrin', *Publication du Centre Européen d'études Bourguignonnes (XIVe-XVIes)*, 41 (2001).
48. *Great Chronicle*, p. 207. Warwick's popular reputation is discussed in Pollard, *Warwick*, pp. 147–66.
49. For a positive account of this process which emphasises Henry's role, see Hicks, *Warwick*, pp. 132–7, and references there cited.
50. The mayor and sheriffs of London poured 5,000 men on to the streets, in order to keep order, and the carrying of weapons was forbidden. The Yorkists were allowed within the city walls, but the Lancastrian lords were encouraged to lodge outside the city, to the west of Temple Bar.
51. A chapel where masses would be said for the souls of those who were killed in the battle.
52. See below, p. 76.
53. 'John Benet's Chronicle for the Years 1400–62', in G.L. and M.A. Harriss *Camden Miscellany*, 24 (1972), pp. 223–4.
54. My account of the ensuing campaign is largely based on Goodman, *Military Activity*, pp. 25–31.
55. For the remainder of this paragraph see Ross, *Edward IV*, pp. 9–11 and references there cited; Commynes, p. 258; Mancini, p. 80.
56. *English Chronicle*, p. 88.
57. Henry was later to be praised by Parliament for his fortitude, 'not sparing for any impediment or difficulty of way, nor of intemperance of weather', and because he 'lodged in bare field sometime two nights together with all your Host in the cold season of the year'. R.E. Horrox (ed.), 'Henry VI: Parliament of 1459, Text and Translation', item 15, *PROME*. Salisbury was pointedly excluded from the pardons, which suggests Henry was particularly angered by the events at Blore Heath. This could have been because the force there had been raised in the name of his son, although perhaps also because they had been given the Lancastrian swan livery, of which Henry was particularly proud.
58. Wavrin, p. 276.

Chapter 2 – Calais, November 1459

1. Wavrin, p. 277, tr. in L. Visser-Fuchs, ' "Warwick, by himself": Richard Neville, Earl of Warwick, "the Kingmaker", in the *Receuil des Croniques D'Engleterre* of Jean de Wavrin', *Publication du Centre Européen d'études Bourguignonnes (XIVe-XVIes)*, 41 (2001), p. 151.
2. Crucially, he recognised and encouraged ability in others, most notably in Andrew Trollope, who acted as the duke's military advisor. Trollope is described by Wavrin as a 'subtle man of war', and appears to have been a wise

choice. Somerset also appears to have won the loyalty of common soldiers. In 1469, five years after the duke's death, one of the men hired by the Pastons to defend Caister was still describing himself as a 'soldier of the Duke of Somerset'. Wavrin, p. 325; Goodman, *Soldiers' Experience*, p. 93.

3. Ironically, much of this fleet was made up of Warwick's own ships, which had been impounded and repaired by the Government. See C.F. Richmond, 'The Earl of Warwick's Domination of the Channel and the Naval Dimension to the Wars of the Roses, 1456–1460', *Southern History* 20/21 (1987–9), p. 8.

4. *PL*, III, p. 204.

5. *Annales*, p. 772.

6. Anthony Goodman was puzzled by Commynes' assertion that Edward was present, on the winning side, on nine occasions. Goodman counts seven battles – Northampton, Mortimer's Cross, Ferrybridge, Towton, Empingham, Barnet and Tewkesbury – and eight including St Albans. The engagement at Newnham Bridge may therefore be Edward's 'missing' battle. Commynes, p. 181, p. 261; Goodman, *Military Activity*, p. 272 n. 92.

7. *Annales*, p. 772.

8. Fogge and Scott were to become two of Edward's most trusted servants. Robert Horne was killed at the Battle of Towton. See below, p. 86.

9. Unless otherwise specified, the next seven paragraphs are based on *English Chronicle*, pp. 90–91; Wavrin, pp. 299–300; Whethamstede, pp. 372–5.

10. For example, see A.W. Boardman, *The Medieval Soldier in the Wars of the Roses* (Stroud, 1998), p. 166.

11. For a good discussion of late medieval continental battle tactics, including the battle plan of Duke John 'the Fearless' of Burgundy, see *The Great Warbow*, pp. 319–25; pp. 339–43.

12. The extent to which military treatises influenced (or reflected) actual practice is a matter for debate, although it should be noted that Christine de Pisan, describing her ideal battle plan, did reflect on the best way to deploy raw levies. They were to be deployed as part of the main, or central battle, on the flanks, protected by a screen of archers. See *The Great Warbow*, p. 319.

13. Whethamstede, p. 374. Translated in R.I. Jack, 'A Quincentenary: The Battle of Northampton, July 10th, 1460', *Northamptonshire Past and Present*, 3 (1960), p. 23.

14. H.T. Evans, *Wales and the Wars of the Roses* (Stroud, 1995, c. 1915), p. 69.

15. Jack, 'Battle of Northampton', p. 24.

16. Quoted in *The Great Warbow*, p. 357.

17. *Annales*, pp. 773–4.

18. Whethamstede, p. 376, tr. in Scofield, *Edward IV*, I, p. 104.

19. Wavrin, pp. 314–15, translated in Visser-Fuchs, 'Warwick, by himself', p. 151.

20. Visser-Fuchs, in her article 'Warwick, by himself', suggests that at this point Wavrin was using a propagandist text – the original no longer exists – that

was designed to promote Warwick's cause on the Continent and to excuse his more controversial actions.

21. A number of historians have considered the possibility that the deposition of Henry VI was the ultimate aim of the Yorkists' invasion in 1460. See especially M.K. Jones, 'Edward IV, the Earl of Warwick and the Yorkist Claim to the Throne', *Historical Research* 70 (1997), and references there cited.

22. Gregory, pp. 209–10.

23. According to the *Short English Chronicle*, Edward spent Christmas at Gloucester, but Shrewsbury seems more likely. The author of *Annales* provides persuasive circumstantial detail; he tells us that Edward stayed at the Friary. *Three Fifteenth-Century Chronicles*, p. 76; *Annales*, p. 775. Shrewsbury was, moreover, a town Edward knew well and which had strong links with the House of York (for this, see, M.A. Hicks, *Edward V* (Stroud, 2003), pp. 102–3). Edward's second son Richard was born at Shrewsbury in 1473.

24. Jasper's father Owen Tudor had married Henry V's widow, Queen Katherine, following a whirlwind romance.

25. Denbigh had been held for the Duke of York during his exile, but had fallen to Pembroke after an extensive siege.

26. Herbert's career is discussed in detail in Evans, *Wales and the Wars of the Roses*.

27. See Goodman, *Soldiers' Experience*, pp. 93–4. Worcester, as the secretary of the famous Sir John Fastolf, a hero of the French Wars, had a natural interest in the fortunes of veteran soldiers.

28. See 'Case Studies' in *Blood Red Roses*, pp. 246–7.

29. Margaret was negotiating support from Mary of Guelders, who had become regent following the death of her husband, James II, in August. For the political situation in Scotland see below, pp. 66–7.

30. Somerset had surrendered Guines to Warwick, who had briefly returned to Calais, in August. Somerset was granted a safe-conduct into France on the promise that he would never take up arms against Warwick again. However, he appears to have set little store by this agreement. *Annales*, p. 774; Wavrin, pp. 306–7.

31. The reasons for the Yorkist defeat are uncertain, although most sources agree that the Lancastrians employed treachery, or at least deception. Wavrin tells us that York was induced to leave the safety of Sandal by Andrew Trollope, whose men were disguised as Yorkists, and that he and his men were then slaughtered by Somerset, who had prepared an ambush. Whethamstede tells us that the Lancastrians broke the terms of a local truce and set upon the Yorkists while they were foraging for supplies. Wavrin, V, pp. 325–6; Whethamstede, p. 382.

32. According to tradition Edmund was killed in cold blood by Lord Clifford, whose father had been killed by the Yorkists at St Albans. Edmund's death

has become famous, through the work of Shakespeare and others, although the Tudor writers transformed it into a melodrama.

33. *Three Fifteenth-Century Chronicles*, p. 77.

34. Although 'kern' – derived from the Gaelic *Ceithernn*, meaning 'warband' – is often used as a generic term to describe Irish troops at this time.

35. A letter to Roger Puleston, quoted in R.A. Griffiths, *The Reign of King Henry VI* (Stroud, 1998, c. 1981), p. 871.

36. R.A. Griffiths, *Making of the Tudor Dynasty*, p. 52.

37. Dafydd ap Llewelyn is better known as 'Davy Gam' ('the lame'). Although he was a proud Welshman, he had opposed Owain Glyndwr's rebellion and died in the service of the English kings at Agincourt. Herbert's was the first generation of his family to take an English name.

38. Although the bards also promoted unity; they were fervently nationalistic and preserved a distinctively Welsh culture. For a valuable introduction to the Welsh bards, including Lewis Glyn Cothi, the greatest bard of this period, see Evans, *Wales and the Wars of the Roses*, especially pp. 1–10.

39. Gregory, p. 207. The Duke of York's town of Newbury was to suffer a similar fate later in the year, which suggests the pillaging at Ludlow may have been systematic. At Newbury, a commission led by Lords Scales, Lord Hungerford and the Earl of Wiltshire descended on the town. A number of York's servants were executed, and the occupants were 'spoiled of all their goods'.

40. D. Seward, *The Hundred Years War: The English in France 1337–1453* (London, 1988), p. 171.

41. *English Chronicle*, p. 99. The three suns are also mentioned in the *Short English Chronicle* (p. 77) and Gregory (p. 213). John Whethamstede also recorded parhelia occurring around this time, along with other extraordinary phenomena such as bloody rain, but did not associate them specifically with Edward (pp. 385–6).

42. See Hughes, *Alchemy*, p. 81.

43. British Library MS Harley 7353. See Plate Section, p. 2.

44. *CSPM*, p. 69.

45. Although H. Stanford notes that 'the sonne shyning' was a royal badge used by Richard II, and that Edward's use of a sun badge was therefore not unique. However, it still appears suggestive that Edward chose to merge the White Rose of York with the sun badge. See H. Stanford, *Royal Beasts* (London, 1956), pp. 30–1. I am grateful to Geoffrey Wheeler for bringing this work to my attention.

46. Michael K. Jones has written extensively about inspirational military leadership in the late Middle Ages, stressing the importance of ritualistic behaviour before battle was joined. Jones's ideas are set out concisely in M.K. Jones, 'The Battle of Verneuil (17 August 1424): Towards a History of Courage', *War in History* 9 (2002). See also his *Bosworth* and *Agincourt 1415* (Barnsley, 2005).

47. 'Here tradition has left two signposts: the cottage called Blue Mantle, still the title of a royal pursuivant or herald, and the rotten stump of the once mighty Battle Oak.' G. Hodges, *Ludford Bridge and Mortimer's Cross* (Almeley, 1989), p. 43. However, other sites are possible. An alternative scenario, for example, might see the Yorkists taking up a position somewhere on the gently rising ground towards Lucton.

48. There has been much debate about the tactical deployment of archers. See, for example, *The Great Warbow*, pp. 287–317. Given the high ratio of archers to men-at-arms and other troops during the Hundred Years' War it makes sense that archers would often, in that theatre, have been deployed along the whole of the battle line, and not only to the flanks. However, whether this scheme can be applied to armies during the Wars of the Roses is not certain.

49. Literally meaning 'knife', the term *skein* encompasses a range of bladed weapons.

50. Drayton's poem is quoted in Hodges, *Ludford Bridge and Mortimer's Cross*, p. 50. For the Irish at Stoke, see D. Baldwin, *Stoke Field: The Last Battle of the Wars of the Roses* (Barnsley, 2006), pp. 63–4. According to Jean Molinet, the lightly armed Irish were 'shot through and full of arrows like hedgehogs'.

51. Gregory, p. 198. 'Gregory' also alleges Wiltshire deserted King Henry's standard – a great dishonour – and according to the 'Dijon Relation' he escaped in disguise (as a monk). The 'Dijon Relation' is printed in C.A.J. Armstrong, 'Politics and the Battle of St Albans', *Bulletin of the Institute of Historical Research* 33 (1960), pp. 63–5.

52. *Annales*, p. 776.

53. For example, a *barbute* – a helmet of Italian design – was discovered in the River Lugg downstream at Lugwardine and may have been lost as a survivor attempted to cross the water. See Hodges, *Ludford Bridge and Mortimer's Cross*, p. 51.

54. *English Chronicle*, p. 99. Although this is surely an exaggeration.

55. Gregory, p. 211.

56. Evans, *Wales and the Wars of the Roses*, pp. 78–9.

57. Edward, as Duke of York, was commissioned to raise troops throughout the Marches and the south-west. *CPR, 1452–61*, p. 659.

58. *English Chronicle*, pp. 97–8; Wavrin, pp. 328–30; Gregory, pp. 212–4.

59. He was probably spared execution because Somerset feared reprisals against his own brother, Edmund, who was then in Yorkist custody.

60. Ross, *Edward IV*, p. 32.

61. For the next two paragraphs see Ross, *Edward IV*, pp. 33–4 and references cited there.

62. Commynes believed that Warwick 'governed King Edward in his youth and directed his affairs'. One Frenchman joked, in a letter to Louis XI, that the English had 'but two rulers, M. de Warwick and another whose name I have forgotten'. *CSP, Milan*, I, p. 63; Pollard, *Warwick*, p. 55.

63. See, for example, Ross, *Edward IV*, p. 33. But see also Pollard, *Warwick*, pp. 48–50, for a more equivocal view.
64. Gregory, p. 215.
65. *Ibid.*

Chapter 3 – London, March 1461

1. *CCR, 1461–8*, pp. 54–6.
2. See Ross, *Edward IV*, p. 35.
3. Scofield, *Edward IV*, I, p. 158.
4. Quoted in Goodman, *Military Activity*, p. 156.
5. Gillingham, p. 45.
6. Wavrin, p. 335.
7. Gregory, p. 214.
8. Warwick's regime in London took active steps to disrupt their supply lines in January and February 1461. Commissions were set up in East Anglia and Cambridgeshire to arrest men and impound ships that were supplying provisions to the Lancastrians. See Goodman, *Military Activity*, p. 156.
9. Whethamstede, p. 389; Ingulph, p. 422.
10. Gillingham, p. 123.
11. *English Chronicle*, p. 97.
12. Gregory, p. 213.
13. Ross, *Edward IV*, p. 35.
14. The Dukes of Exeter and Somerset; the Earls of Devon, Northumberland and Shrewsbury; Viscount Beaumont; Lords Clifford, Randolph Dacre, FitzHugh, Grey of Codnor, Lovell, Neville, Rivers, Roos, Rugemont-Grey, Scales, de la Warre, Welles and Willoughby. See C.F. Richmond, 'The Nobility and the Wars of the Roses, 1459–61', *Nottingham Medieval Studies* 21 (1977), p. 75.
15. See the attainder passed later in the year: R.E. Horrox (ed.), 'Edward IV: Parliament of 1461, Text and Translation', item 20, *PROME*.
16. Goodman, *Military Activity*, p. 51.
17. *CSPM*, p. 64; 'John Benet's Chronicle for the Years 1400–62' in G.L. and M.A. Harriss *Camden Miscellany*, 24 (1972), p. 230.
18. For example, Ross, *Edward IV*, p. 36.
19. The Duke of Norfolk, the Earl of Warwick, Viscount Bourchier, Lords Clinton, Dacre (Richard Fiennes), Fauconberg, Grey of Ruthin and Scrope of Bolton. See Richmond, 'The Nobility and the Wars of the Roses', p. 175.
20. An excerpt is printed in *Blood Red Roses*, Appendix A, p. 198.
21. Wavrin, pp. 336–42.
22. *CSPM*, pp. 60–5.
23. *Annales*, pp. 777–8; 'Brief Latin Chronicle' in *Three Fifteenth Century Chronicles*, p. 178; Ingulph, pp. 424–6; Gregory, pp. 216–7; 'Hearne's

Fragment', in J.A. Giles (ed), *Chronicles of the White Rose of York* (1843), p. 9; Whethamstede, pp. 408–10.

24. Hall, pp. 254–6.

25. Although Gravett notes that a gorget was not usually worn in the 1460s. C. Gravett, *Towton 1461: England's Bloodiest Battle* (Oxford, 2003), p. 38.

26. F. de Reiffenberg (ed.), *Memoirs de Jacques du Clercq* (Brussels, 1835), III, p. 118; British Library MS Harley 4424, f. 158. Hall provides an almost literal translation, although in the Continental sources Warwick's speech occurs later in the conflict, and Warwick responds to an attack by Somerset rather than Clifford.

27. *The Great Warbow*, p. 345. Although Clifford's actions also evoke the daring exploits of men such as Henry Percy, 'Hotspur', accompanied by *his* northern horsemen: 'Henry was called Hotspur by the Scots and the French, because in the silent watches of the night, while others slept, he rode tirelessly upon his enemies as though he would make his spurs hot.' *Knighton's Chronicle 1337–1396* ed. G.H. Martin (Oxford, 1995), p. 401.

28. For the construction of a pontoon bridge in France during the period see Commynes, p. 95.

29. Perhaps the Lancastrian army camped in and around the village of Towton, although more comfortable billets would have been available a few miles further north at Tadcaster.

30. As above, note 15.

31. For the rest of this paragraph see 'English Heritage Battlefield Report: Towton 1461' (1995), available at http://www.english-heritage.org.uk. See also V. Fiorato, 'The Context of the Discovery' in *Blood Red Roses*, especially pp. 4–11.

32. Castle Wood and Renshaw Woods to the west, and Carr Woods and Towton Spring to the east, are listed as ancient semi-natural woodlands. The name 'Carr' implies the area is likely to have been marshy.

33. For example, Somerset was singled out for particular attention in a letter that was written to the Lancastrians by Coppini. Furthermore, in February 1461, when the Lancastrians had threatened London, frightened citizens daubed a portcullis on their doors (the portcullis was an emblem used by the Beauforts). *CSPM*, p. 39; Scofield, I, p. 148.

34. We have already seen that the Lancastrian leaders may have struggled to enforce discipline on the large forces under their command. Moreover, although the effective partnership between Somerset and Trollope is well attested, we know little for certain about Somerset's relationships with the other young Lancastrian leaders such as Northumberland and Clifford. At the Battle of Agincourt, when there was a high concentration of noble leaders on the French side, similarly in the absence of their king, there were tensions between the various nobles and ultimately a failure of command. See *The Great Warbow*, pp. 331–2.

35. Gunpowder would be transported in its constituent parts – charcoal, saltpetre and sulphur – and then finely crushed and blended together close to the time of the battle. However, *mealed* powder was extremely susceptible to moisture from the air. This prompted experiments in the production of *corned* (granulated) gunpowder, which was used increasingly as the fifteenth century progressed. B.S. Hall, *Weapons and Warfare in Renaissance Europe: Gunpowder, Technology and Tactics* (Baltimore, 1997), pp. 69–73.

36. There is, however, some circumstantial evidence. Over ten years later, at the Battle of Tewkesbury, Edward was deeply concerned about an area of woodland to the west of his position, because he feared it might conceal an ambush. Was Edward thinking of his experience at Towton? See below p. 130. For this, and further discussion of the 'ambush', see also A.W. Boardman, *The Battle of Towton* (Stroud, 2000, *c.* 1994), pp. 113–7.

37. Otherwise it is impossible to understand how many defeated armies were pursued for miles, as many sources attest. See below; p. 60, p. 136.

38. The notable exception, of course, is Michael K. Jones. He argues that, at Bosworth, Richard III's famous last charge was pre-meditated. Jones believes Richard was inspired by King Ferdinand of Aragon's victory at Toro, in 1476, in which a charge by heavy cavalry won the battle. Jones, *Bosworth*, esp. pp. 138–40. For the renewed importance of heavy cavalry in other parts of Europe during the later fifteenth century, see M.G.A. Vale, *War and Chivalry: Warfare and Aristocratic Culture in England, France and Burgundy at the End of the Middle Ages* (London, 1981), pp. 100–28. Anthony Goodman considers that 'the Wars of the Roses probably produced a revival of English cavalry fighting', although his discussion of this point is necessarily limited to circumstantial evidence. Goodman, *Military Activity*, pp. 178–81, quote at p. 179.

39. Commynes, p. 71. Commynes also notes that, at the Battle of Barnet, the Earl of Warwick was counselled by his brother John, 'a very courageous knight', to dismount and fight on foot. Apparently this was contrary to Warwick's usual practice, although this is uncertain. Commynes, p. 195.

40. Perhaps Warwick was overtly targeted by the powerful Percy retinue; many smaller battles were being fought within the larger conflict. I owe this suggestion to Scowen Sykes.

41. A. Curry, *Agincourt: A New History* (Stroud, 2006), pp. 235–6.

42. *Historia Roffensis*, quoted in *The Great Warbow*, p. 453 n. 123.

43. See J. Waller, 'Combat Techniques' in *Blood Red Roses*, esp. pp. 149–50.

44. *The Great Warbow*, pp. 335–7.

45. Curry, *Agincourt*, p. 256; S.A. Novak, 'Battle Related Trauma' in *Blood Red Roses*, pp. 90–102. Of the twenty-eight men whose skulls were able to be analysed, only one had not suffered a head wound. Many of the wounds were sustained to the left-hand side of the face, which suggests they were inflicted by right-handed opponents who were facing them.

46. A.W. Boardman, *The Medieval Soldier in the Wars of the Roses* (Stroud, 1998), pp. 53–60.
47. Moreover, during the ensuing conflict in the north there were occasions when warfare was strictly limited in accordance with the law of arms. See below, esp. pp. 70–2.
48. C. Given-Wilson and F. Bériac, 'Edward III's Prisoners of War: The Battle of Poitiers and its Context', *English Historical Review* 116 (2001), p. 808.
49. As suggested in Gravett, *Towton*, p. 88.
50. By this time the bodies had apparently been moved to hallowed ground, in Saxton churchyard, on the orders of the local Hungate family.
51. John Davey has demonstrated that the main road to Towton is likely to have followed the line of the modern A162, not the 'Old London Road', as is generally assumed, which was never more than a local track. J. Davey, 'The Battle of Towton, 1461: A Reassessment', in Idem, *Penbardd* (Las Vegas, 2007), pp. 45–56.
52. Gravett, *Towton*, p. 73.
53. 'Gregory', for example, asserts that 35,000 were killed.
54. *PL*, III, pp. 267–8.
55. When the grave at Towton Hall was first discovered it was initially suggested the dead men must have been executed, or, more optimistically, that the bones were those of wounded soldiers who were killed as an act of mercy.
56. Quoted in Holmes, *Acts of War*, p. 187. Anecdotal evidence suggests that mercy killings have remained a feature of modern conflicts, although this is not officially condoned. Holmes considers that, when wounded men wish for death, it takes 'great moral courage to accede to such a request'. Holmes, *Acts of War*, pp. 187–8, quote at p. 188.

Chapter 4 – York, March 1461

1. Beverley, for example, was assessed by John Fogge, now a knight and the Treasurer of Edward's household. The citizens were required to send twenty-four men-at-arms and a company of archers. Scofield, I, p. 167.
2. He had been captured at Cockermouth, attempting to reach exile in Scotland.
3. *The Politics of Fifteenth-Century England: John Vale's Book*, eds. M.L. Kekewich *et al* (Stroud, 1995), pp. 171–2. Warwick also noted that a powerful artillery train would be required.
4. Hastings was appointed to this office in the summer of 1461 and held it until the end of the reign. Ross, *Edward IV*, p. 73.
5. Herbert became chief justice and chamberlain in South Wales. Ross, *Edward IV*, p. 76.
6. See Hughes, *Alchemy*, especially chapters 4 and 5, pp. 77–161. A key text is the *Illustrated Life of Edward IV*, cited above at p. 56.

7. See Scofield, I, p. 192.
8. Although the defenders were severely outgunned, using approximately a quarter of the 'gunstones' and ammunition that was used by the Yorkists. Grummitt, 'Defence of Calais', p. 259.
9. See Scofield, I, pp. 205–6 and references there cited. Blount's experience at Calais illustrates the financial problems faced by Edward's fledgling regime. Blount came over to England several times in 1461–2 to complain to Edward and his council about the garrison's poverty. In March 1462 he received £2,000 from the chancery, although this money had to be borrowed from Italian bankers. Even so, as late as 1464 Blount was still owed £1,849 for the wages of the soldiers who had served at the siege of Hammes.
10. Scofield, I, p. 187. As well as artillery – bombards and serpentines with saltpetre – Harveys was also responsible for the purveyance of bows, arrows and bowstrings.
11. Somerset's planned role was to solicit support from his friend the Count of Charolais. For the relationship between Somerset and Charolais see below, p. 75.
12. Quoted in Scofield, I, p. 193.
13. Scofield, I, p. 199, quoting *Ricart's Kalendar*.
14. R.E. Horrox (ed.), 'Edward IV: Parliament of 1472, Text and Translation', item 31, *PROME*.
15. *PL*, III, p. 312.
16. Duke Philip's support was vital to Edward in the early years of his reign. In early 1462, when Philip fell ill, Edward ordered his subjects to pray for the duke's recovery and took part in religious ceremonies himself. Scofield, I, pp. 234–5.
17. J. Hardyng, *The Chronicle of John Hardyng*, ed. H. Ellis (London, 1811), p. 378.
18. For much of the later Middle Ages the 'Black' Douglases had been one of the greatest families in Scotland. However, in 1452 James II murdered Earl James's elder brother, William Earl of Douglas. Earl James was allowed to succeed his brother, but he soon rose in rebellion and was forced into exile: the power of the Black Douglases was broken.
19. *Annales*, p. 779. Somerset, by now released from French custody, had returned to Scotland in March. However, according to *Annales*, his presence was unwelcome. Mary is said to have sent another of her (alleged) lovers, Lord Hailes, to intercept Somerset and kill him.
20. *Warkworth's Chronicle*, p. 2.
21. It is unclear whether Somerset joined Margaret's army in France or Scotland. See Scofield, I, p. 253 n. 2.
22. 'Brief Notes' in *Three Fifteenth-Century Chronicles*, p. 157.
23. *Warkworth's Chronicle*, p. 2.
24. Possibly measles. *Great Chronicle*, p. 200.

25. See below, p. 79.
26. All of those inside a besieged castle or town, including non-combatants, would be subject to the same savage rules. Hence, for example, when the Black Prince massacred the townspeople of Limoges in 1370, he surely considered himself to be within his rights to do so, even though Froissart was critical. For the massacre at Limoges see J. Froissart, *Chronicles*, ed. G. Brereton (London, 1978), pp. 175–9. For the laws governing sieges see M.H. Keen, *The Laws of War in the Late Middle Ages* (Oxford, 1993, *c*. 1965), pp. 119–33.
27. *PL*, IV, pp. 59–61. Spelling and grammar modernised following Gillingham, p. 144.
28. *Annales*, p. 780. Although according to *Annales* they were not able to obtain such favourable terms, notably concerning the restoration of their lands.
29. *Warkworth's Chronicle*, p. 2.
30. *Annales*, p. 781.
31. 'Brief Latin Chronicle' in *Three Fifteenth-Century Chronicles*, p. 176.
32. Vegetius was a Roman writer whose work on military organisation was regarded to be a classic work during the Middle Ages. Manuscripts proliferated throughout Europe: see C. Allmand, 'The *De Re Militari* of Vegetius in the Middle Ages and the Renaissance', in C. Saunders, F. Le Saux and N. Thomas (eds.), *Writing War: Medieval Literary Responses to Warfare* (Cambridge, 2004). A translation in English was provided for Henry VI by Viscount Beaumont. R. Dyboski and Z.M. Arend (eds.), *Knyghthode and Bataile* (Early English Text Society, 1935). However, Clifford Rogers has offered a forceful critique of the notion, *pace* Philippe Contamine (and others), that 'medieval strategy does indeed appear to have been dominated by ... fear of the pitched battle.' C.J. Rogers, 'The Vegetian "Science of Warfare" in the Middle Ages', *Journal of Medieval Military History* (2002), pp. 1–19, quoting Contamine at p. 19.
33. See below, pp. 125–6.
34. The command was given instead to Sir John Astley, a knight of the garter and a noted jouster. However, Astley was a southerner with no obvious ties to Northumberland. Grey, on the other hand, was a local man, whose ancestral seat was at Chillingham in Northumberland. He may have fought for Henry VI at Towton, but had thereafter fought for the Yorkists in the north. He had previously been in command at Alnwick, albeit briefly.
35. E.g. Chastelain, IV, pp. 278–9.
36. Gregory, pp. 220–1.
37. Scofield, II, Appendix I, pp. 461–2.
38. 'Brief Latin Chronicle', p. 177; *Warkworth's Chronicle*, p. 3.
39. Chastelain, IV, p. 66.
40. Gregory, p. 206; *Annales*, p. 781.
41. See above, p. 157, n. 30.

42. For Ross, it was 'one of those political blunders which mars Edward's record as a statesman'. Ross, *Edward IV*, pp. 51–2, quote at p. 51.

43. R.E. Horrox, 'Edward IV: Parliament of 1463, Text and Translation', item 28, *PROME*.

44. M.K. Jones, 'Edward IV and Beaufort Family: Conciliation in Early Yorkist Politics', *The Ricardian* (1983), p. 260.

45. *PL*, IV, p. 52. It would have also been Warwick, of course, who negotiated with Somerset at Bamburgh and received his surrender on Edward's behalf.

46. Gregory, p. 219.

47. As Jaeger explains, 'ennobling love is primarily a public experience, only secondarily private ... it is primarily a way of behaving, only secondarily a way of feeling ... it is a form of aristocratic self-representation. Its social function is to show forth virtue in lovers [sic], to raise their inner worth, to increase their honor and enhance their reputation'. C.S. Jaeger, *Ennobling Love: In Search of a Lost Sensibility* (Philadelphia, 1999), p. 6.

48. See N. Offenstadt, 'The Rituals of Peace during the Civil War in France, 1409–19: Politics and the Public Sphere', in T. Thornton (ed.), *Social Attitudes and Political Structures* (Stroud, 2000), esp. pp. 92–4.

49. Ross, *Edward IV*, p. 274.

50. See R. Barber, 'Malory's *Le Morte d'Arthur* and Court Culture under Edward IV' in J.P. Carley and F. Riddy (eds.), *Arthurian Literature XII* (Cambridge, 1993), pp. 133–55.

51. See S. Anglo, 'Anglo-Burgundian Feats of Arms: Smithfield, June 1467', *Antiquaries' Journal* (1967), pp. 271–2. At one tournament in the late 1460s, for example, Anthony Woodville appeared dressed as a monk.

52. Susan Crane has studied the use of disguise during this period, at tournaments and on the battlefield, both in romances and historical texts, and her conclusions have clear implications for this episode: 'the pivotal function of chivalric incognito ... is to establish or revise the perception of others concerning the disguised knight's merits. That is, incognito is not significantly self-concealing and self-protecting but the reverse: the disguised knight draws the curious and judgemental eye and stands clear of his past to be measured anew.' S. Crane, *The Performance of Self: Ritual, Clothing and Identity During the Hundred Years War* (Philadelphia, 2002), pp. 107–39, quote at p. 132.

53. If there is any truth in the stories of ill-feeling between Somerset and Mary of Guelders (see above, p. 164, n. 19), then her death may also have offered Somerset hope that he might now be more likely to receive help from the Scots.

54. A number of other northern nobles who Edward had pardoned, including Sir Henry Bellingham and Sir Humphrey Neville, had also returned to their former allegiance.

55. Wavrin, pp. 440–1.

56. As argued in M.A. Hicks, 'Edward IV, the Duke of Somerset and Lancastrian Loyalism in the North', *Northern History* 20 (1984), pp. 23–37.

57. Gregory, p. 223.

58. Gregory, p. 224.

59. Gillingham, p. 152.

60. Gregory, p. 224.

61. See *Warkworth's Chronicle*, pp. 37–8, quoting from a MS in the College of Arms transcribed by the editor. Spelling and grammar has been modernised following Gillingham, p. 153.

62. The *Dijon* and the *London* were brought by sea from Calais for use during this campaign. The *London* was melted down in 1472–3, at a time when Edward was attempting to update his stock of gunpowder weapons. See Grummitt, 'Defence of Calais', p. 260. Also see below, p. 143.

63. R.E. Horrox (ed.), 'Edward IV: Parliament of 1463, Text and Translation', item 28, *PROME*.

64. *Warkworth's Chronicle*, pp. 38–9. There were precedents for Grey's treatment. The ritual disgrace that was planned for Grey was almost identical to that inflicted on Sir Andrew Harclay in 1323. See M.H. Keen, 'Treason Trials under the Law of Arms', *Transactions of the Royal Historical Society*, 12 (1962), pp. 88–90.

65. Gillingham, p. 154.

66. Cited in Goodman, *Soldiers' Experience*, p. 192.

Chapter 5 – Reading, September 1464

1. Possibly Duchess Jacquetta had become pregnant before the marriage, which explains why the couple married in haste. See A. Okerlund, *Elizabeth Wydeville: The Slandered Queen* (Stroud, 2005), p. 43.

2. See D. Santiuste, ' "Puttyng downe and rebuking of vices": Richard III and the *Proclamation for the Reform of Morals*', in A.S. Harper and C. Proctor (eds.), *Medieval Sexuality: A Casebook* (New York, 2008), esp. pp. 137–9.

3. Gregory, pp. 226–7.

4. Hicks, *Warwick*, pp. 256–7.

5. Pollard, *Warwick*, pp. 76–80.

6. *PL*, IV, p. 275.

7. Pollard, *Warwick*, p. 57.

8. *Crowland Chronicle*, p. 115.

9. It is perhaps a measure of the strength of Edward's position, as well as of his character, that Henry VI was not put to death (although Henry was publicly humiliated: he was led through the streets of London with his feet tied to the stirrups of his horse. *Warkworth's Chronicle*, p. 5).

10. See, for example, Chastelain, V, pp. 455–6.

11. Chastelain, V, p. 453.

12. Charles is said to have discovered Exeter, virtually destitute, on the streets of Bruges. According to Commynes, Exeter was barefoot and clad in rags. Commynes, p. 180.
13. Commynes, p. 145; *Crowland Chronicle*, p. 115.
14. Scofield, I, p. 429.
15. *Warkworth's Chronicle*, p. 4.
16. Wavrin, p. 545.
17. *CSPM*, p. 121.
18. For example, *Crowland Chronicle*, pp. 132–3. For a sympathetic account of Clarence's career, see M.A. Hicks, *False, Fleeting, Perjur'd Clarence 1449–78* (Gloucester, 1980).
19. Although by now they had two daughters: Elizabeth, born in February 1466, and Mary, born in August 1467.
20. The dispensation was necessary because Clarence and Isabel were related within the degrees prohibited by the Church.
21. *Annales*, p. 788.
22. Scofield, I, p. 434.
23. See Ross, *Edward IV*, p. 112.
24. *PL*, IV, p. 298.
25. Quoted in H.T. Evans, *Wales and the Wars of the Roses* (Stroud, 1995, *c*. 1915), p. 89.
26. Evans, *Wales and the Wars of the Roses*, p. 100.
27. Ross, *Edward IV*, p. 113.
28. *Warkworth's Chronicle*, p. 12.
29. According to the 'Brief Latin Chronicle', in *Three Fifteenth-Century Chronicles*, ed. J. Gairdner (Camden Society, 1880), p. 183. However, the sources for the northern risings are contradictory and confusing. See K. Dockray, 'The Yorkshire Rebellions of 1469', *The Ricardian*, 6 (1983), pp. 246–57.
30. Unless otherwise specified, for the rest of this paragraph and the next see Ross, *Edward IV*, p. 129 and references there cited.
31. The true identity of Robin of Redesdale is discussed in Dockray, 'The Yorkshire Rebellions of 1469', pp. 253–4. According to *Warkworth's Chronicle*, p. 6, Robin was Sir William Conyers of Marske. However, Dockray shows that the chronicle is not always reliable with regard to names, and concludes that Sir John Conyers is a much more likely candidate. A.J. Pollard has recently suggested a third candidate though, who was also involved in the rising: Robert, Lord Ogle, who was the Lord of Redesdale. Pollard, *Warwick*, p. 119.
32. The marriage took place at Calais because it was outside the jurisdiction of Cardinal Bourchier, Archbishop of Canterbury.
33. Printed in *Warkworth's Chronicle*, pp. 46–9.
34. Although Warwick's strategy, if this was so, was extremely ambitious within the context of medieval warfare. See Y.N. Harari, 'Inter-frontal Cooperation in the Fourteenth Century and Edward III's 1346 Campaign', *War in History*,

6 (1999), pp. 379–95. Harari notes that 'inter-frontal' co-operation was extremely difficult in the Middle Ages. This was because of the lack of accurate maps, and also because communication times between forces were usually measured in days or even weeks. This meant the overall commander would need to delegate considerable autonomy to his subordinates on other fronts. The best he could usually hope for was that his subordinates could be trusted to make good decisions, and that some of his enemies would be 'tied down' thereby making it impossible for them to concentrate their forces effectively. However, in both of these respects Warwick's strategy succeeded admirably.

35. For accounts of the battle see 'Hearne's Fragment' in *Chronicles of the White Rose of York*, ed. J.A. Giles (London, 1845), p. 24; *Warkworth's Chronicle*, pp. 6–7; Wavrin, V, pp. 581–3. See also Evan, *Wales and the Wars of the Roses*, pp. 102–7. Hall, who may again have amplified his sources, adds the 'romantic' detail (p. 274) that the earls quarrelled over a woman who worked in one of the inns.

36. Pollard, *Warwick*, p. 119.

37. *Warkworth's Chronicle*, p. 7.

38. Richard Duke of Gloucester gained custody of the young King Edward V at Stony Stratford in similar circumstances in 1483, even though Edward had at his disposal an escort of 2,000 men.

39. P.M. Kendall, *Richard III* (New York, 2002, *c*. 1955), p. 86.

40. The title of his chapter which discusses Warwick's first rebellion is 'Lion into Fox.' Kendall, *Richard* III, pp. 81–8.

41. Hicks, *Warwick*, p. 278.

42. *Crowland Chronicle*, p. 117.

43. *PL*, V, p. 63.

44. *Crowland Chronicle*, p. 117.

45. Henry Percy had been a prisoner in London since 1464.

46. 'Chronicle of the Rebellion in Lincolnshire', ed. J.G. Nichols, *Camden Miscellany*, 1 (1847), p. 6.

47. Goodman, *Military Activity*, p. 71.

48. *Ibid.*

49. *Warkworth's Chronicle*, p. 8.

50. The battle has become traditionally known as 'Losecoat Field'. It is usually assumed this is a reference to the rebels discarding liveries and equipment as they ran. However, in fact 'Losecoat' is the name of a local field, which is probably derived from the Old English *hlose-cot*, meaning 'pigsty cottage'. See P. Morgan, 'The Naming of Battlefields' in D. Dunn (ed.), *War and Society in Medieval and Early Modern Britain* (Liverpool, 2000), p. 41.

51. 'Chronicle of the Rebellion', p. 10.

52. For discussion see Ross, *Edward IV*, Appendix V, pp. 441–2; Hicks, *Warwick*, pp. 282–4.

53. For the rest of this paragraph see 'Chronicle of the Rebellion', pp. 14–6.
54. *PL*, V, p. 71.
55. Sir William Parr, for example, who carried the messages between Edward and the rebels, had already made his peace with Edward by this time.
56. 'Chronicle of the Rebellion', pp. 16–7.
57. *CPR, 1467–77*, pp. 218–9.
58. According to *Warkworth's Chronicle*, p. 9, for this Worcester 'was greatly hated among the people'.
59. Commynes, p. 183.
60. Hicks, *Warwick*, p. 287.
61. The so-called *Manner and Guiding*, printed in *The Politics of Fifteenth-Century England: John Vale's Book*, eds. M.L. Kekewich *et al* (Stroud, 1995), pp. 215–7.
62. When Edward was barely thirteen, a Milanese ambassador was concerned that the young prince 'talks of nothing but cutting off heads or making war, as if he had everything in his hands or was the god of battles'. *CSPM*, p. 117.
63. Commynes, p. 186.
64. Chastelain, V, pp. 492–3, quoted and translated in Ross, *Edward IV*, p. 148.
65. Ross, *Edward IV*, pp. 147–9.
66. The master of the *Trinity*, John Porter, was rewarded with a substantial annuity.
67. Hicks, *Warwick*, p. 291.
68. *PL*, V, p. 80.
69. *Ibid*.
70. For example: Gillingham, pp. 182–3; Goodman, *Military Activity*, p. 75.
71. *Warkworth's Chronicle*, p. 10.
72. *Ibid*.
73. See below, p. 112.

Chapter 6 – Texel, The Netherlands, October 1470

1. In 1467, following a number of diplomatic disputes, Edward had temporarily revoked the League's commercial privileges. A number of German merchants who were resident in London had been imprisoned. See Scofield, *Edward IV*, I, pp. 465–9.
2. Commynes, p. 189.
3. This paragraph is based on L. Visser-Fuchs, '*Il n'a plus lion ne lieppart, qui vouelle tenir de sa part*: Edward IV in exile, October 1470 to March 1471', *Publication du Centre Européen d'études Bourguignonnes (XIVe-XVIes.)*, 35 (1995), pp. 95–6.
4. Certainly, Norton's biographer found it difficult to explain why he had not warned Edward of the danger he was in, concluding the only possible explanation was that 'some great fault in the King letted it'!

5. Much of the next two chapters is based on this account (although many useful details of the ensuing campaign are also supplied by Commynes, *Warkworth's Chronicle* and by a newsletter written by a German merchant resident in London, Gerhard von Wesel). Harpisfield's career is discussed in L. Visser-Fuchs, 'Nicholas Harpisfield, clerk of the signet, author and murderer', *The Ricardian*, 7 (1985–87), pp. 213–19.

6. Edward later ordered a number of Flemish manuscripts. See Scofield, I, *Edward IV*, p. 566.

7. Commynes, p. 193.

8. Beaufort had absented himself from the celebrations of Charles's wedding with Margaret, but he had soon returned to court and remained high in Charles's favour.

9. Commynes, pp. 190–3.

10. Although Commynes does tell us he received a cool reception. Although Wenlock's behaviour was courtly as ever, it was quite clear how the land lay.

11. See Visser-Fuchs, 'Il n'a plus lion ne lieppart', p. 91. Certainly, at the least, his chronology appears to be suspect. At this time Commynes was a counsellor of the Duke of Burgundy, but he was later to defect to Louis of France, who was to become the 'hero' of his historical work.

12. See R. Vaughan, *Charles the Bold* (Woodbridge, 2002, *c.* 1973), p. 71.

13. Ironically these troops may have included Englishmen, professional soldiers who had taken service with the Duke of Burgundy. Goodman, *Soldiers' Experience*, p. 106.

14. Hughes, *Alchemy*, p. 216.

15. *CSPM*, p. 151. This was in a letter from the Milanese ambassador to France, written from Beauvais on 9 April. It therefore postdates Edward's landing in England, but it is likely to reflect general expectations of the expedition on the Continent, rather than being a specific response to later news from England.

16. *Warkworth's Chronicle*, p. 11.

17. *Ibid.*

18. See Pollard, *Warwick*, p. 71. The extent of popular support for Warwick is confirmed by Yorkist proclamations and propagandist verse which condemn the 'blindness' of the commons.

19. Ross, *Edward IV*, p. 156. In addition to the restoration of his former offices he became Chamberlain and Admiral. He also took the wardship of the young Duke of Buckingham's lands in South Wales, which had previously been held by William Herbert.

20. *Arrivall*, p. 10.

21. Quoted in Hicks, *Warwick*, p. 306.

22. Ross, *Edward IV*, p. 157. Commissions of the Peace – crucial to the maintenance of law and order – also show that the Readeption Government quickly abandoned attempts to be inclusive. Prominent Yorkists, such as Sir John Howard and Lord Ferrers, were removed from the bench.

23. Warwick told Henry Vernon that Edward had 2,000 men (see Ross, *Edward IV*, p. 160, n. 4). *Warkworth's Chronicle*, however, puts Edward's force at 1,200, consisting of 900 English and 300 Flemish handgunners. The *Great Chronicle* puts Edward's strength at only 1,000, including 500 English and 500 Flemings.

24. *Arrivall*, pp. 3–4.

25. *Arrivall*, p. 4.

26. For the events at York see *Arrivall*, p. 5. See also *Warkworth's Chronicle*, p. 14, where it is said that Edward entered York wearing the ostrich feather badge of Prince Edward and shouting 'A King Harry!'

27. For this paragraph see *Arrivall*, pp. 6–7.

28. Although, again, we should note the difficulties of maintaining effective communication between separated forces during this period (see above, pp. 168–9, n. 34).

29. *Arrivall*, p. 9.

30. *Arrivall*, p. 11.

31. Clarence was kept well informed of developments by Henry Vernon, a Derbyshire gentleman who had famously rejected Warwick's own desperate plea for support: 'Henry, I pray you fail not now as ever I may do for you.' Quoted in Hicks, *Warwick*, p. 308.

32. *Arrivall*, p. 11.

33. *Arrivall*, p. 12.

34. *Arrivall*, pp. 13–14.

35. During the dissolution of the monasteries Henry VIII's agents sought, with some success, to prove that many such 'miracles' were in fact produced by man-made 'engines, vices and crafty conveyances'. See P. Marshall, 'The rood of Boxley, the blood of Hailes and the defence of the Henrician church', *The Journal of Ecclesiastical History* (1995), p. 694, quoting a contemporary treatise known as the 'The Declaration of Faith'.

36. See P.W. Hammond, *The Battles of Barnet and Tewkesbury* (Gloucester, 1990), p. 68.

37. *Great Chronicle*, p. 215.

38. Sir Thomas Cook – who had been deputising for Mayor John Stockton – may have fled to France as early as 7 April (Stockton had diplomatically taken to his bed with illness).

39. See Scofield, *Edward IV*, I, p. 575.

40. *Great Chronicle*, p. 216.

41. Scofield, *Edward IV*, I, p. 576, quoting a letter written by Duchess Margaret of Burgundy.

42. Commynes, p. 194.

43. Unless otherwise specified, this and the next seven paragraphs are based on *Arrivall*, pp. 19–21; H. Kleineke, 'Gerald Von Wesel's Newsletter from England, 17 April 1471', *The Ricardian* 16 (2006), pp. 77–83; *Warkworth's Chronicle*, pp. 15–17.

44. The Elizabethan chronicler Holinshed situated Warwick's position on Gladmore Heath, and most historians have followed suit. Gladmore Heath (now called Hadley Green) lies just to the north of Barnet. The cross-ridge here would certainly have appealed to a commander who had the opportunity to choose his ground. See A.H. Burne, *The Battlefields of England* (Barnsley, 2005, *c*. 1950), pp. 263–5; Hammond, *Barnet and Tewkesbury*, pp. 72–3.

45. Goodman, *Military Activity*, p. 159.

46. Goodman suggests Edward may have been consciously imitating Henry V's policy on the night before the Battle of Agincourt. Goodman, *Soldiers' Experience*, pp. 159–60.

47. Although the *Great Chronicle*'s account has been followed by later chroniclers and historians. See, for example, Burne, *Battlefields of England*, p. 260.

48. Von Wesel, who saw the Yorkist muster, gives them 15,000. Wavrin, relying on a short French version of the *Arrivall*, gives the Lancastrians 20,000.

49. Grummitt, 'Defence of Calais', pp. 262–3. Between April 1471 and April 1472 the Calais victualler bought 223 brass handguns at Antwerp, which were intended for the use of the Calais garrison.

50. B.S. Hall, *Weapons and Warfare in Renaissance Europe: Gunpowder, Technology and Tactics* (Baltimore, 1997), p. 132.

51. Although, perhaps surprisingly, Edward is praised by the second Crowland Continuator for 'behaving rather in response to immediate necessity than foolish propriety'. *Crowland Chronicle*, p. 125.

52. See Holmes, *Acts of War*, p. 124: although the attacker's soldiers are also at a 'metabolic low', they have been awake long enough to make physiological adjustments.

53. A British military study of 1980 reports that after forty-eight hours without sleep 'responses to simulated attacks [. . .] were bad, with most soldiers over-reacting and misunderstanding orders, which were not always clearly given by the section commander'. Quoted in Holmes, *Acts of War*, p. 125.

54. Some of those who fled did not stop until they reached London, where they began to spread alarming (although erroneous) news of a Yorkist defeat.

55. According to Von Wesel '3,000 of King Edward's people fled from the rear, yet neither party noticed because of the fog'. Von Wesel also reports that at one stage Warwick's men succeeded in gaining custody of Henry VI, although he was afterwards recaptured.

56. Von Wesel, p. 81. Anthony Earl Rivers was also wounded.

57. Geoffrey Wheeler has raised some interesting points about this episode. Warkworth clearly states that 'the Earl of Oxford's men had upon them their lord's livery, both before and behind'. This means that the two badges appeared on the *soldiers*, not on the *banners* as is usually supposed. We do not know how elaborate livery badges would have been, although in the Middle Ages the sun was often drawn like a *molet* (star) with seven or eight points, which could easily be mistaken for Oxford's five-pointed molet. However,

if the *colours* of the two badges – presumably gold and silver respectively – were featured then this makes the confusion harder to understand. G. Wheeler, 'The Battle of Barnet: Heraldic Complications and Complexities', *Ricardian Bulletin* (December, 2000), pp. 43–8.

58. Oxford fled into exile. He launched an abortive invasion in 1472 which achieved nothing except the temporary capture of St Michael's Mount. He spent the rest of Edward's reign in prison, but he was then released by his gaolers and led Henry Tudor's victorious army at Bosworth.

59. Exeter was imprisoned in the Tower until 1475, when he was released to accompany Edward on his expedition to France. However, he drowned at sea.

60. Warwick's depiction in continental sources has been comprehensively studied by Livia Visser-Fuchs. See, for example, '*Sanguinis Haustor* – Drinker of Blood: A Burgundian View of England, 1471', *The Ricardian*, 7 (1985–87), pp. 213–19.

61. Pollard, *Warwick*, p. 1.

Chapter 7 – London, April 1471

1. *Arrivall*, p. 21.
2. For the meeting at Cerne, see *Arrivall*, p. 23.
3. *CSPM*, p. 154.
4. *Arrivall*, p. 23.
5. *Arrivall*, p. 23.
6. The Bishop of Bath and Wells later received a pardon for the loss of the prisoners (25 February, 1472). See P.W. Hammond, *The Battles of Barnet and Tewkesbury* (Gloucester, 1990), p. 82.
7. *PL*, V, p. 100.
8. M. Mercer, 'The Strength of Lancastrian Loyalism during the Readeption: Gentry Participation at the Battle of Tewkesbury', *Journal of Medieval Military History*, 5 (2007), pp. 84–98.
9. See Scofield, vol. I, p. 583. On the same day the City of London granted Edward 1,000 marks for the defence of the realm. Scofield, vol. I, p. 584.
10. *Arrivall*, pp. 23–4.
11. H. Kleineke, 'Gerald Von Wesel's Newsletter from England, 17 April 1471', *The Ricardian* 16 (2006), p. 69.
12. *CPR 1467–77*, pp. 283–5. The majority of Edward's army seems to have come from the Home Counties and the Midlands; Clarence was particularly prominent in the commissions of array.
13. *Arrivall*, p. 24.
14. *CPR 1467–77*, p. 259. William Bygge and John Brymston received similar responsibilities the following day.
15. See Ross, *Edward IV*, p. 274.
16. Edward paid 3,436 archers after the battle. See C. Gravett, *Tewkesbury 1471: The Last Yorkist Victory* (Oxford, 2003), p. 28.

17. *Arrivall*, p. 24.
18. *Arrivall*, p. 25.
19. *Arrivall*, p. 27.
20. Estimates vary as to the marching speed of medieval armies, which was, of course, dependent on a bewildering range of factors. Bachrach has calculated the eighth-century armies of Pepin the Short were capable of marching 30 kilometres per day (about 18.5 miles). See H. Nicholson, *Medieval Warfare: The Theory and Practice of War in Europe 300–1500* (Basingstoke, 2004), p. 125. Von Clausewitz expected a nineteenth army largely consisting of infantry to march 15 miles per day during 'normal' conditions, 30 miles during a forced march. See Holmes, *Acts of War*, pp. 117–18.
21. For some evocative modern descriptions of infantry on the march see Holmes, *Acts of War*, p. 117.
22. *Arrivall*, p. 28.
23. Quoted in J. Keegan, *The Mask of Command: A Study of Generalship* (London, 1999, *c*. 1987), p. 65.
24. Mancini, p. 64.
25. *Arrivall*, pp. 27–8.
26. Evans, *Wales and the Wars of the Roses*, p. 114.
27. Named as the Lancastrians' 'field' in the near contemporary 'Tewkesbury Abbey Chronicle', excerpt printed in Kingsford, *English Historical Literature*, pp. 376–8.
28. *Arrivall*, p. 29.
29. S. Goodchild, *Tewkesbury: Eclipse of the House of Lancaster* (Barnsley, 2005), p. 46.
30. *Arrivall*, p. 29.
31. *Arrivall*, p. 29.
32. For example, Hammond, *Barnet and Tewkesbury*, p. 93.
33. See Goodchild, *Tewkesbury*, pp. 148–50.
34. See above, p. 156, n. 11.
35. This was the role for small arms that was later advocated by Machiavelli in his *Art of War*. See B. Cassidy, 'Machiavelli and the Ideology of the Offensive: Gunpowder Weapons in the "Art of War",' *Journal of Military History* 67 (2003), pp. 387–8.
36. *Arrivall*, p. 29.
37. *Arrivall*, p. 29.
38. A.H. Burne, *The Battlefields of England* (Barnsley, 2005, *c*. 1950), p. 281.
39. Gravett, *Tewkesbury*, p. 77.
40. Goodchild, *Tewkesbury*, p. 53.
41. *Warkworth's Chronicle*, p. 40.
42. Goodman suggests auxiliaries, probably youths, may have replenished the archers' stocks of arrows, 'dodging like ballboys at a tennis match'. Goodman, *Soldiers' Experience*, p. 139.

43. *Arrivall*, p. 29.
44. J. de Bueil, *Le Jouvencel*, quoted and translated in C.J. Rogers, 'The Bergerac Campaign (1345) and the Generalship of Henry of Lancaster', *Journal of Medieval Military History*, 2 (2004), p. 106, n. 59.
45. P. Vergil, *Three Books of Polydore Vergil's English History*, ed. H. Ellis (Camden Society, 1844), p. 152.
46. Hall, p. 300.
47. For Formigny, see *The Great Warbow*, pp. 358–60.
48. According to an enquiry in June 1472, on the authority of the Bishop of Worcester, the church had been 'notoriously polluted by violence and shedding of blood'. A completely new church was built six years later by the Abbot of Hailes, although whether this was in response to the events after Tewkesbury is unclear. See Hammond, *Barnet and Tewkesbury*, p. 99.
49. Vergil, p. 152.
50. *Arrivall*, p. 30.
51. *Warkworth's Chronicle*, p. 18.
52. *Warkworth's Chronicle*, pp. 18–19; 'Tewkesbury Abbey Chronicle', pp. 376–7.
53. *Arrivall*, p. 31.
54. *Arrivall*, p. 31.
55. Grummitt, 'Defence of Calais', p. 262.
56. Margaret was 'ransomed' by Louis XI in 1476, although she was forced to resign any rights to her family's lands in France. Thereafter she lived a quiet life, living on a meagre pension provided by Louis. Margaret died on 25 August, 1482. Ross, *Edward IV*, pp. 237–8.
57. *Arrivall*, p. 38.
58. *CSPM*, p. 157.
59. *Warkworth's Chronicle*, p. 22.
60. The Mayor of Canterbury, Nicholas Faunt, was one of the most prominent victims. He had been captured and held in the Tower, but was taken to Canterbury to undergo punishment.

Chapter 8 – Epilogue

1. C. Carpenter, *The Wars of the Roses: Politics and the Constitution in England, c. 1437–1509* (Cambridge, 1997), p. 205.
2. Mancini, p. 64.
3. Carpenter, *Wars of the Roses*, pp. 190–6, which focuses on Edward's rule in the localities, especially Warwickshire.
4. Although Carpenter offers a damning assessment of Richard's actions in 1483. Carpenter, *Wars of the Roses*, p. 204, pp. 209–10.
5. If King James III of Scotland had not been thwarted in his desire to meet the English in battle, by his own nobles, it is possible (although of course not certain) that Richard might have been able to strike an even greater blow.

6. Although, according to Mancini (p. 62), Richard of Gloucester held the Woodvilles responsible and swore that he would one day avenge his brother's death.
7. *Crowland Chronicle*, p. 146.
8. Mancini, p. 66.
9. For discussion see Ross, *Edward IV*, pp. 414–6.
10. D. Santiuste, 'Edward V: King or Pawn?' *The Medelai Gazette*, 10 (2003), pp. 6–12.
11. Ross, for example, criticises Edward for his 'failure to make early and deliberate provision for the succession in the event of his own premature death'. Ross, *Edward IV*, p. 426.
12. For some recent views of Richard see: A. Carson, *Richard III: The Maligned King* (Stroud, 2008); M.A. Hicks, *Richard III* (Stroud, 2003); Jones, *Bosworth*; D. Santiuste, ' "Puttyng downe and rebuking of vices": Richard III and the *Proclamation for the Reform of Morals*', in A.S. Harper and C. Proctor (eds.), *Medieval Sexuality: A Casebook* (New York, 2008); Paul Kendall's powerful biography remains a classic text – P.M. Kendall, *Richard III* (New York, 2002, *c*. 1955). But the historiography is now vast. Useful reading lists are available at the websites of the Richard III Foundation, Inc. (http://www.richard111.com) and the Richard III Society (http://www.richardiii.net).
13. Unless otherwise specified the next six paragraphs are based on: D. Grummitt, 'The French Expedition of 1475 and What the Campaign Meant to Those Involved', available at http://www.richardiii.net; M.A. Hicks, *Edward IV*, pp. 132–42; M.K. Jones, '1477 – the Expedition That Never Was: Chivalric Expectation in Late Yorkist England', *The Ricardian*, 12 (2001), pp. 275–92; J.R. Lander, 'The Hundred Years War and Edward IV's 1475 Campaign in France', A.J. Slavin ed., *Tudor Men and Institutions* (Baton Rouge, 1972), pp. 70–100; Ross, *Edward IV*, 205–38; A.F. Sutton and L. Visser-Fuchs, '*Chevalrie [. . .] in som partie is worthi forto be commendid, and in some part to be amendid*: Chivalry and the Yorkist Kings', C.F. Richmond and E. Scarff, eds., *St George's Chapel, Windsor, in the Late Middle Ages* (Windsor, 2001), esp. pp. 116–18.
14. Grummitt, 'Defence of Calais', pp. 263–5.
15. Many of the new guns were expected to be used in the field. For example, the serpentine provided by van Meighlyn was mounted on a cart with four wheels shod with iron. This gun, along with the *Great Edward*, was part of the English army in 1475.
16. *CSPM*, p. 194.
17. *Crowland Chronicle*, pp. 136–7.
18. Commynes, p. 258, p. 359, p. 361.
19. Most of the English noblemen in the army accepted gifts from Louis, in addition to the terms agreed at Picquigny.

20. Commynes, p. 261.
21. Some of Edward's soldiers joined the army of Charles of Burgundy.
22. Catherine Nall's doctoral thesis, which will be published in due course, is concerned with the reception and dissemination of military texts in the aftermath of the Hundred Years' War. Several owners of manuscripts of Vegetius, Chartier and Pisan annotated passages which linked internal peace and outward war.
23. The first Crowland Continuator reports how Edward visited the Abbey and 'passed the night a well-pleased guest. On the morrow, being greatly delighted with the quietness of the place and the courtesy shown to him, he walked on foot through the streets to the western outlet of the village [...] praising in high terms of commendation the plan of the stone bridge and the houses'. Ingulph, p. 445.
24. Quoted in A. Lynch, ' "Peace is good after war": The Narrative Seasons of English Arthurian Tradition', in C. Saunders *et al*, eds., *Writing War: Medieval Literary Responses to Warfare* (Cambridge, 2004), p. 144. In this article Lynch surveys a number of medieval English Arthurian romances, and his conclusions are suggestive. 'Too much' war is seen as an evil, although peace is almost never seen as a good in itself.
25. As noted in Sutton and Visser-Fuchs, 'Chivalry and the Yorkist Kings', p. 117.
26. Commynes, p. 353.

Bibliography

Allmand, C.T., 'The *De re militari* of Vegetius in the Middle Ages and the Renaissance', in Saunders *et al* (eds.), *Writing War: Medieval Literary Responses to Warfare*.

—— (ed.), *Society at War: the Experience of England and France During the Hundred Years War* (Woodbridge, 1998, *c.* 1973).

An English Chronicle, 1377–1461: edited from Aberystwyth, National Library of Wales MS 21068 and Oxford, Bodleian Library MS Lyell 34, ed. W. Marx (Woodbridge, 2003).

Anglo, S., 'How to Win at Tournaments: The Technique of Chivalric Combat', *Antiquaries' Journal* 68 (1988).

——, 'Anglo-Burgundian feats of arms: Smithfield, June 1467', *Guildhall Miscellany* 2:7 (1965).

'Annales Rerum Anglicarum', *Letters and Papers Illustrative of the Wars of the English in France*, ed. J. Stevenson, vol. II part 2 (Rolls Series, 1864).

Armstrong, C.A.J., 'Politics and the Battle of St Albans', *Bulletin of the Institute of Historical Research* 33 (1960).

Baldwin, D., *Stoke Field: The Last Battle of the Wars of the Roses* (Barnsley, 2006).

Barber, R., 'Malory's *Le Morte d'Arthur* and Court Culture under Edward IV', *Arthurian Literature* 12 (1993).

Boardman, A.W., *The Battle of Towton* (Stroud, 2000, *c.* 1994).

——, *The Medieval Soldier in the Wars of the Roses* (Stroud, 1998).

Burley, P., M. Elliot and H. Watson, *The Battles of St Albans* (Barnsley, 2007).

Burne, A.H., *The Battlefields of England* (Barnsley, 2005, *c.* 1950).

Calendar of State Papers and Manuscripts [. . .] of Milan, ed. A.B. Hinds, vol. I (London, 1912).

Calendar of the Close Rolls.

Calendar of the Patent Rolls.

Carpenter, C., *The Wars of the Roses: Politics and the Constitution in England, c.* 1437–1509 (Cambridge, 1997).

Carson, A., *Richard III: The Maligned King* (Stroud, 2008).

Cassidy, B., 'Machiavelli and the Ideology of the Offensive: Gunpowder Weapons in the *Art of War*', *Journal of Military History* 67 (2003).

Caudrey, P. 'William Worcester, *The Boke of Noblesse*, and Military Society in East Anglia', *Nottingham Medieval Studies* 52 (2008).

Chastelain, G. *Oeuvres*, ed. K. de Lettenhove, 8 vols (Brussels, 1863–6).

'Chronicle of the Rebellion in Lincolnshire 1470', ed. J.G. Nichols, *Camden Miscellany* 1 (1847).

Chronicles of London, ed. C.L. Kingsford (Oxford, 1905).

Chronicles of the White Rose of York, ed. J.A. Giles (London, 1845).

Commynes, P. de, *Memoirs: The Reign of Louis XI 1461–83*, tr. M.C.E. Jones (Harmondsworth, 1972).

Crane, S., *The Performance of Self: Ritual, Clothing and Identity During the Hundred Years War* (Philadelphia, 2002).

The Crowland Chronicle Continuations 1459–86, eds. N. Pronay and J.C. Cox (Gloucester, 1986).

Curry, A., *Agincourt: A New History* (Stroud, 2005).

Davey, J., 'The Battle of Towton, 1461: A Reassessment', *idem, Penbardd* (Las Vegas, 2007).

Dockray K (ed.), *Henry VI, Margaret of Anjou and the Wars of the Roses: A Sourcebook* (Stroud, 2000).

——, 'Edward IV: Playboy or Politician?' *The Ricardian* 10 (1995).

——, 'The Yorkshire Rebellions of 1469', *The Ricardian* 6 (1983).

Duclercq, J., *Mémoires de Jacques du Clercq*, ed. F. de Reiffenberg (Brussels, 1835).

Dyboski, R., and Z.M. Arend (eds.), *Knyghthode and Bataile* (Early English Text Society, 1935).

'English Heritage Battlefield Report: Towton 1461' (1995) available at http://www.english-heritage.org.uk (details correct on 7 February, 2009).

Evans, H.T., *Wales and the Wars of the Roses* (Stroud, 1995, *c.* 1915).

Fiorato, V., A. Boylston and C. Knüssel (eds.), *Blood Red Roses: The Archaeology of a Mass Grave from the Battle of Towton AD 1461* (Oxford, 2000).

Froissart, J., *Chronicles*, ed. G. Brereton (London, 1978).

Gillingham, J., *The Wars of the Roses* (London, 1981).

Given-Wilson, C., *Chronicles: The Writing of History in Medieval England* (London, 2004).

Given-Wilson, C., and F. Bériac, 'Edward III's Prisoners of War: The Battle of Poitiers and its Context', *English Historical Review*, 116 (2001).

Goodchild, S., *Tewkesbury: Eclipse of the House of Lancaster* (Barnsley, 2005).

Goodman, A.E., *The Wars of the Roses: The Soldiers' Experience* (Stroud, 2005).

——, *The Wars of the Roses: Military Activity and English Society, 1452–97* (London, 1981).

Gransden, A., *Historical Writing in England II, c.* 1307 to the Early Sixteenth Century (London, 1982).

Gravett, C., *Tewkesbury 1471: The Last Yorkist Victory* (Oxford, 2003).

——, *Towton 1461: England's Bloodiest Battle* (Oxford, 2003).

The Great Chronicle of London, eds. A.H. Thomas and I.D. Thornley (London, 1938).

'Gregory's Chronicle', *Historical Collections of a Citizen of London*, ed. J. Gairdner (Camden Society, 1876).

Griffiths, R.A., and R.S. Thomas, *The Making of the Tudor Dynasty* (Gloucester, 1985).

——, *The Reign of King Henry VI* (Stroud, 1998, *c*. 1981).

Grummitt, D., 'The Defence of Calais and the Development of Gunpowder Weaponry in England in the Late Fifteenth Century', *War in History* 7 (2000).

Grummitt, D., 'The French Expedition of 1475 and What the Campaign Meant to Those Involved', available at http://www.richardiii.net (details correct on 7 February 2009).

Hall, B.S., *Weapons and Warfare in Renaissance Europe: Gunpowder, Technology and Tactics* (Baltimore, 1997).

Hall, E., *Hall's Chronicle*, ed. H. Ellis (London, 1809).

Hammond, P.W., *The Battles of Barnet and Tewkesbury* (Gloucester, 1990).

Harari, Y.N., 'Inter-frontal Cooperation in the Fourteenth Century and Edward III's 1346 Campaign', *War in History* 6 (1999).

Hardyng, J., *The Chronicle of John Hardyng*, ed. H. Ellis (London, 1811).

Harvey, I.M.W., 'Was there Popular Politics in Fifteenth-Century England?' R.H. Britnell and A.J. Pollard (eds.), *The McFarlane Legacy: Studies in Late Medieval Politics and Society* (Stroud, 1995).

Hicks, M.A., *Edward IV* (London, 2004).

——, *Edward V* (Stroud, 2003).

——, *Richard III* (Stroud, 2003).

——, *English Political Culture in the Fifteenth Century* (London, 2002).

——, 'Bastard Feudalism, Overmighty Subjects and Idols of the Multitude during the Wars of the Roses', *History* 85 (2000).

——, *Warwick the Kingmaker* (Oxford, 1998).

——, 'Idealism and politics', in *idem, Richard III and his Rivals: Magnates and their Motives in the Wars of the Roses* (London, 1991).

——, 'Edward IV, the Duke of Somerset and Lancastrian Loyalism in the North', *Northern History* 20 (1984).

——, *False, Fleeting, Perjur'd Clarence 1449–78* (Gloucester, 1980).

Historie of the Arrivall of Edward IV in England and the Finall Recouerye of his Kingdomes from Henry VI. A.D. M.CCCC.LXXI., ed. J. Bruce (Camden Society, 1838).

Hodges, G., *Ludford Bridge and Mortimer's Cross* (Almeley, 1989).

Holmes, R., *Acts of War: The Behaviour of Men in Battle* (London, 2003, *c*. 1985).

Horrox, R.E (ed.), *Fifteenth-Century Attitudes: Perceptions of Society in Late Medieval England* (Cambridge, 1994).

Hughes, J., *Arthurian Myths and Alchemy: The Kingship of Edward IV* (Stroud, 2002).

Ingulph's Chronicle of the Abbey of Croyland, ed. H.T. Riley (London, 1854).

Jack, R.I., 'A Quincentenary: The Battle of Northampton, July 10th, 1460', *Northamptonshire Past and Present* 3 (1960).

Jaeger, C.S., *Ennobling Love: In Search of a Lost Sensibility* (Philadelphia, 1999).

'John Benet's Chronicle for the Years 1400–62', G.L. and M.A. Harriss (eds.), *Camden Miscellany* 24 (1972).

Jones, M.K., *Agincourt 1415* (Barnsley, 2005).

——, *Bosworth 1485: Psychology of a Battle* (Stroud, 2002).

——, 'The Battle of Verneuil (17 August 1424): Towards a History of Courage', *War in History* 9 (2002).

——, '1477 – the Expedition That Never Was: Chivalric Expectation in Late Yorkist England', *The Ricardian*, 12 (2001).

——, 'Edward IV, the Earl of Warwick and the Yorkist Claim to the Throne', *Historical Research* 70 (1997).

——, 'Somerset, York and the Wars of the Roses', *English Historical Review* 104 (1989).

——, 'Edward IV and the Beaufort Family: Conciliation in Early Yorkist Politics', *The Ricardian* 6 (1983).

Kaeuper, R.W., *Chivalry and Violence in Medieval Europe* (Oxford, 1999).

Keegan, J., *The Mask of Command: A Study of Generalship* (London, 1999, *c.* 1987).

Keen, M.H., *Chivalry* (Yale, 1984).

——, *The Laws of War in the Late Middle Ages* (Oxford, 1993, *c.* 1965).

——, 'Treason Trials under the Law of Arms', in *Transactions of the Royal Historical Society* 12 (1962).

Kendall, P.M, *Richard III* (New York, 2002, *c.* 1955).

Kingsford, C.L., *English Historical Literature in the Fifteenth Century* (Oxford, 1913).

Kleineke, H., 'Gerald Von Wesel's Newsletter from England, 17 April 1471', *The Ricardian* 16 (2006).

Knighton's Chronicle 1337–1396, ed. G.H. Martin (Oxford, 1995).

Lander, J.R., 'The Hundred Years War and Edward IV's 1475 Campaign in France', in A.J. Slavin (ed.), *Tudor Men and Institutions* (Baton Rouge, 1972).

Laynesmith, J.L., 'Constructing Queenship at Coventry: Pageantry and Politics at Margaret of Anjou's "Secret Harbour"', L.S. Clark (ed.), *The Fifteenth Century, III, Authority and Subversion* (Woodbridge, 2003).

'Le livre des faicts du Mareschal de Boucicaut', in *Nouvelle collections des Mémoires pour server a l'histoire de France*, eds. Michaud and Poujoulat, vol. II (Paris, 1836–9).

Lynch, A., ' "Peace is good after war": The Narrative Seasons of English Arthurian Tradition', in C. Saunders *et al* (eds.), *Writing War: Medieval Literary Responses to Warfare* (Cambridge, 2004).

Mancini, D., *The Usurpation of Richard III*, ed. and tr. C.A.J. Armstrong (London, 1969).

Marshall, P., 'The rood of Boxley, the blood of Hailes and the defence of the Henrician church', *The Journal of Ecclesiastical History* 46 (1995).

Mercer, M., 'The Strength of Lancastrian Loyalism during the Readeption: Gentry Participation at the Battle of Tewkesbury', *Journal of Medieval Military History* 5 (2007).

More, T., *The History of King Richard III*, ed. R.S. Sylvester (Yale, 1963).

Morgan, P., 'The Naming of Battlefields', in D. Dunn (ed.), *War and Society in Medieval and Early Modern Britain* (Liverpool, 2000).

Mortimer, I., 'York or Lancaster: who was the rightful heir to the throne in 1460?' *Ricardian Bulletin* (Autumn, 2008).

Myers, A.R (ed.), *The Household of Edward IV: the Black Book and the Ordinance of 1478* (Manchester, 1959).

Nicholson, H., *Medieval Warfare: The Theory and Practice of War in Europe 300–1500* (Basingstoke, 2004).

Offenstadt, N. 'The Rituals of Peace during the Civil War in France, 1409–19: Politics and the Public Sphere', in T. Thornton (ed.), *Social Attitudes and Political Structures* (Stroud, 2000).

Okerlund, A., *Elizabeth Wydeville: The Slandered Queen* (Stroud, 2005).

Orme, N., *From childhood to chivalry: the education of the English kings and aristocracy 1066–1530* (London, 1984).

The Parliament Rolls of Medieval England, ed. C. Given-Wilson *et al*, CD-ROM (Leicester, 2005).

The Paston Letters, ed. J. Gairdner, 6 vols in 1 (Gloucester, 1993, *c.* 1904).

The Politics of Fifteenth Century England: John Vale's Book, eds. M.L. Kekewich *et al* (Stroud, 1995).

Pollard, A.J., *Warwick the Kingmaker: Politics, Power and Fame* (London, 2007).

Rawcliffe, C., 'Richard, Duke of York, the King's "obessant liegeman": a new source for the protectorate of 1454 and 1455', *Historical Research* 60 (1987).

Registrum Abbatiae Johannis Whethamstede Abbatis Monasterii Sancti Albani, ed. H.T. Riley, vol. I (Rolls Series, 1872–3).

Richmond, C.F., 'The Earl of Warwick's Domination of the Channel and the Naval Dimension to the Wars of the Roses, 1456–1460', in *Southern History* 20/21 (1987–9).

——, 'The Nobility and the Wars of the Roses, 1459–61', in *Nottingham Medieval Studies* 21 (1977).

Rogers, C.J., 'The Bergerac Campaign (1345) and the Generalship of Henry of Lancaster', *Journal of Medieval Military History* 2 (2004).

——, 'The Vegetian "Science of Warfare" in the Middle Ages', *Journal of Medieval Military History* 1 (2002).

——, 'The Efficacy of the English Longbow: A Reply to Kelly DeVries', *War in History* 5 (1998).

Ross, C.D., *Edward IV* (London, 1974).

Santiuste, D., ' "Puttyng downe and rebuking of vices": Richard III and the *Proclamation for the Reform of Morals*', in A.S. Harper and C. Proctor (eds.), *Medieval Sexuality: A Casebook* (New York, 2008).

————, 'Edward V: King or Pawn?' *The Medelai Gazette* 10 (2003), pp. 6–12.

——, ' "Fighting fulle manly": The Wars of the Roses in *Gregory's Chronicle*' (Unpublished).

Saunders, C., Le Saux, F. and Thomas, N. (eds.), *Writing War: Medieval Literary Responses to Warfare* (Cambridge, 2004).

Scofield, C.L., *The Life and Reign of Edward IV*, 2 vols (London, 1923).

Seward, D., *The Hundred Years War: The English in France 1337–1453* (London, 1988).

Six Town Chronicles, ed. R. Flenley (Oxford, 1911).

Stanford, H., *Royal Beasts* (London, 1956).

Strickland, M.J., and R. Hardy, *The Great Warbow: From Hastings to the Mary Rose* (Stroud, 2005).

Sutton, A.F. and Visser-Fuchs, L. '*Chevalrie [. . .] in som partie is worthi forto be commendid, and in some part to be amendid*: Chivalry and the Yorkist Kings', C.F. Richmond and E. Scarff, eds., *St George's Chapel, Windsor, in the Late Middle Ages* (Windsor, 2001).

Three Fifteenth-Century Chronicles, ed. J. Gairdner (Camden Society, 1880).

Vale, M.G.A, *War and Chivalry: Warfare and Aristocratic Culture in England, France and Burgundy at the End of the Middle Ages* (London, 1981).

Vaughan, R., *Charles the Bold* (Woodbridge, 2002, *c*. 1973).

Vergil, P., *Three Books of Polydore Vergil's English History*, ed. H. Ellis (Camden Society, 1844).

Visser-Fuchs, L., ' "Warwick, by himself": Richard Neville, Earl of Warwick, "the Kingmaker" ', in the '*Receuil des Croniques D'Engleterre* of Jean de Wavrin', *Publication du Centre Européen d'études Bourguignonnes (XIVe–XVIes)* 41 (2001).

——, '*Il n'a plus lion ne lieppart, qui vouelle tenir de sa part*: Edward IV in exile, October 1470 to March 1471', *Publication du Centre Européen d'études Bourguignonnes (XIVe–XVIes)* 35 (1995).

————, '*Sanguinis Haustor* – Drinker of Blood: A Burgundian View of England, 1471', *The Ricardian* 7 (1985–87).

——, 'Nicholas Harpisfield, clerk of the signet, author and murderer', *The Ricardian*, 7 (1985–87).

Warkworth's Chronicle: A Chronicle of the First Thirteen Years of the Reign of Edward IV, by John Warkworth, ed. J.O. Halliwell (Camden Society, 1839).

Watson, P.J., ' "May God have Pity at the Wretched Spectacle": A Review of the Sources for the Battle of Barnet, 14 April 1471', in *The Ricardian* 12 (2000–2002).

Watts, J.L., *Henry VI and the Politics of Kingship* (Cambridge, 1996).

Wavrin, J. de, *Receuil des Croniques et Anchiennes Istoires de la Grant Bretaigne*, ed. W. Hardy, vol. V (Rolls Series, 1864–91).

Wheeler, G., 'The Battle of Barnet: Heraldic Complications and Complexities', *Ricardian Bulletin* (December, 2000).

Index